Japan to 1600

Japan to 1600

A Social and Economic History

William Wayne Farris

University of Hawai'i Press
Honolulu

22 21 20 19 18   6 5

Library of Congress Cataloging-in-Publication Data

Farris, William Wayne.
   Japan to 1600 : a social and economic history /
William Wayne Farris.
      p. cm.
   Includes bibliographical reference and index.
   ISBN 978-0-8248-3325-1 (hardcover : alk. paper) —
ISBN 978-0-8248-3379-4 (paper back : alk. paper)
1. Japan—Social conditions—To 1600.   2. Japan—Economics
conditions—To 1868.   I. Title.
   HN723.F36 2009
   952'.01—dc22
                                        2008056151

Designed by the University of Hawai'i Press production staff

Printed by Sheridan Books, Inc.

To Penelope Niven-McJunkin

Contents

Preface

History consists of stories about the past, intended to be true. Because no one can ever recapture a bygone era "exactly as it was," historians rely on sources of various types to reconstruct bygone times. Sometimes these materials are plentiful and there is general agreement on how to interpret them, whereas in other cases they are nonexistent and historians make differing inferences to fill in gaps in what is known.

Sources are plentiful for Japan to 1600, perhaps even more so than for medieval Europe, yet writing a social and economic history of this long epoch presents special problems. First, because such history deals primarily with commoners, the overwhelming majority of whom were illiterate, written records often refer obliquely—if at all—to these people. Sources for Japan until 1600 include law codes and their interpretations, court histories written by chroniclers with their own agendas, and documents of practice set down for a particular purpose. There are also aristocratic diaries whose authors cared little about social inferiors, and literature that may often be a product of the imagination and reflect the historical context only indirectly. For these reasons, writing social and economic history presents a challenge, but not an insuperable one.

The archaeological boom beginning in Japan around 1960 and continuing to the present has been a great aid in filling in holes in our understanding about pre-1600 society and economy. Archaeologists have uncovered city layouts and remains such as tools, weapons, village foundations, bits of clothing, and other artifacts of everyday life that have greatly increased our understanding of commoner life. Archaeology also helps us know about the environment and how it has changed over the centuries. Unfortunately, the dating system preferred by Japanese archaeologists is neither scientific nor widely used outside of Japan, a fact that engenders confusion and controversy. Japanese archaeology, as important as it is for the study of everyday life, has its shortcomings, too.

Finally, I would like to add a word about the quantitative statistics used in this book. Relatively speaking, again, Japan has a wealth of statistical materials. Figures on yields, prices, and population have been remarkably well preserved for even the

Chronology of Periods in This Book

Standard Chronology	Periodization of This Book, Corresponding to Chapters
PALEOLITHIC: 35,000–15,000 BP **JŌMON: 15,000 BP—900 BCE** **YAYOI: 900 BCE–250 CE** **TOMB: 250 CE–600 CE**	Origins to 600. Chapter 1. *The Building Blocks of Japan:* social and economic growth
ANCIENT ERA, 500–1185 Asuka, 552–645: Age of Reform Hakuhō, 645–710 Nara, 710–784	600–800. Chapter 2. *An End to Growth:* onslaught of epidemics; dispersed agriculture; pyramid-like social structure; high status of women
Heian, 784–1185	800–1050. Chapter 3. *State and Society in an Age of Depopulation:* "the era of microparasitism"; agricultural contraction; increasingly unbalanced social pyramid; continuing high status of women
	1050–1180. Chapter 4. *Rising Social and Political Tensions in an Epoch of Minimal Growth:* development of trifunctional elite; lessening effects of epidemics; mild agrarian and commercial revival; decline in elite women's power
MEDIEVAL ERA, 1185–1600 Kamakura, 1185–1333	1180–1280. Chapter 5. *Economy and Society in Age of Want:* rise of the warrior; the great famines; minimal agrarian, industrial, and commercial improvements; apocalyptic "Latter Day of the Buddhist Law"
Muromachi (Ashikaga), 1333–1573	1280–1450. Chapter 6. *The Revival of Growth:* agricultural and commercial boom; increasingly differentiated classes; origins of structured social organizations; further decline in the status of women
Warring States, 1467–1568 Azuchi-Momoyama, 1568–1600: Age of Unification	1450–1600. Chapter 7. *Uneven Expansion in an Age of Endemic Warfare:* continuing but fitful agrarian, industrial, and commercial boom; more subclasses; more tightly knit social organizations; decline in political power and social standing of women
TOKUGAWA (EDO) ERA: 1600–1868 Genroku, 1675–1725	1600–1720. Epilogue. *The Seventeenth Century in Historical Perspective:* massive growth and social differentiation

distant past. For most periods, however, such quantitative figures are the product of inference, based upon fragmentary or indiscriminate sources. Although all figures cited in this book have been corroborated by diverse methods, students should realize that even these represent merely best-guess estimates; they should not be taken as literal facts. In the end, history is never a "given" from on high but always open to reinterpretation and revision.

This book is a social and economic history of Japan to 1600, and the periodization schema that I have adopted is fitting to that approach. Such a chronology, however, varies considerably from the standard temporal divisions found in most textbooks. As may be noted in the table, the conventional periodization derives primarily from elite cultural trends or the presumed location of the capital. Although it continues to serve historians well, there is nothing particularly sacrosanct about it.

In contrast, my social and economic periodization is based on a combination of interdependent factors. They include population trends; agricultural, industrial, and commercial development; the differentiation of social classes; the formation of tightly knit social units; and variations in gender relations. The reader should be made aware that these components often do not change in the same way or at the same rate. The periodization table juxtaposes the standard chronology with my own to permit students to move easily between the two.

Acknowledgments

I would like to acknowledge the influence of two revered scholars in the conception and writing of this book. The first is David Herlihy, professor of medieval European social and economic history at several institutions, most notably Harvard and Brown universities. During 1974–1975, I was fortunate enough to audit his survey class at Harvard, and it changed my life. The world of demography and social and economic history came so alive in his fascinating and often humorous classes that eventually I decided to dedicate my life to bringing the same perspectives to early and medieval Japan. This book is unthinkable without the inspiration, knowledge, and support of this great scholar.

The second is Jeffrey Mass, Yamato Ichihashi Professor of Japanese History and Civilization at Stanford University. I can still remember the excitement with which I took up his first monograph, *Warrior Government in Early Medieval Japan*, in the autumn of 1974. At the time, almost no one ventured into the arcane world of pre-1600 Japanese history, and there was even some doubt as to whether Anglophone scholars could write intelligently about that era. Jeffrey Mass not only "did the impossible," but also produced a bevy of young scholars who have expanded upon his work in countless ways.

Tragically, both these fine men died far too young, while still at the height of their careers. I can only hope that each would look upon this project with approval.

Introduction

This book examines the social and economic history of Japan from earliest times until 1600. Social and economic history encompasses numerous and diverse topics, including population and factors affecting mortality and fertility, specifically war, famine, disease, marriage, birth control, diet, and migration. The social and economic historian also investigates how people make a living and the technologies by which they do so. This book therefore addresses topics such as silk, cotton, and salt making; agriculture and fishing; ceramics; and construction. Another important economic sector includes commerce, markets, and money. Social history means the study of how society is organized and the relations among its members. It is concerned with class and family structures and experiences, life in villages and cities, gender relations, and the condition of children. Finally, social history takes into account material culture as represented by housing, sanitation, clothing, modes of transportation, and other ordinary hallmarks of everyday life. Taken together, these phenomena helped form the basis of daily life for people of all classes and regions in Japan from the prehistoric era through 1600. They interacted in complex ways with religious beliefs, political institutions, and ties to the outside world. The perspective of social and economic history on pre-1600 Japan is important in its own right, but also offers the basis for a more complete understanding of later periods. More broadly, it adds to human knowledge about the nature and diversity of global social and economic patterns.

English-language surveys of this long epoch in Japanese history have largely approached their subject through either elite cultural or political-institutional narratives. Although these approaches have contributed valuable insights, they offer, by virtue of their emphasis on the life of the privileged few, only a partial view of Japan's distant past. Fortunately, Japanese, American, and many other scholars have created a repository of excellent data and research on social and economic history, and I draw on this material to fill out the picture of Japan's society and economy.

In the following pages, I will trace two main themes, one economic and one social. In terms of the Japanese economy, I will describe how the residents of the archipelago gradually moved from a forager-collector mode of subsistence to a more predominately agrarian base, supplemented by sophisticated industries and an advanced commercial economy. The transition from foraging to farming took place over many centuries, as persons moved back and forth from settled agriculture to older forager-collector regimes in response to ecological, political, and personal factors. Even in 1600, there remained a substantial portion of the population that never settled down to farm wet rice, as the governing elite desired.

At the level of society, this book will show how, as the population expanded over the last three thousand years, the social structure became increasingly complex, and occupational specialization and status divisions more intricate. In some ways, Japan has always been a land of diverse social categories, reflecting the islands' rich variety of landforms and flora and fauna and thus possibilities for subsistence. Particularly between 1300 and 1600, as the population grew relatively rapidly, the social structure became ever more elaborate. Along with this expanded social specialization came trends toward more tightly knit corporate organizations, whether in the village, city, market, or family. Along with this tendency toward higher levels of organization came transformations in gender relations and the situation of children.

The focus of this book is on continuity and change in social and economic structures and experiences in Japan until 1600. But, because the political approach has so dominated the historical narrative and because the economy, society, and political systems are so interwoven, I will begin most chapters with an outline of developments in the political system of that period. Readers will note that as the economy became more agrarian and commercial, and the social structure more complex, political organization also grew larger and more intricate so that, by 1600, the political elite was able to count on a bigger surplus of commoner produce and labor than ever before.

I will also take into account cultural phenomena, particularly religious beliefs. Just as culture is a reflection of social, economic, and political circumstances, religious sensibilities to some degree affect and are affected by the nature of the society and economy. There is never a simple relationship among all the various factors that make up history, whether material, institutional, or intellectual. Finally, I will address the growing connectedness between the residents of the archipelago and the rest of the world. It was once the conventional wisdom that Japan produced a unique culture because of its isolation. Today, it is generally acknowledged that it can be more helpful to conceive of Japan as a place where peoples, materials, and ideas—as well as other living things—converged and mixed. Residents of Japan constantly influenced and were influenced by neighbors and forces near and far, since prehistoric times.

I begin, as most historical surveys do, with the period leading up to about 600 common era (CE), tracing the development of certain basic structures—so-called building blocks—that were to last for a millennium and longer. Here I will examine the shifting geographical and ecological context, the advent of hunter-fisher-gatherer society, the gradual and incomplete transition to agriculture (particularly wet-rice cultivation), and the slow evolution of a political consciousness under the Yamato confederation centered in the Kyoto-Osaka-Nara region (the Kinai). I next look at the epoch from the early 600s until 800, a stressful time that witnessed a gradual cessation of socioeconomic growth due to numerous factors, including foreign wars and the threat of invasion, the arrival of an East Asian pandemic, the shortcomings of early agriculture, and galloping inflation by century's end. The population of approximately six million formed a social structure resembling a pointed pyramid, with the political and social elite at the top and a hard lot for commoners and slaves on the bottom. For society as a whole, kinship was flexible. Households were typically nuclear, and the customs of marriage ill defined, commonly allowing for multiple sexual liaisons for most males and females. Women played critical roles both at home and at work.

Quantitative standstill was the rule for the next two phases, the first covering 800–1050 and the second 1050–1180. Both were ages of declining or stable population, in part because of the ongoing effects of repeated plagues. This demographic situation was exacerbated by a hot and often drought-ridden climate and extensive ecological damage to the forests of the Kinai. These environmental drawbacks left many fields without water and caused harvests to fail about once every three years. A shortage of workers encouraged the adoption of labor-saving technologies in industry, cities shrank or disappeared, and the economy demonetized, especially during the initial phase. Under these pressures, the social structure became increasingly unbalanced, with a larger and more exalted elite created by rank inflation and differential mortality rates. The expanded ruling group tried, often in vain, to secure its tribute items from a disproportionately small, mobile, and uncooperative commoner class. During 1050–1180, the ruling class grew even larger to comprise a full-fledged trifunctional elite—civil aristocracy, religious organizations, and a military class. These groups functioned within a reformed political system headed by a retired emperor. Except for signs of a rebound in commerce due to the stimulus of a dynamic Chinese economy, the islands' economy and society—agriculture, industry, fertility, mortality, life expectancy, kinship, the family, gender relations, and material culture—remained much as before.

The century from 1180 to 1280 was another stressful transitional time, featuring trends that were both familiar and novel. Strains were evident in all sectors, but perhaps most striking in the collapse of the unbalanced social pyramid during the civil war of 1180–1185, which created a warrior government in Kamakura. The climate became harsher, causing three major famines each lasting for multiple years. Warriors became secure rent collectors whose abuse of cultivators provoked protests and led peasants to abscond from their lands. War, famine, and debt created a large class of slaves, and many impoverished families disintegrated or were forced to abandon their children. Ecological and economic stresses and the political and social upheaval during this time gave rise to an uneasy sense among some that the last chance for religious salvation was slipping away ("The Latter Age of the Buddhist Law"). Not all trends, however, were negative. Especially after 1250, there were new, more salutary approaches to farming, epitomized by the spread of double-cropping and more productive use of dry fields and a steady expansion and monetization of the commercial network, giving rise to more cities and markets.

Beginning about 1280 and lasting until 1600, socioeconomic growth and change were the watchwords, taking place in two stages. Population grew by sixty-seven percent, to about ten million in 1450 and then to between fifteen and seventeen million around 1600. Political instability marked these growth stages, especially during the Warring States' Era from 1450 through 1590. The all-out warfare dominating this latter period was especially costly. Mortality climbed in many places, provoked by harvest failure and the arrival of at least one new disease (syphilis). Many women, especially those in the elites, slowly lost their previously high status, as well as the ability to inherit and manage property, in male-dominated stem households. Greater wifely security, though, may have compensated for the loss of status, to a degree. Agrarian growth was evident in better irrigation engineering, the more widespread employment of double cropping, and the introduction and diffusion of a hardier species of rice from Southeast Asia. During this time, the proportion of "floating" people, or foragers, dropped to the lowest percentage ever in Japan. Evidence of the benefits to society can be seen in the incorporation of tightly knit villages, increasingly stable peasant families with a considerable patrimony, and lower infant mortality. The development of a full-fledged money economy was but one factor contributing to marked gains in most peoples' material life. Beginning in 1590, the settlement negotiated by the political elite with the peasantry and other social classes, which had resisted the armies and their tactics of pillage and plunder, led to the greatest political stability the residents of the archipelago had ever known. The Tokugawa system laid the groundwork for the beginning of a new era, marked initially by continued population increase, economic prosperity, and further social specialization.

Years of research in Japanese primary and secondary sources, along with teaching experience, inform the content of this textbook. I have benefited greatly from the growing and sophisticated corpus of work by my English-speaking colleagues in different disciplines. Many observations made throughout this volume originated with others, and I have tried to synthesize these with my own understanding of how Japan's society and economy developed. Because of my desire to create a simple narrative appealing to students and general readers, I have not cited specific references at all points. Only where I use another scholar's ideas, or otherwise owe a substantial debt to another's work, have I provided a citation. For further guidance, readers may consult the brief essay at the end of the book suggesting specific English-language readings.

1 The Building Blocks of Japan, Origins to 600

Geography and Ecology

Human history unfolds within a specific geographical and ecological context. In Japan's case, that context has greatly influenced its economy and society. Japan consists of a long string of islands, extending from 45 degrees north latitude to 31 degrees south, roughly equal to the distance between Montreal and the Florida Keys. This archipelago is pressed between two giants, the world's largest ocean (the Pacific) and its most massive continent (Asia). Most residents live on one of four main islands. To the southwest is Kyushu, the gateway to East Asia. Shikoku is a small, peripheral island that, together with Kyushu, helps form the Inland Sea, Japan's equivalent to Europe's Mediterranean. Honshu is the largest landmass and home to most of the population. From prehistoric times, the northernmost island of Hokkaido served as the archipelago's link to northern Asia, but it was unexplored frontier for most of the centuries examined in this book. In addition, there are hundreds of small islets scattered throughout the chain. In total, Japan is about the size of Montana, or half again the area of Great Britain.

Historians have made much of Japan's supposed isolation from its neighbors, but in fact peoples, materials, ideas, and other living things converging from three directions have profoundly influenced the islands. In the north, humans, animals, and plants have migrated from Siberia through Kamchatka, Sakhalin, and the Kuriles, on to Hokkaido, aided by the Arctic Current. To the west, there has been near-constant interaction with Korea, China, and other states of East Asia, via scattered islands connecting southern Korea and Kyushu. Although the distance there is more than one hundred miles, a few hours' ride on a modern ferry reveals that ancient seafarers remained within sight of land along the entire journey, making the voyage safer than it otherwise might seem. To the south, Japan is connected to Southeast Asia through Kyushu and the Ryukyus. The Black Current, carrying warm waters from the equator to the eastern coast of Japan, has undoubtedly encouraged migration from the south.

Japan is a land of mountains, which cover about eighty percent of its area.

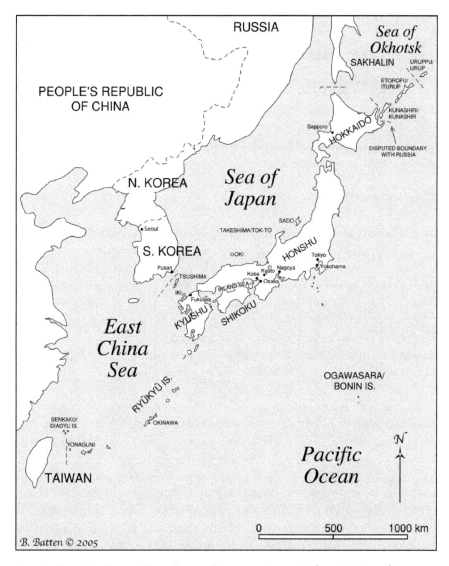

Japan in East Asia: Source: Bruce Batten, *Gateway to Japan: Hakata in War and Peace, 500–1300* (Honolulu: University of Hawai`i Press, 2005), p. 7.

Young, jagged peaks (the Japan Alps) stand about 10,000 feet tall in central Honshu, dividing the archipelago into eastern and western halves. Where heavily forested, the mountains tend both to collect moisture—making Japan one of the wettest areas in the world—and to discharge that moisture rapidly, causing frequent flooding and erosion of cultivated lands. The mountainous terrain has also meant that rivers in Japan are short and generally not navigable. About sixty of the peaks are active volcanoes, and when they fill the sky with ash, smoke, and other debris, the result is cool, wet weather that leads to crop failure. Earthquakes have been common in Japan, as it sits astride the junctures of four tectonic plates: the Pacific and Philippine oceanic and the Eurasian and North American continental.

Along with the mountainous terrain, the country consists of three major plains and innumerable small flatland basins suitable for farming. Historically, the two most important plains have been the Kanto (the metropolitan Tokyo region of about 5,000 square miles) and the Kinai (the Kyoto-Nara-Osaka area of around 1,250 square miles). Throughout Japanese history, the residents of these large plains—located in eastern Honshu and central Japan, respectively—have maintained an adversarial relationship, with both the population and political center shifting back and forth. A third defining landform is a coastline of more than 17,000 miles that gives Japan a maritime outlook despite the relative lack of good harbors.

Japan's climate is intimately related to atmospheric conditions over the Asian landmass. In the winter, cold air from Siberia dominates and produces temperatures in the low thirties (Fahrenheit) in central Honshu and drops substantial snowfall along the Japan Sea littoral. In the spring and summer, the atmosphere warms up, moisture arrives from the south, and Japan experiences its monsoon season between late May and mid-July. The monsoons produce about seventy percent of the moisture for these rain-soaked islands, and are essential for the agricultural cycle and Japan's lush and variegated vegetation.

Japan's resource base has been a critical factor in the development of its society and economy. The archipelago was originally home to ubiquitous stands of broadleafs and conifers and these timbers supplied most of the building materials for the Japanese as late as the twentieth century. The soil is generally gravelly, acidic, and lacking in the nutrients and vegetable detritus helpful in sustaining agriculture, even in the flatlands. Japan has a few minerals—notably sulfur, silver, gold, and copper— but lacks substantial deposits of iron, a fact of crucial importance throughout the archipelago's history.

Three points stand out about Japan's geographical and ecological context for students of Japan's society and economy to 1600. First, the combination of mountainous terrain, torrential rains, and generally poor soil has meant that farming was slow to develop, thus promoting diverse means of subsistence for the population in the mountains and along the seashore. Second, this forbidding landscape has engendered high costs for transportation and commerce and a strong sense of regionalism, with both settlements and families scattered over the landscape. Third, Japan has served as a point of convergence for diverse transportation routes. It has derived much of its material culture from other parts of the world while at the same time sending its traders, armies, and tourists throughout much of Asia.

The Age of Foraging and Collecting: 35,000 BP–900 BCE

THE PALEOLITHIC, 35,000–15,000 BP

No one can be sure when humans first set foot in the archipelago, but the current consensus is that habitation is remarkably recent, likely no earlier than 35,000 years ago. For comparison's sake, consider that the proposed "first" human ancestor, Lucy, whose remains Donald Johansson discovered in eastern Africa in the mid-1970s, was deemed to have lived 3.5 million years ago. Even in China, human occupation dates back almost two million years. In fact, according to present fossil evidence, none of humanity's distant ancestors, such as *Homo erectus*, ever lived in the islands. From the beginning *Homo sapiens* represented humankind in Japan.

Fluctuations in global climate resulted in periods of cooling and warming throughout what is known as the Pleistocene era (about one million years ago). When the earth cooled, northern oceans froze over and seawaters receded, as huge glaciers covered much of the globe's surface. During the last glacial period, about eighteen thousand years ago, temperatures were seven or eight degrees colder than at present, and the main islands of Kyushu, Shikoku, and Honshu were joined to one another, although not linked to Korea. Hokkaido, however, was joined to Sakhalin and the Asian mainland, perhaps indicating a north Asian origin for these earliest inhabitants. The cold climate turned Hokkaido into tundra, and northern and much of western Japan became home to coniferous forests, which today are limited to the north.[1]

The typical site from paleolithic times is a stone workplace where people made hand axes, flakes, and, eventually, microblades, or small, chipped, knife-shaped tools set in bone or antler shafts. From about twenty thousand years ago, humans fashioned more sophisticated points for composite spears, and the consequent improvement in hunting technology helped the population grow. Archaeologists believe that large migratory mammals, such as Naumann's elephant, were common game, but hunters also pursued easier-to-catch small- and medium-sized mammals, such as deer, boar, rabbit, and monkey. Like most early hunting societies, paleolithic humans seemed to have lived in caves at first, moving to surface dwellings toward the end of the era. These settlements are known through clusters of burnt, rounded stones two or three meters in diameter and often caked with animal fat. Paleolithic hunters kept on the move and stored little.

Almost nothing is known about paleolithic society, but a late site has revealed stone "dolls." Measuring less than ten centimeters in height, these artifacts are cylindrical with a rounded head and slits for the eyes and mouth. Archaeologists have discovered similar figures all over Siberia, which may suggest the origins of the first *Homo sapiens* to come to the islands. Why these dolls were made and what they meant remain a mystery.

THE JŌMON AGE, 15,000 BP–900 BCE

The Jōmon era may encompass the most materially affluent hunter-gatherer society known to the modern world. As such, Japan's last great age of foraging had a strong impact on later periods, including the development of livelihoods still practiced in the twentieth century; aspects of material culture including housing, ceramics, and textiles; and a preoccupation with age hierarchy and fertility. It is important to note that, even after the introduction of other technologies, Jōmon occupations and material culture continued to be significant.

A major cause for this age of affluence arose from shifts in the environment. The cold climate of the paleolithic warmed from about eighteen thousand years ago, and the Japanese archipelago took its current shape about 15,000 BP. After another brief cool spell beginning about thirteen thousand years ago, temperatures rose until about 6,000 BP, obtaining an "optimum warm" with sea levels at two to six meters higher than today. Even then, however, violent shifts in the environment could make life hard. About 7,300 years ago, for example, one of the largest volcanic eruptions in Japanese prehistory, along with associated earthquakes and tsunamis, left Kyushu nearly uninhabited for centuries.[2]

Where did these Jōmon people come from? The concentration of the population in eastern and northern Japan suggests a north Asian origin, but DNA and cranial evidence indicates some affinity with the peoples of Southeast Asia. One theory has it that in about 7,000 BP a continent called Sundaland, located in what is today Indonesia and the Philippines, collapsed in a giant earthquake, creating thousands of refugees, many of whom followed the Black Current to Japan and added to the Jōmon stock.

The term "Jōmon," which literally means "rope-pattern," has been adopted as the name for this period because it helps to describe a critical invention: pottery. Brownish-orange Jōmon earthenware, dated at about 13,000 years BP, is considered to be the earliest in the world—comparable cultures in contemporary Korea and China produced nothing like it until thousands of years later. The term "rope pattern" refers to the textured surface of these pots, which may be highly ornamental. The makers built these ceramics by hand and fired them at a relatively low temperature in the open air, oxidizing the clay minerals. The pieces are often pointed at the bottom and do not hold liquid well because the low firing temperature prevented the clay minerals, of which the pots were made, from congealing completely. These vessels, however, represented a major advance for human subsistence because people could cook and store food in them, decreasing the risk of starvation.

The development of pottery went hand in hand with marked improvements in ways to make a living. Jōmon hunters increased their efficiency by learning to make the bow and arrow, which flies about ten times as far as a thrown spear. The dog, with its keen sense of smell and hunting instincts, also made its way to Japan about 9,200 BP. Those Jōmon who lived near shorelines or shallow estuaries used bone and horn harpoons and hooks, as well as nets equipped with clay weights, to obtain shellfish and other riches of the sea, including seaweed. In northeastern Honshu, fishermen depended upon large runs of salmon. The gathering of tubers, berries, and nuts such as acorns, chestnuts, and walnuts was an important job done by women. Skeletal evidence indicates that they developed strong arm muscles and elongated clavicles from pounding nuts and tubers. Jōmon people may even have planted stands of trees deep in the mountains from which they harvested nuts. Residents of the mid-Jōmon period may also have practiced small-scale horticulture, planting millet, beans, barley, burdock, and melons, perhaps in slash-and-burn style. The different peoples who composed the Jōmon stock probably could not survive by specializing in any one pattern of subsistence for too long. Rather, they moved around from a central location and collected food seasonally. They pursued fishing and marine mammals in the summer, headed for the mountains to gather nuts in the autumn, hunted in the winter, and migrated back to the sea to take shellfish in the spring.

The Jōmon invented or improved upon other technologies of daily life. Unlike paleolithic toolmakers, the Jōmon learned to polish their stone implements. A polished Jōmon hand ax can fell a tree almost as rapidly as a modern steel one. The Jōmon sewed together strands of hemp, ramie, or mulberry bark to make clothing that though itchy provided some protection from the cold. Besides gathering seaweed, they learned to boil down seawater in large pots to make salt, a technology that remained unchanged until the end of the eighth century. They also collected the sap of the sumac tree to make lacquer for baskets, cloth, and other articles. With these diverse occupations and technologies, it should come as no surprise that the Jōmon developed short- and long-distance exchange networks for such commodities as obsidian, jade, asphalt, salt, amber, and exotic shells. To facilitate trade, they learned to hollow out logs for use as boats, a basic form of transportation predominating until the 1300s.

With all these improvements, the population grew rapidly, reaching at least 261,000 by 6,300 BP. Some experts believe that as many as 350,000 people may have lived in the islands at the height of the Jōmon, testimony to the richness and diversity of non-agricultural occupations in these islands. This population was concentrated in Hokkaido and northern and eastern Japan, with those living in

The Jōmon people buried their dead with arms and legs in flexed position. The missing teeth have been pulled as part of a coming-of-age ritual. *Source:* Kodama Kōta, ed. *Zusetsu Nihon bunka shi taikei.* Vol. 1 (Shōgakkan, 1956), p. 109.

western Japan settled sparsely, perhaps because their resource base for foraging was poorer. Fortunately for archaeologists, Jōmon villagers frequently buried their dead in or near heaps of refuse such as shell mounds or piles of animal bones. Shells and bones are chemically basic, neutralizing the acidic character of Japanese soil and preserving about five thousand skeletons contained in more than four thousand shell mounds.

The skeletons, often buried in flexed positions, reveal much about Jōmon society. The average height of a Jōmon man was 5 feet 3 inches and of a woman 4 feet 11 inches. Life expectancy for adults was short, only twenty-four years for females and thirty-four for males. When infant mortality is factored in, however, life expectancy at birth dipped to a mere sixteen or seventeen years. X-rays of these bones also betray periods of near-fatal malnutrition. The data show that, even with improvements in subsistence, life was hard and humans often just barely managed to reproduce. Furthermore, skeletal evidence shows that apparently most Jōmon people were in dire need of dentists. Teeth full of cavities have been linked to a diet rich in nuts and other high-calorie foods. Finally, burials almost never disclose markers for class distinction, which suggests a fundamentally egalitarian society with little surplus to expend for a ruling elite.

Just as in their pursuit of livelihood, the Jōmon were inventive when it came to living arrangements. They developed the housing unit preferred by the overwhelming majority of Japanese throughout history: the pit dwelling. After digging a floor about seventy to eighty centimeters below ground level, they set four posts in the earth and thatched the frame with grasses. The entire structure was about ten meters square. These pit dwellings had a campfire in the middle and several hollows in the floor used for storing food. The typical Jōmon village consisted of about five to eight dwellings, with an average of five residents each. Many villages had a central open space around which the dwellings were set.

The huge Sannai-Maruyama site located at the northern tip of Honshu is the most famous excavation from the Jōmon age.[3] People lived at Sannai-Maruyama, a protected estuary offering numerous opportunities for trade and collecting seafood, during the height of the Jōmon age, from 5,900 to 4,000 BP. Excavated in the 1990s, Sannai-Maruyama contained numerous pit dwellings, large holes for timbers for sizable structures, along with garbage heaps, storage pits, and burial jars. The site is circular, with a large space for group activities. At any one time it contained forty or fifty pit dwellings with a population of four hundred to five hundred. Two human-made mounds served as garbage dumps. The northern one contained pottery shards, a bone sword, ornamental stones, clay earrings, lacquerware, and human and animal bones, whereas the southern hill had some eight hundred clay figurines, numerous shards, and pieces of jade, amber, and lacquered plates, bowls, and combs. Residents also built a road about fifteen meters wide. Two rows of adults' graves flanked the road; infants had their own cemetery. The site was also home to numerous structures with raised floors, one as long as thirty-two meters, perhaps serving as a community center or home for a chieftain. These large buildings suggest a level of community development never before attributed to the Jōmon. Sannai-Maruyama was part of several trade networks in amber, obsidian, asphalt, and lacquerware, among other things.

Sites such as Sannai-Maruyama reveal much about the spiritual life of the Jōmon. Many skeletons have had some of their healthy adult teeth pulled or filed, either to distinguish between village insiders and outsiders or as a coming of age ritual. Taboo and magic were important, as shown by clay figurines (*dogū*). Jōmon people may have employed these miniatures, which are often missing an arm or a leg, as sympathetic magic to heal fractures. Presumably, they believed that by transferring the injury to one of these figures, the patient could be magically healed. More likely, these figures were part of fertility rites, as indicated by the many females with exaggerated breasts or large with child. From the middle and late Jōmon, female sex organs were graphically represented and stone phalluses appeared.

The emphasis on fertility was well placed, as the population slowly began to shrink toward the end of the era. By 3,300 BP it had dropped to 160,000; by 2,900 BP, the population was a mere 76,000. The number of ritual objects, such as clay masks, stone circles, and female fertility figures, increased, as did interments of infants. What was responsible for this crisis of the late Jōmon? Some point to a decline in average temperature and increase in the amount of rainfall. These climatic changes would have been felt keenly in eastern and northern Japan, the most populated areas. Other scholars think that stored nuts were improperly prepared and became poisonous, killing off large numbers of foragers. The gradual reversal of fortunes for the Jōmon reminds us that every system of subsistence is prone to decline.

The Advent and Spread of Agrarian Society

YAYOI PHASE, 900 BCE–250 CE

The name "Yayoi" was taken from a section of downtown Tokyo where the first pottery from this age was discovered. The diffusion of farming and metallurgy from the Yang-tze basin of China through Korea to the islands, however, is the real story of this prehistoric phase. It is often portrayed as a revolution, and in some respects it certainly was. The population increased many times over; numerous residents took up cultivation, especially paddy rice; iron tools began to replace those of stone, bone, and wood; and by the end of this phase, a political consciousness had asserted itself in many communities. In conceptual terms, the contrast between the prior forager regimes and agriculture could not have been more pronounced. Agriculture involves far more manipulation of the environment than foraging. Agrarian society is essentially a human-centered biological community in which certain plants and animals become as dependent on humankind for survival and propagation as humans do on them.

Toward the end of the Jōmon epoch, inhabitants of the archipelago probably began to cultivate the seed-bearing grasses that constitute the basis of agriculture. Most scholars focus on the arrival of paddy rice (*Oryza sativa japonica*) from southern China, either directly or through southern Korea. Indeed, various sites contain evidence of paddies, irrigation ditches and dikes, postholes for raised storehouses, numerous farm tools, and carbonized rice grains. One of the first rice-growing communities ever discovered may be seen today at Toro, located in central Honshu along the Pacific Ocean. It was home to twelve dwellings, two raised storehouses, plentiful wooden farm tools, and 17.4 acres of rice fields. The settlement supported about sixty people in 200 CE. Toro reveals that Yayoi rice farming often took place in lands that were low lying and swampy, and the sluices and ditches found there were employed by farmers to siphon off excess water, not to usher it in. Paddies carved out of low-lying lands constituted a form of rice

Pit dwellings like the one shown here reconstructed at Toro served as the basic unit of rural housing until the nineteenth century. *Source: Tokubetsu shiseki Toro shiseki* (Shizuoka City: Shizuoka shiritsu Toro hakubutsukan, 1992) p. 6.

cultivation that endured for centuries because farmers did not need to expend the effort to build ponds or dig ditches through natural river levees. Instead, they merely relied upon the annual rainfall to water their lands. Even on small, flat stretches above the water table, simple techniques of irrigation and reliance upon precipitation predominated in the Yayoi phase.

At first, cultivators broadcast rice seeds over their minimally prepared fields, perhaps in some cases digging holes. The rice grew up among reeds and other weeds, and farmers typically harvested their rice one sheaf at a time with a crescent-shaped stone or bone blade held in the palm of the hand. Spades and hoes were almost all wooden, and threshing was done in a wooden mortar with a pestle. These simple methods meant that yields were feeble, only ten to twenty percent by today's standards. Yayoi farmers possessed no domesticated cattle or horses, and did all the back-wrenching work themselves.

Under these circumstances, it is not surprising that rice farming diffused only gradually over the Yayoi age, and its effects varied by region. From northern Kyushu, where the first sites have been found, along the Inland Sea and across to the Kinai, the new agrarian regime took hold quickly and expanded rapidly, partly because the older Jōmon livelihoods had been so unproductive. From central to northeastern Honshu, where Jōmon foraging was highly successful, residents resisted agriculture and continued to consume large amounts of salmon and nuts. Rice farming did not reach this part of the island until near the end of the Yayoi period. In southern Kyushu and Hokkaido, there are no signs of agriculture throughout the Yayoi era. Even where rice farming flourished, people continued to hunt, fish, and gather to supplement their diets. The conversion of the entire Japanese archipelago to an essentially agrarian society required hundreds of years of refinement of agricultural techniques by thousands of people. It was still ongoing in the 1600s.

Living in an age when new technology is eagerly adopted, we might ask why the progress of wet-rice farming was slow. After all, rice is the most calorific of all grains, leading to large populations wherever it is eaten. In Japan, though, the poor soil and easy chances of erosion did not favor farming. Moreover, in many places foraging was successful and there may have been little incentive to try anything new. Finally, rice cultivation is typically down-on-your-knees, backbreaking labor, more akin to gardening than what Americans and Europeans think of as farming. Why invest such effort in a crop that might fail?

Despite the risks inherent in rice farming, it did eventually pay dividends. There is sound evidence that at some point during the Yayoi era—possibly even from the beginning—some tillers engaged in a more advanced form of artificially irrigated rice cropping. In this method, farmers flooded small paddies located above the water table with river run-off and transplanted to the fields seedlings that had sprouted in separate seedbeds, just in time for the monsoon season. Under this regime, cultivators could more easily manage weeds and when it came time to harvest the rice, they used iron sickles to cut the plant off at the root.

Other innovations made farming more lucrative. Wooden mashers may have been available to crush plant matter for fertilizer. The construction of raised warehouses for grain also showed that the Yayoi people had markedly improved storage techniques over the small pits of the Jōmon age. Some believe that Yayoi tillers also cultivated beans and fruit, as well as dry fields with grains such as barley, millet, wheat, soybeans, and buckwheat. In the mountains the Yayoi practiced slash-and-burn tillage. In addition, the pig was domesticated. Throughout the millennium of the Yayoi, farmers gradually improved their yields, and thus their chances of survival, through the greater use of transplantation, iron tools, green manure, and more capacious storehouses.

As agrarian technology improved, there was a gradual and sizable effect on population. From a low of about seventy-six thousand at the end of the Jōmon age, population soared to between six hundred thousand and three million by 250 CE, an increase of ten- to forty-fold, proportional gains unequaled in Japanese history. Most of the expansion took place in western Japan, where rice cultivation had been quickly and firmly adopted, and the distribution of population soon reversed the Jōmon pattern of eastern and northern dominance. Moreover, considerable in-migration from Korea and the Asian continent fueled demographic growth. As many as three thousand people per year may have moved from the continent to Japan over the Yayoi phase. These immigrants likely related to the indigenes through intermarriage and war, usually settling together and only rarely segregating themselves. By the end of the Yayoi age, however, the waves of new people from the continent had overwhelmed the older stock. It is therefore not surprising that modern Japanese share more genetic, biological, and linguistic traits with Koreans than with any other Asian people.

To be sure, there was considerable continuity with Jōmon material culture. Yayoi pots include more vessel shapes not nearly as decorative as those built by the Jōmon, but they are also earthenware, made and fired in the same way as their predecessors. Jōmon livelihoods remained critical even in northern Kyushu and the Kinai, where gathering, hunting, and fishing—often using new tools such as barbed iron hooks and wooden octopus traps—were essential. The technologies for housing, salt making, lacquerware, and stone tools were basically the same. Clothing was still made of hemp or ramie, woven on the many spindles and looms now recovered from that era. The Yayoi also knew of silk.

The importation of metallurgical techniques also had a gradual but growing impact by 250 CE. Yayoi Japan reversed the standard historical sequence of the Bronze followed by the Iron Age: ferrous tools entered Japan first about 300 BCE, before technology shifted to bronze. These two metals had very differing meanings and uses: iron was for functional tools, such as the sickle, chisel, plane, and shoes for spades and hoes, while bronze was for ceremonial items.

Even though the Yayoi age is customarily considered the beginning of iron working in Japan, few sites yield ferrous artifacts until those of the last centuries of the period. One reason for the scarcity of iron use is that the Yayoi were unaware that most iron in Japan is to be found in granules at the bottoms of riverbeds. The iron used by Yayoi people was likely imported from Korea, where rich deposits were known by 300 BCE. Then, too, iron does not last long in Japan's acidic soil. Undoubtedly another reason for the lack of ferrous artifacts is that iron, being so rare and valuable, tended to be recycled as soon as a tool had worn out. Even though finds of iron have been relatively few, by 250 CE it provided sickle blades and metal coverings for spades and hoes, as well as chisels and point planes to support lathe-working.

Bronze is an alloy of copper and tin, combined in the proportion of ten parts to one, respectively. It could not be forged on an anvil like iron but was cast in molds. The technology came directly from Korea, with the first immigrants, early in the Yayoi period. Soon wandering specialists made a living casting bronze items.

The most prominent artifacts include huge bronze bells buried in large caches in the Kinai and western Honshu, and oversized double-edged swords, halberds, and spear blades found mainly in northern Kyushu. In effect, both the bells and weapons seem to have served as instruments symbolizing the communal cohesion of scattered villages ruled by separate elites. The existence of these two relatively distinct regions, therefore, may indicate areas inhabited and defended by different peoples. The bells were used for farming rituals and typically show scenes from everyday life, including fishing, hunting, and threshing grain. Archaeologists have discovered the out-sized bronze weapons purposely buried in large numbers in chiefly graves.

This ritual interment of large armaments seems to have signified a society that worshiped weapons. Indeed, Yayoi society was constantly at war, as historians have known from brief citations about the islands in Chinese annals. For example, of the five thousand skeletons surviving from the Jōmon era, practically none suggests a violent death, whereas among the one thousand skeletons preserved from Yayoi times, about one hundred betray signs of gruesome ends, including beheading and piercing with a dozen or more arrowheads. Iron and stone arrowheads are among the most common finds in Yayoi sites, and by the middle and late Yayoi, iron arrowheads were heavier and more deadly than ever.

Settlement location and structure also imply that Yayoi society was violent. Scattered throughout upland areas, highland settlements for just a few people probably served as lookouts for attackers. Some of these hamlets have pits containing ash, which suggests a system of smoke signals. On the flatlands, one and sometimes two moats with a V-shaped cross section encircle large settlements; as of 1998, about eighty moated villages have been found for the Yayoi period. At Ōtsuka in the Kanto, a trench measured twenty by one hundred thirty meters and was two meters deep. At Ōgidani near Kyoto, there were two ditches one kilometer in length; it is estimated that it would have taken one thousand ten-ton dump trucks to haul away the earth. Many moated settlements also used stakes, twisted branches, and earthen walls as barricades.

Why did the Yayoi resort to war so frequently? The reason is probably related to the importation of agriculture, which, even though it diffused slowly over the archipelago, soon produced classes of haves and have-nots. Villagers resorted to violence when their harvest was inadequate or when they wanted to take over a neighbor's surplus grain and the lands that had produced them. The discovery of similar moated and walled settlements around the world from an analogous period, when agriculture was just underway, also supports such a view.

The invention of war went along with famine to comprise new ways for agrarian peoples to die. Malnutrition had been a problem under forager regimes, of course, but with the advent of agriculture and the consequent population growth, many more people were dependent on a new subsistence system and liable to starve to death. Known as the "spring hungers," famine usually beset a family or village whose crop had failed or whose reserves of grain had been exhausted by the late winter. Along with the greater chance of extensive famine came war, which was really just theft organized on a village-wide scale. Every system of subsistence has its advantages and disadvantages.

Yoshinogari located in northern Kyushu is currently the most famous moated settlement from Yayoi times. It was a double-ditched, twenty-five-hectare village of about one thousand to fifteen hundred residents perched on the highest point of a low hill. In addition to the two moats with V-shaped cross sections, there was an earthen embankment encompassing fifteen thousand square meters. Watchtowers guarded the approaches. It was most densely populated during the last three centuries of the Yayoi age, and probably had one hundred pit dwellings at any one time. There were also storage pits and fifty granaries with raised floors. A forty-by-thirty-meter burial mound held in six chambers the remains of about twenty members of the village elite, evidenced by the headdress, daggers, and the red chemical vermillion found there. Another cemetery, for commoners, contained almost 2,500 burial jars, cists, coffins, and pits. Residents at Yoshinogari also possessed beads, silk and hemp cloth, stone, bone, and iron tools, and molds for bronze casting. The inhabitants of Yoshinogari traded with places as distant as the Ryukyus.

Yoshinogari was one station in the trade networks criss-crossing the islands. Stone tools, salt, cloth, iron, beads, and even rice were popular items for exchange. Itinerant bronze makers probably followed trade routes fanning out from a central production location, such as Yoshinogari, to neighboring villages. Finally, all the iron, copper, and tin were imported from the continent. This finding suggests that residents of the archipelago made frequent trips in their dug-out craft.

A good deal is known about Yayoi social arrangements. Based upon the size of dwellings, the typical Yayoi family was nuclear, with five to ten members. At least in western Japan, kinship was probably bilateral. In other words, families could trace descent through either the father's or mother's line. Prospective mates moved in with the chosen man or woman, often from another village, based upon the availability of resources, especially land. This highly flexible kinship form would remain the rule throughout much of the archipelago for hundreds of years. Yayoi women undoubtedly had a significant, perhaps even equal, role in work, raising the family, and managing lands.

Like their Jōmon counterparts, Yayoi people had a rich ceremonial life. For instance, Yayoi society reveals abundant signs of age consciousness and differentiation within villages. According to custom, the deceased were interred first when they died and later their bones were unearthed and reburied when every member of their generation had passed on. We know that the Yayoi practiced divination by heating animal bones and making judgments based on the resulting cracks. Shamanism was prevalent, as suggested by an elderly female skeleton found buried with a wooden bird, ready to fly up to heaven for inspiration. The Yayoi buried their dead in segregated cemeteries and in many forms, using wooden or stone coffins, simple earthen pits, or two large earthenware jars placed end-to-end. Chinese written sources state that a mourning period was observed.

By the end of the Yayoi era, the growth of agriculture had given birth to a small ruling class, which, like the twenty individuals at Yoshinogari, were distinguished by separate interment in mounds with a few grave goods, such as jade beads, a single sword, or part of a mirror. Moreover, members of the Yayoi elite displayed their lofty status by slicing seashells to form bracelets and armbands worn beginning in childhood. These ornaments restricted bicep growth, signifying those who did not do manual labor. Compared to later epochs, Yayoi chiefains and chieftainesses were few and relatively poor, but the establishment of a more complex social structure represented the wave of the future.

Society and Economy during the Tomb Era, 250–600 CE

The third and final stage that laid the building blocks of early Japan occurred during the Tomb age, which derives its name from the approximately ten thousand tumuli—some of them gigantic—that were constructed during these years. These burial mounds are the most outstanding feature of the period and indicate a dramatic increase in the economic and demographic resources available to society. A growing elite consumed a larger portion of the more plentiful surplus than ever before and new industries were introduced from Korea especially for the benefit of the ruling class.

Economic growth continued nearly unabated during these centuries. Demographic increase was sizable, and by 600 CE five million or more persons dwelt in the islands, doubling or trebling the number of residents at the end of the Yayoi era. What is more, in-migration from East Asia in general, and the Korean peninsula in particular, helped fuel the expansion. One measure of the increase in population is the amount of labor needed to construct the tombs and their moats, totaling about four million worker-days for a large tumulus.

The continued spread of Yayoi agrarian and metallurgic techniques certainly propelled the economy forward. More widespread use of iron tools, methods of transplanting, green manure, and dry crops were all part of the story. In addition, new ideas and technologies imported through Korea were responsible for the expansion. Most of the improved materials and tools introduced by immigrants from the peninsula embraced all social classes, but some were especially important for two new groups: locally powerful notables and members of a courtly elite.

The first and most fundamental technology was in better iron-working methods, dependent on an ever-growing amount of iron ore imported from southern Korea. Even during the late Yayoi era, iron was a relatively rare commodity in the islands. Within a century, however, giant tombs reveal enormous caches of iron weapons and woodworking and farming tools. At Ariyama Tomb near Osaka, for instance, archaeologists have uncovered 85 swords, 8 pike points, 1,542 arrowheads, 134 hand ax blades, 201 sickles, 49 U-shaped shovel or spade fittings, and 90 chisels, all dated to the mid-fifth century. The source for all this iron had to be continental, and most likely Korean, because residents of the islands did not discover their meager deposits of iron sand and ore until after 500. Even the Chinese noted that southern Korea produced iron and that the people living there and in the western archipelago traded for it.

Not only did iron ore from the peninsula find its way into Japan, but smithies also became more efficient and productive. Archaeologists have found large pliers, scissors, mallets, chisels, and anvils, all identical to those used on the peninsula. In Japan and Korea small furnaces called bloomeries were used to heat the ore to about 1,200° C and separate out the slag. After cooling, blacksmiths hammered and forged iron implements and weapons on an anvil. Iron was so valuable that inhabitants of the archipelago and the peninsula used iron ingots as cash, each measuring about ten to fifty centimeters in length and often weighing several hundred grams.

The improved ferrous industry had many spin-offs. Tool making showed marked improvement, with new and better chisels, saws, awls, and blades for sickles and hand axes. For the first time, inhabitants of the islands could produce finely detailed luxury goods and large wooden structures such as houses or boats with boards attached to the sides to enhance their seaworthiness. Even more significant was the importation from southern Korea of U-shaped edges for shovels and hoes. These new thicker and stronger blades could bite more deeply into the earth and facilitated the opening of more land to cultivation.

Building dams and irrigation ponds also became easier, which provided a steadier supply of water for lands located on the flat stretches of Japan's many small basins. For example, at Furuichi in Osaka, archaeologists have uncovered a large canal, about nine meters wide, five meters deep, and ten kilometers long, probably dating to the fifth century. The moats surrounding the fourth-century tombs also suggest the advent of better irrigation methods. Many of the engineers and workers building these new ditches, dams, and ponds were Korean immigrants.

These two refinements in agrarian technology—sturdier shovels and spades and improved ditch- and pond-digging methods—helped continue the expansive trend in land under cultivation throughout the Tomb era. In eastern Honshu, farmers began to convert the flatlands around the Tone River (Hitachi) into productive fields. In western Honshu, they opened more paddies in Kibi (Bizen); an early eighth-century source lists sixteen ponds built during this era in Izumo. By the end of the Tomb era, peasants had established an agrarian base that was to last for the next several centuries.

As they produced more grain, Tomb-era farmers also learned to build bigger raised-floor storehouses laid out according to advanced surveying techniques. Following a north-south orientation and ranging in floor space from sixty to ninety square meters, warehouses were between three and ten times larger than those of Yayoi times. These new buildings not only contained grain, but also cloth, salt, and armaments.[4]

The pit dwelling was still the basic housing unit, although moated settlements disappeared at the end of the Yayoi period. There was, however, an improvement in cooking and heating for pit dwellings located in western Japan: the three-legged boiler. Made of clay or terra cotta, it was cylindrical with a semicircular hole cut out on one side to permit the user to tend the fire. The cook placed dishes on top of the open upper end of the cylinder, directly above the flames. Residents cut a hole out of the wall against which the boiler was placed to let smoke exit. The boiler represented an advance over Yayoi campfires because they contained heat more effectively and safely, produced less smoke, and were easier to cook with. The boiler would remain the basic heating and cooking implement in western Japan for centuries.

A new type of hand-formed earthenware also appeared at this time. Called Haji ware, it was reddish to pale orange, and was used for storing, boiling, steaming, and serving food. Specialists from the Haji family supervised local residents who molded the jars, bowls, vats, and pedestals in various areas in the Kinai. At first used exclusively by the elite, Haji ware eventually served all classes.

Tomb-era villages were quite different from their Yayoi predecessors. Settlements came in various sizes, dependent upon such factors as the topography and the availability of cultivated land. People lived dispersed over the landscape, with wasteland and fields intermingled with dwellings. Villages might range from ten to sixty or more pit dwellings, along with several storehouses, and residences might be grouped in units of two or three, suggesting that they contained extended families. In larger settlements, archaeologists have uncovered the remains of sizable wooden structures, sometimes surrounded by a moat or stone wall. The floors in these buildings were laid at surface level, occasionally using boards. These separate homesteads were undoubtedly the property of a powerful local family dominating the village.

Tomb-age families seem to have continued the patterns of the Yayoi period. Most families were nuclear and kinship was bilateral. Women played an especially

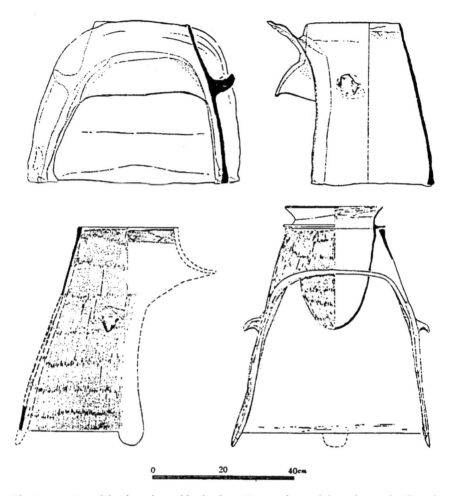

The importation of the three-legged boiler from Korea enhanced the safety and utility of food preparation beginning about 500 CE. Source: Hayashi Hiromichi, "Kamado shutsu-gen ni kansuru ni san mondai," *Tsuchi to mizu no kōkogaku* (Jōyū City: Kōyū kai, 1973), p. 105.

prominent role in work and politics. When archaeologists tabulated the sex of tomb occupants, about half were female, which suggests the political power and economic resources commanded by women. They also controlled transportation and access to iron and fought in Tomb-age armies in numbers approximately equal to men. Women supervised agricultural work and may even have been the prime sake brewers in the islands.[5]

A final aspect of life shared by people of all classes and both sexes was spiritual (often mistakenly called Shinto). Both the tombs and mythology suggest that there was belief in an afterlife, either dark and polluting or maritime and subliminal. Women apparently had special powers to communicate with the realm beyond, and mountains comprised sacred routes to the other world. Most people held animistic beliefs that gods and goddesses inhabited nature. Believers sought to mollify nature—its floods, droughts, or the falling of spirit-possessing trees—through entreaties and petitions. Finally, beliefs were profoundly this-worldly and focused on pragmatic concerns such as the prevention of disease and death, prayers for rain to water the crops, or taboos surrounding the safe delivery of children. Even with the introduction of Buddhism in the mid-sixth century, people overwhelmingly desired practical benefits in this lifetime.

While the entire Tomb-age populace shared many of the new technologies, living arrangements, familial and kinship patterns, and beliefs about the spirit world, some new imports carried to Japan by Korean immigrants remained exclusively in the hands of local and courtly elites. One was a new and improved variety of ceramics called Sue ware. Unlike previous earthenware pots, this grayish stoneware was wheel-thrown and fired at a higher temperature in a closed kiln resembling a tunnel running up the side of a hill. Instead of oxidizing the minerals in the clay, these ceramics were chemically reduced by cooking with moist foliage near the end of baking. Moreover, Sue stoneware was nonporous and opaque. By the sixth century, the production of stoneware was an important industry for the elite of the islands, particularly in western and central Japan.

The flourishing iron industry affected warfare, beginning in the fifth century. New weapons included better spear and pike points, the ring-pommeled sword, and iron armor in the shape of a cuirass or sheets of thin plates attached with leather thongs. Undoubtedly the most terrifying new weapon was the horse, imported into the archipelago from Korea during the mid-fifth century. From the beginning, the horse did not serve to pull a plow, but was the near-exclusive possession of local notables and certain court families who had both the time and resources to afford the beasts and learn to ride and fight from them. Japanese soldiers rode these small mounts, using iron stirrups, bits, and decorations to control and display their animals.

In addition to these new sources of elite power, other technologies arrived from Korea especially for the benefit of rulers. They included better methods of shaping and fitting large stones, first imported into northern Kyushu in the fifth century. The improved techniques made tomb building so much easier and less expensive that local notables adopted the practice, leading to an explosion in the number of these smaller side-entrance tombs, beginning in the 500s. Another accoutrement for the fifth- and sixth-century elite was gold jewelry—earrings, crowns, caps, shoes, and belt buckles—requiring expertise in gilding and inlaying.

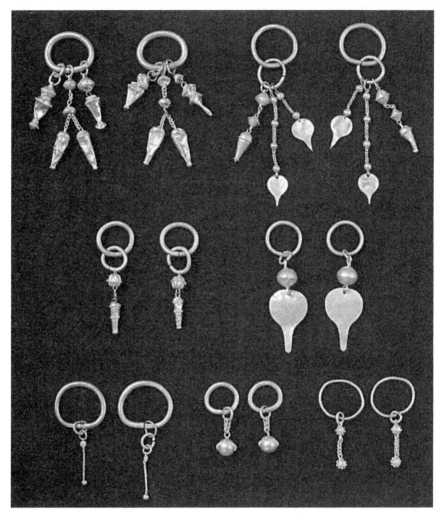

Golden earrings like the ones seen above functioned as markers of prestige and rank among the aristocracy. Gyeongsang National University Museum. *Source: Kaya—Ancient Kingdoms of Korea* (Asahi shinbun, 1992), p. 51.

The final item was silk, probably woven by families of Korean descent. The wearing of silk by the elite increased markedly after 500.

By 600, a relatively complex society and economy had taken root in Japan: the foraging livelihoods of the Jōmon epoch, the new agrarian regimes and metallurgical skills of the Yayoi period, and the diverse new technologies and industries of the Tomb era all combined. Groups specializing in each of these areas traded among themselves as well as with their neighbors on the Asian continent. The class structure ranged from chieftains able to command hundreds of workers to poor foragers and peasants with just a few fields farmed in slash-and-burn style. The family was an ill-defined entity, sometimes extended, usually nuclear. Kinship was bilateral. As in the earlier era, women ran businesses, oversaw rice farming, and served as warriors and leaders. The evolution of a political consciousness and structure inevitably accompanied the development of such a complex social structure.

The Emergence of the Yamato State

Between 238 and 265 CE, residents of the western archipelago and the Chinese court exchanged gifts and ambassadors at least four times, resulting in the first detailed written description of the people living in Japan, the "Account of the Wa." The Chinese visited the Wa, a derisive term meaning "dwarf people," because they were searching for prospective allies in their own politically divided empire. In their report, the Chinese envoys described the land, society, and economy of the Wa in striking detail. Politically, they portrayed Japan as a land of "countries" ruled by "kings," occasionally united in confederations.[6] The only known large political organization was named Yamatai, ruled by a mature single woman called Himiko.

Although the precise location and size of Yamatai remain controversial, the picture the "Account of the Wa" gives of political organization in Japan at the end of the Yayoi age combines with the archaeological record to present a fairly clear picture. The standard political unit centered on a large moated settlement, like Yoshinogari, with smaller satellite villages attached. Taken together, these "countries" averaged about 100 to 150 square kilometers.[7] The elite of Yoshinogari led their region and heads of satellite villages probably came to pay their respects. This political unit also comprised a trade sphere in bronze ceremonial items and other goods.

By the last three centuries of the Yayoi phase, such "countries" could be found all over the archipelago, particularly in the population center of Japan reaching from northern Kyushu to the Kinai. These units fought, exchanged commodities, and distributed among themselves ceremonial goods such as Chinese mirrors, glass beads, and other signs of legitimacy. According to the Chinese envoys who purportedly visited Yamatai, these units were linked together in a confederation of as many as thirty "countries."[8]

The "Account of the Wa" gives other clues about political life. Inferiors squatted to convey respect to superiors, a clear sign of the development of class distinctions. Moreover, officials oversaw trade and enforced law and order. Throughout the late second century CE, however, conflict raged among the petty village-states of Wa.

Then Himiko appeared and by occupying herself with magic and sorcery bewitched the populace, returning the land of Wa to peace. She kept a thousand female attendants, but her brother was virtually the only person to see her and acted as medium of communication. Himiko resided in a palace protected by watchtowers and armed guards. Toward the end of her reign, Yamatai was at war, and upon Himiko's death, "a great mound was raised, more than a hundred paces in diameter."[9] A man tried to replace the queen, but disorder prevailed until a thirteen-year-old girl related to Himiko became the new chieftainess.

This all-too-brief account of politics in the land of Wa leaves several questions unanswered. The oldest debate surrounds the location of Yamatai: was it confined to northern Kyushu, or did the confederation stretch from the Kinai down the Inland Sea to the southwestern island? Various arguments have been advanced supporting one position or the other, and, although there is a growing consensus in favor of the larger Kinai confederation, no one can be sure. What is clear about the Wa's political development as of 250 CE is that an ethnic group (the Wa) populated western Japan, and possibly even resided in southern Korea. Local power was predominant, and the best that Himiko or any other leader could manage was to bind the myriad "countries" of the Wa into a rather ephemeral confederation. Finally, leaders ruled primarily through "magic and sorcery" and diplomacy with Chinese emperors.[10] Even at the end of the Yayoi age, the ruling elite was tiny and not very powerful.

The "Account of the Wa" states that Himiko was buried in a large mound, and that statement is one reason that archaeologists date the beginning of the Tomb epoch at 250 CE. Unfortunately, Chinese sources do not report on the land of the Wa for the next one hundred seventy years, and three conflicting types of evidence make the time from 250 until 350 into "the century of mystery." First, there are materials compiled by the Japanese court in the early eighth century, *The Record of Ancient Matters* and *The Chronicles of Japan*. Because the myths and genealogies they were based on were not written down until at least the sixth century, the story they tell of the origins of what would later be called the Japanese imperial line is highly suspect. The presumed "first emperor" Jinmu supposedly ascended the throne in 660 BCE, descended from the sun goddess. The stories of his conquests have a ring of authenticity, but the next eight "emperors" have all been proven to be fictitious. More conquerors followed, with the story of Empress and Regent Jingū especially interesting. She supposedly ordered a fleet to Korea and forced the peoples there to submit to her rule. At the time of her embarkation, she was pregnant, but postponed the birth of her royal son by blocking her birth canal with stones until she had finished her war.

The second source is the giant tombs themselves, especially the one hundred twenty or so shaped like giant keyholes. The round end of the tomb contains the burial chamber, and the rectangular area is believed to have been the ritual space where the next leader was consecrated. Because the Imperial Household Agency designated them in the nineteenth century as containing the remains of the ancestors of the current occupants of the Japanese throne, however, almost none has been excavated. Yet their size alone is testimony to the growth of a larger and much more powerful elite. For example, the tomb attributed to Empress Jingū measures two hundred seventy-five meters in length. Those few that have been excavated held large quantities of iron implements and weapons and other grave goods, showing the wealth of their occupants. Most of the keyhole-shaped tombs are found in the Kinai, especially near the modern cities of Nara and Osaka, but they also exist in many other regions of Japan. Some believe that differences in the relative size of the mounds and in the distribution of grave goods such as bronze mirrors indicate the existence of a status hierarchy among regional leaders. It is just as easy, however, to imagine several loose confederations centering on Kibi, Yamato, Izumo, and northern Kyushu.

The third source consists of Korean records, some included in the eighth-century sources, in combination with the archaeological record of South Korea and Japan. This evidence has led some to propose that nomadic Central Asian horse riders galloped down the peninsula and went on to the islands, founding kingdoms as they went. Although there is no positive evidence for an invasion, there can be little doubt that the peoples of Korea and Japan were closely bound together through immigration, trade, diplomacy, and war.

When we reach the late fourth century, the political situation in East Asia is one of disunity: China into Northern and Southern Dynasties, Korea into four kingdoms called Koguryŏ, Paekche, Silla, and Kaya, and Japan into innumerable "countries."

War prevailed in China and Korea, undoubtedly serving as a stimulus for residents to move to the archipelago with their advanced technologies. In Korea, at first the northern state of Koguryŏ was the strongest and applied pressure to Paekche and Silla, especially between 391 and 407. Wa troops intervened to preserve allies Paekche and Kaya, but were humiliated.

The Wa states participating in that war had changed considerably from Yayoi times. Chinese sources tell of five monarchs reigning between about 390 and 480, all of them associated with mammoth keyhole tombs as large as four hundred by six hundred meters. This early kingship was militaristic, with horse trappings, iron weapons, and armor as grave goods. These "kings" claimed to rule "countries" ranging from eastern Honshu to southern Korea, but no one knows how authentic their claims were.[11] In fact, what would later be known as the Yamato

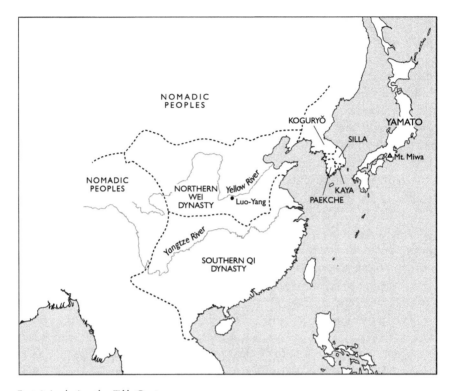

East Asia during the Fifth Century

monarchy probably did not come into being until the reign of Yūryaku in the late fifth century.

These kings had few firm institutions of rule, and the death of one ruler usually led to an interregnum during which the corpse of the preceding king was displayed while contenders for the throne jockeyed for power behind the scenes. The five kings did, however, make some lasting contributions to the political structure. They developed the tradition of recognizing one family as the marital line for the monarchy. Families named Wani or Katsuragi provided consorts and heirs and wielded considerable power. These kings also began to develop a nobility to advise and serve them. Early on, surnames (*uji*) revealed the function of each family, such as Kashiwade for cooks, Nakatomi for priests, and Mononobe for the military, but as the court grew, titles (*kabane*) were necessary to distinguish wellborn nobles from their inferiors. Finally, the five kings borrowed from Paekche the idea of designating certain groups of specialists to provision the king and his court with cloth, weapons, fish, grain, and labor. These units (*be*) were scattered over the islands, mostly in western Honshu, and belonged to royal and aristocratic families as their own property. They did not constitute a systematic way to gather tribute items, however. In some cases, as residents of the peninsula migrated to Japan with their new skills, they were simply named haphazardly as a provision group. Scribes were one such immigrant group, introducing writing to Japan by the late fourth century.

Yūryaku, the last of the five kings, probably ruled near the sacred Mount Miwa in Yamato in the late fifth century, and his death was followed by conflict. In the early sixth century, a satisfactory royal candidate was brought in from the outside, but foreign and domestic crises confronted the new king and his descendants. In Korea, an increasingly powerful and hostile Silla gradually gobbled up the independent kingdom of Kaya, haughtily claimed by the Yamato court as one of its "countries." Paekche, Yamato ally and source of so many skilled immigrants, was also losing territory quickly. The new kings tried to send military aid, but to little avail.

At home, a northern Kyushu chieftain named Iwai rebelled in the 520s. While the revolt was eventually suppressed, it emphasized the need for a stronger military and more effective institutions of control. The new dynasty of the sixth century developed various ways to strengthen its grip in response to the revolt. The king designated the conquered rebel's territory to be royal demesne, or land under the complete and direct control of the Yamato sovereign. Soon there were patches of such territory stretching from northern Kyushu to the Kanto. The Yamato kings also extended titles to a growing number of local notables, about one hundred twenty by 600. These regional magnates formed a widespread confederation under the monarch, providing material support and, more important, the bulk of fighters for the king.

The sixth century also witnessed the rise of a new marital line for the king. The Soga were probably of Korean ancestry and were devotees of a new religion introduced to the court from Paekche—Buddhism. Members of the court, tied to the old animistic beliefs, were hostile to Buddhism and tried to destroy both the Soga and the symbols of their religion. In 587, war broke out between the Soga and Nakatomi priests and their allies, but the Soga won and Buddhism began to receive government support in return for ceremonial bolstering of the regime. Members of the service nobility also established family temples. By the end of the sixth century, the Soga were firmly in control of the Yamato court, placing a female relative (Suiko) on the throne and dominating decision making through powerful kinsmen Soga no Umako and Prince Umayado, later to be known as Shōtoku Taishi.

The Soga continued to define the new government and its symbolic basis. They adopted Korean-style cap ranks, given not to groups but to individuals, to define the status of members of the service nobility more precisely. Different colors of headgear distinguished the various ranks. The Soga also served as keepers of written records and the royal regalia providing legitimacy to the Yamato state. In essence, these symbols—a sword, mirror, and possibly beads—helped the Soga and their monarch Suiko lay claim to divine origins through the sun goddess and the fictitious Jinmu. This source of legitimacy was to serve Japan's sovereigns well, even into the twentieth century.

Japan's Society and Economy in 600

By 600, the social and economic building blocks of Japan were in place. The population was dense and growing, and the area of land under cultivation was expanding. Industries such as salt making, ceramics, lacquerware, metallurgy, stone carving and fitting, weapon and tool making, and woodworking were all established. The inhabitants of the islands practiced an impressive variety of occupations, including several types of rice agriculture, unirrigated cropping, fishing, trading, hunting, and gathering. Important artifacts of daily life, such as the pit dwelling, hemp and silk clothing, storage warehouses, and a new boiler were widely used.

Socially, the crucial change was the dramatic expansion of the population from the hundreds of individuals of the paleolithic epoch to five million or more by 600. The growth in population stimulated the elaboration of a more complex class system, until by 600 there were from top to bottom a tiny courtly elite, local notables, commoners, and slaves taken as war captives or debtors. Villages came in many sizes, were spread all over the landscape, and showed signs of individual distinctions based on age and place of origin. Families, too, seem to have been both large and small, but kinship was bilateral, at least in western Japan. Women worked alongside men, brewing sake, cultivating rice, and enjoying a high status socially and politically. Beliefs aimed at pragmatic benefit, peasants seeking rain for their crops and nobles petitioning for relief from disease and death. Politically, confederation with the monarch as *primus inter pares* would become the typical structure. Altogether, these social and economic underpinnings predominated for at least seven hundred years, and in some cases, through to 1600.

2 An End to Growth, 600–800

The Creation of a New Political Structure

A Looming East Asian Crisis

In 589, Yang Jian, a general of mixed Chinese and nomadic blood, reunited the Chinese empire and the diplomatic situation in East Asia changed overnight. For the last 350 years, China had been divided between nomadic dynasties in the northern China plain and Han Chinese kingdoms based in the south. It mattered that Yang, who named his new dynasty the Sui (589–618), was from northern China because, during the centuries of disunity and strife, his land had suffered continuous upheaval from nomadic incursions, bouts with lethal epidemics, and refugees fleeing to the south seeking a better life.

For these reasons, Yang adopted an aggressive foreign policy designed to pacify the borders and keep China's enemies at bay. In the south, the Sui reestablished control over Viet Nam; to the west, they conquered a mixed nomadic-Tibetan state; to the north, they forced troublesome Turkish peoples to acknowledge their suzerainty. Unfortunately for the Yang clan, Jian's son carried these aggressive policies too far when he tried repeatedly to conquer the stubborn northern Korean state of Koguryŏ in the early seventh century. Giant Chinese armies were so badly mauled that the empire disintegrated and the emperor was assassinated.

There followed a short struggle for power, but once again a general of mixed Chinese and nomadic ethnicity from northern China, Li Shi-min (later the second Emperor Taizong), won; he founded the Tang dynasty (618–907). In many respects, Li followed the policies of the preceding Sui dynasty, including its aggressive, expansionist foreign policy. Eventually, the Tang ruled an immense territory ranging from southern Siberia to Southeast Asia and from the Pacific Ocean to northern India.

News of Chinese reunification and expansionist foreign policy reached the ears of the leaders of the Korean and Yamato monarchies and caused consternation in those squabbling kingdoms. Battles among Koguryŏ, Silla, and Paekche

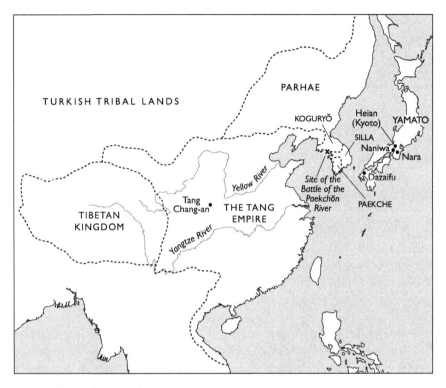

East Asia during the Seventh Century

had continued during the late sixth and early seventh centuries, with the Yamato court frequently intervening on the side of Paekche and against Silla. What if the Tang decided to invade Korea, too? To forestall attacks previously, the Korean and Japanese states had sent missions to the Sui capital, but, while the Korean states acknowledged Chinese suzerainty, the Yamato ambassadors of 607–608 accepted no titles and insulted the Sui court by claiming equality as "the land where the sun rises."[1]

In 631, Taizong decided to resume the Sui policy of attacking the warlike state of Koguryŏ by sending an expedition to gather the bones of Chinese troops who had perished during earlier campaigns. Tang soldiers also pillaged Koguryŏ villages, throwing that kingdom into an uproar. The presence of massive Chinese armies on Koguryŏ soil also profoundly affected the political outlook in Paekche, Silla, and Yamato. When the Tang assaulted Koguryŏ again in 641, the elites in Paekche, Koguryŏ, Yamato, and Silla panicked. Between 641 and 647, militaristic, centralizing coups rocked each kingdom, as conspirators hoped to assemble the resources and troops necessary to fend off the coming Tang invasion.

In Japan, what is known as the Taika Reform took place in 645, concentrating leadership in the hands of a coterie of disenchanted royals (Princes Naka and Karu) and nobles (Nakatomi, later Fujiwara, no Kamatari). After killing off the Soga before the eyes of a startled monarch during a banquet, the rebels announced their intentions to take control of all the land and human resources of the islands, using institutions modeled after successful Chinese precedents. In other words, the best way to repel the Chinese was to copy their advanced political system and use it against them. Members of the cabal moved immediately to secure all weapons and arsenals, especially in the Kanto, home to the majority of mounted fighters. For the next fifteen years, the leaders of the Taika palace revolution struggled to play local leaders off against each other so as to concentrate power in their own hands.

The conflict in Korea, however, kept forcing its attention on the Taika leaders. After all, Paekche was a Yamato ally and a source of invaluable materials, ideas, and immigrants. Between 621 and 650, Yamato's long-time enemy, Silla, sent envoys to the Tang court, and eventually the two cemented an alliance. Tang wanted the accord because its direct assaults on Koguryŏ were proving no more effective than those of the Sui, and the court needed an ally located at Koguryŏ's rear. Finally, Tang and Silla decided that the best way to destroy Koguryŏ was to first conquer Paekche, a feat accomplished in 660 with an army of more than one hundred thousand. Most of the Paekche royal house fell into the hands of the alliance, but some escaped to Japan.

Beginning in 661, the Yamato court sent flotillas of small vessels to join Paekche guerillas fighting to revive their fortunes. By 663, more than twenty-five thousand Yamato troops were on erstwhile Paekche soil. At this time, a Yamato embassy was visiting the Tang court, but Taizong decreed that he had "determined . . . to take administrative measures in regard to the lands east of the sea, and you, visitors from Wa, may not return."[2] The envoys were locked in prison for months to prevent them from giving away Taizong's plans. Later that year, the Tang navy and Silla army crushed the Yamato troops and Paekche partisans at the Battle of the Paekch'ŏn River. It was one of the most decisive engagements in Japanese history.

Prince Naka and his supporters were now faced with a true emergency. Naka ascended the throne as the monarch Tenji and ordered beacons and Korean-style mountain fortifications erected from northern Kyushu, up the Inland Sea, to the Kinai. He withdrew his court to Ōtsu, guarded by mountains and safer from the looming threat. Meanwhile, the Tang-Silla alliance advanced from victory to victory, smashing Koguryŏ in 668. It is amazing that, although Tenji's centralizing policies had met resistance from the beginning and he was now branded as a loser for the defeat in Korea, he managed to reform the bureaucracy and attempted to implement a census in 670.

When Tenji died in 671, he was unpopular with most local notables because they had lost men in Korea. He pressed his son Prince Ōtomo to succeed him, but Tenji's brother, Prince Ōama, secluded in the Yoshino Mountains to the south, had other ideas. In a brief civil war, Ōama routed his nephew and took the title of Tenmu, "the Heavenly Warrior Emperor" (*tennō*). Born in 631, Tenmu had witnessed the Taika coup as a boy and the Battle of the Paekch'ŏn River as a youth. He knew that to resist an invasion he had to have a strong, stable government capable of calling on the material and human resources of the entire archipelago. If Tenmu needed any further persuasion, Silla, which had implemented modified Chinese institutions, unified the peninsula, and then terminated its alliance with the Tang and chased the Chinese armies out of Korea. Fear of invasion consumed the Japanese court for several decades, and relations with Silla (668–935) were hostile for most of the 700s.

A New Political Structure

Holding unprecedented power as the charismatic victor in a civil war, Tenmu set about centralizing and militarizing his government. He established a new system based on Chinese guidelines for ranking, appointing, promoting, and dismissing members of the old service nobility. Tenmu also abolished and then reorganized the independent economic bases (*be*) of the service nobility so that government officials intervened between wellborn aristocrats and the land and people from which they collected labor and materials. He prevailed over intransigent local notables by playing them against each other and subdividing their jurisdictions with more loyal lieutenants. In 600, there had been one hundred twenty members of a Yamato confederacy; by 700 there were five hundred fifty ranked local officials serving the court. Militarily, Tenmu shipped soldiers to northern Kyushu to resist any invasion.

The "Heavenly Warrior" sovereign died in 686, but his consort Jitō and grandson Monmu helped finish what Tenmu had started. Commencing in 690 under Jitō (r. 686–697), the court implemented its first set of civil statutes written in Chinese. She then carried out a comprehensive registration of the population to draft soldiers and collect revenues. To symbolize the new polity, Jitō finished Japan's first Chinese-style capital built at Fujiwara, due south of Nara (694–710).

Monmu (r. 697–707) built upon this legacy. He ordered the compilation of the court's first comprehensive set of penal and civil statutes, the Taihō Code of 701, which defined in elegant Chinese the structure, functions, and rituals of the new state. By 710, the court had begun to execute Monmu's plans for a new capital at Nara. Together, the Taihō Code and Nara were the crowning achievements of the new Chinese-style polity.

At the apex of the new government was the Heavenly Sovereign, a sage-king legitimized by the ruler's supposed divine ancestry and Daoist and other theories adopted from China. He was the main actor in a "theater state," implementing courtly rituals for all occasions. A large court bureaucracy numbering seven to ten thousand supported the Heavenly Sovereign, with the Taihō Code stipulating the terms of official employment. The elite of the bureaucracy held the First through the Fifth Court ranks and formed the Council of State advising the sovereign. Almost all officials came to their rank and post through their bloodlines, not by examination.

There were two tiers of local administration: provincial government and district magistracy. Governors oversaw about sixty provinces and were appointed from among the capital aristocracy for four-year terms. While their powers were broad in the abstract, the real kingpins in the local regions were the district magistrates, born and raised in the territory they administered. To co-opt former notables into serving the capital elite, the court granted each several perquisites, such as lifetime tenure, a large parcel of land, and the ability to pass their positions down to an heir. Moreover, their relatives held the chief religious and military posts in each district. In essence, the new polity ratified an alliance between capital aristocrats and local magnates. Without the cooperation of these district magistrates, administration of the countryside was nearly impossible.

To finance the government, the authors of the Taihō Code modified three interrelated Chinese institutions. Officials registered the populace at a fixed residence every six years in a census, granted a minimal area of rice paddies to sustain them for life, and then extracted poll taxes from adult males. The adoption of these three linked institutions was no accident but was drawn from the experiences of the dynasties reigning in north China, where war, disease, and out-migration had made it difficult to locate and tax peasants and other producers. Japanese rulers also struggled to pin down a mobile and often uncooperative populace, and so the new institutions made perfect sense.

This system functioned relatively well until the early ninth century. Between 702, when the Taihō Code was implemented, and 729, strong sovereigns and their relatives were in control of the court. The symbol of the new Chinese-style state was the system of dual capitals located at Nara and the old port of Naniwa. The Tenpyō era (729–749) witnessed the ascendancy of Heavenly Sovereign Shōmu and his Fujiwara consort Kōmyō; their reign was rocked by a severe epidemic and rebellion in Kyushu. Following these disasters, the court desperately tried to encourage agriculture, tightened restraints on migration, and reformed provincial finances. At the same time, they poured even more tax revenues into Buddhist projects such as the grand temple Tōdaiji, petitioning the Buddha to protect their realm. Between 749 and 769, factionalism and strife wracked the court, as it spent

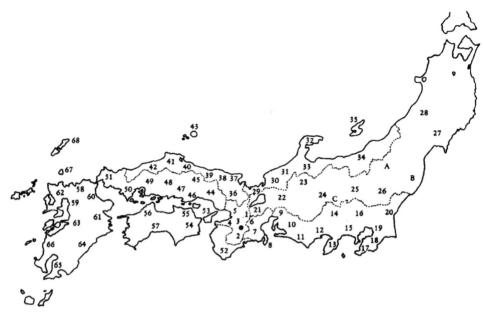

The Provinces of Eighth-Century Japan: *Source:* William Wayne Farris, *Population, Disease, and Land in Early Japan, 645-900,* Harvard Yenching Institute Monograph Series, 24 (Cambridge, Mass.: Harvard University, Council on East Asian Studies, 1985), pp. xvii–xix. Copyright 1985 by the President and Fellows of Harvard College.

KEY:

Kinai:
1. Yamashiro
2. Yamato
3. Kawachi
4. Izumi
5. Settsu

Tōkaidō:
6. Iga
7. Ise
8. Shima
9. Owari
10. Mikawa
11. Tōtōmi
12. Suruga
13. Izu
14. Kai
15. Sagami
16. Musashi
17. Awa
18. Kazusa
19. Shimōsa
20. Hitachi

Tōsandō:
21. Ōmi
22. Mino
23. Hida
24. Shinano
25. Kōzuke
26. Shimotsuke
27. Mutsu
28. Dewa

Hokurikudō:
29. Wakasa
30. Echizen
31. Kaga
32. Noto
33. Etchū
34. Echigo
35. Sado

San'indō:
36. Tanba
37. Tango
38. Tajima
39. Inaba
40. Hōki
41. Izumo
42. Iwami
43. Oki

San'yōdō
44. Harima
45. Mimasaka
46. Bizen
47. Bitchū
48. Bingo
49. Aki
50. Suō
51. Nagato

Nankaidō:
52. Kii
53. Awaji
54. Awa
55. Sanuki
56. Iyo
57. Tosa

Saikaidō:
58. Chikuzen
59. Chikugo
60. Buzen
61. Bungo
62. Hizen
63. Higo
64. Hyūga
65. Ōsumi
66. Satsuma

Islands:
67. Iki
68. Tsushima

A. Iwashiro
B. Iwaki
C. Suwa

more and more resources on Buddhist and other projects. From 770 until 805, re-form and retrenchment were the order of the day. The Heavenly Sovereign Kanmu (r. 782–805) was so ambitious that he tried to construct two new capitals, first Nagaoka and then Heian, and launched mammoth expeditions against the residents (*emishi*) of northern Honshu. Mostly as a result of Kanmu's policies, in 805 the central government in effect declared bankruptcy. The days of untrammeled growth were over.

Population and Economy

Population

Between 600 and about 730, Japan's population continued to expand, reaching a high of about 6.4 million. Most people lived in western Japan, concentrated from northern Kyushu along the Inland Sea to the particularly densely settled Kinai. Central and eastern Honshu was more sparsely populated, and for most of this period the northern half of Honshu was beyond court control. At 6.4 million, the Japanese archipelago joined its Asian neighbors China and India as one of most populous areas in the world, easily supporting more people than any medieval European state.

It would be a mistake to think of the archipelago's inhabitants as belonging to a homogeneous ethnic group. Even in western and central Japan, there was undoubtedly considerable variation, although most people probably derived their ancestry from the Wa or Yamato peoples. At least a third were descendants of Korean immigrants. In southern Kyushu, non-Yamato peoples known as the Hayato and Kumaso resided; they may have been remnants of the old Jōmon stock or of Southeast Asian ancestry. In northeastern Japan and Hokkaido, another non-Yamato group, the *emishi,* predominated, giving the Nara court all it could handle in wars fought between 774 and 812. The *emishi* may have been the ancestors of the modern Ainu; skeletons unearthed from Hokkaido for this period are more like the Ainu than the Yamato. The *emishi* were excellent equestrians, and many lived by the old Jōmon livelihoods of fishing, gathering, and hunting as well as agriculture, but they also knew of iron and stoneware.

Eighth-century Japan was still an overwhelmingly rural place. There were three major urban centers in the 700s: Nara, its port/co-capital Naniwa, and Dazaifu in northern Kyushu. Nara was home to an estimated seventy to one hundred thousand, with Naniwa and Dazaifu adding perhaps another fifty thousand.[3] In addition, each of the sixty-odd provincial capitals housed about six hundred officials and other occupants. Numbering about two hundred thousand, urbanites amounted to about three percent of the total population. Small though they may seem to us today, these cities played a crucial role in both demographic and economic trends. They provided fertile breeding grounds for microbes and also spurred commerce, with large numbers of consumers. Cities also drew many migrants from the countryside.

Census data from northern Kyushu and central Honshu permit computation of the vital statistics of residents of those areas. Birth rates were very high, meaning that women must have spent much of their time either pregnant or bearing children. Birthing and menstruation were secretive experiences usually taking place in a parturition hut to conceal the woman from prying male eyes. Life expectancy was about twenty-five at birth, mostly because infant mortality for those aged five and under was fifty to sixty percent. Miscarriages and stillbirths were common, and malnutrition and diseases such as dysentery undoubtedly carried away many young. Those who survived infancy could expect to live to about age forty. Such vital statistics may be difficult for modern people to comprehend, but they are in line with the general experience of most ancient and medieval societies: frequent births, high infant mortality rates, and short life spans. For comparison, people living a thousand years later in the Tokugawa era (1600–1868) could expect to survive only to about forty, and Europeans during the Renaissance to ages thirty to thirty-five.

Commencing around 730, however, the dramatic demographic increase that had lasted for sixteen hundred years came to a halt. The population trend shifted from growth to stasis for several reasons. First, immigration from the Asian continent slowed to a trickle. With the end to civil strife in China and Korea and the formation of stable regimes there, continentals had less reason to come to Japan. Instead of relying upon the skills of immigrants, the Japanese court now sent missions to China and Korea to learn the latest in technology and culture.

More significant than the end to immigration was the combination of forces driving the death rate up and the birth rate down. The most lethal of these was epidemic disease, devastating Japan as part of a wider East Asian pandemic. To elaborate, microorganisms have always accompanied humanity, but the types of contagious infections spread by contact between the sick and groups of susceptibles have a relatively recent history, because they require a certain number of hosts for the pathogen to thrive. Infectious diseases were not consistently recorded until the rise of densely populated, civilized states—specifically, the Roman Empire in the Mediterranean and the Later Han dynasty (25–220 CE) in China. Each region sustained its own unique pool of diseases until around the first century CE, when Rome and the Later Han began to trade and communicate along the Silk Roads. Because contact was haphazard, it was not until the second century CE that both Rome and the Later Han dynasties began to exchange disease agents with each other and suffer from epidemic outbreaks that "took a ferocious toll in human lives."[4]

One cause for the collapse of the Later Han dynasty was disease, as a particularly harsh plague raged during 161–162 CE. Later, in 317, Chinese histories noted the first outbreak of humanity's most lethal nemesis, smallpox. Little did the Chinese know that these epidemics would start a period of depopulation and then stasis lasting until the fall of the Tang in 907. Today these infections—smallpox, measles, dysentery, influenza, the mumps, and possibly the plague—have been largely tamed thanks to modern medicine. For these ancient Chinese encountering the pathogens for the first time without immunity, however, the effect was disastrous, and because survivors could not convey their immunities to their children, it took some centuries before antibodies developed among the Chinese populace and pestilence ceased to take its grim toll.

From China, the deadly mix of microbes eventually spread to become an East Asian pandemic. It seems to have taken several centuries before the infections were consistently conveyed eastward from China, probably because Korean and Japanese contacts with a politically divided Chinese Empire were so infrequent before unification in 589. There were, for example, only fourteen Japanese missions to the Middle Kingdom between 250 and 600 CE, and twelve occurred in the fifth century. Residents of the archipelago had neither the political impetus nor the advanced nautical technology to travel regularly to epidemic-riddled China. And, of course, the Chinese never visited Japan after the third century CE.

Even so, the wars raging in Korea encouraged large numbers of peninsular peoples to migrate to Japan, so it is not surprising that in 552 and again in 585, when the Paekche court introduced Buddhism to Japan, the envoys also brought along smallpox: "Our bodies are as if they were burnt, as if they were beaten, as if they were broken," and so lamenting they died. Old and young said privately to one another, "Is this a punishment for burning the Image of the Buddha?"[5] Unfortunately, these events are virtually our only clues about epidemics in Japan until the late seventh century.

When Tang armies invaded Korea in the mid-seventh century, however, they carried smallpox and other infections into the peninsula directly, setting off plagues among the numerous susceptible hosts there. By 698, the Japanese government had begun to complain frequently about pestilence. The reason for these repeated epidemics was that both Japan and Korea suffered from a similar dilemma: their populations were dense enough to sustain major die-offs concentrated in a few years, but not large and compact enough to allow the microbes to survive indefinitely as endemic maladies. The result was that in both areas an epidemic would rage for a year or two, killing off large numbers of persons of every age, and then run out of the most susceptible members of the population, only to reappear from abroad a decade or two later, claiming another round of victims. This demographic cycle—a lethal pestilential visitation, followed by gradual recovery, only to lead to another bout with the same infection among a whole new generation with no immunities—obtained in Korea until at least 940, and in Japan until about 1150.

Between 698 and 800, there were at least thirty-six years of plagues in Japan, or about one every three years. The most well-documented epidemic—and to judge by the mortality and its social, economic, and political effects, the most significant—was a smallpox outbreak during 735–737. It started in northern Kyushu, a certain sign of its foreign origin, but by 737 the virus had spread up the Inland Sea and on to eastern Honshu, aided, ironically enough, by the improved network of roads linking the capital and provinces. To its credit, the court tried to apply pragmatic principles to treat the symptoms of the disease, but to little effect. Statistics from various provinces scattered from northern Kyushu to eastern Honshu suggest that mortality was about twenty-five percent, meaning that a million or more persons may have succumbed. As a result of the depopulation, an entire layer of village administration was abolished. Another irony was that the death rate among the exalted aristocracy—living crowded together in the capital at Nara—was even higher, a full thirty-nine percent. At the end of 737, chroniclers wrote, "Through the summer and fall, people . . . from aristocrats on down have died one after another in countless numbers. In recent times, there has been nothing like this."[6] In the wake of the epidemic, government revenues plunged by more than twenty percent, even more draconian measures were implemented to stem cultivator flight from the land, and a guilt-ridden Shōmu approved large expenditures for Buddhist temples, statues, and other religious icons.

Epidemics certainly helped to reverse the long demographic expansion of the last several centuries, but two other factors contributed to population stasis. The first was crop failure and widespread famine, occurring about every third year between the late seventh and eighth centuries. Causes for bad harvests were complex, but various climate data indicate that the eighth century was one of the hottest and driest in Japanese history. In Western Europe, where there was a "medieval warm" at this time, the effect was to dry out water-logged soils and encourage the expansion of agriculture; in Japan, where farmers often depended upon rainfall as the only way to irrigate their paddies, the result was frequent crop failure and hunger. At ten to fifteen percent, mortality from a severe famine was lower than an epidemic, but, like pestilence, malnutrition also reduced fertility. Even in years when the harvest seemed adequate, the populace frequently went hungry in the spring when their supplies of grain were exhausted. More sophisticated means of watering rice paddies may have remedied the problem, but they were either unavailable or not applied.

A second factor leading to population stasis was the ecological degradation besetting the Kinai, the richest and most financially important region in the eighth century. Altogether, the government sponsored the construction of six capital cities and countless temples, shrines, and aristocratic mansions from 690 to 805. All these structures were built from timber harvested in the Kinai and adjacent provinces, and most had roof tiles requiring baking with charcoal in a kiln. During the second half of the eighth century, the shortage of lumber became so critical that planners began to recycle used timbers and roof tiles from older capitals, such as Fujiwara and Naniwa. When the court left Nara for Nagaoka in 784, for example, they used recycled lumber and tiles almost exclusively.

By the late eighth century, tile bakers were relying upon red pine to fire their kilns, a secondary forest cover that typically grows in nutrient-poor soil. Furthermore, the government began to note that the bald mountains in the Kinai and vicinity produced less rain and more erosion. In essence, the stripping of the forests throughout central Japan exacerbated the effects of the hot, dry climate and encouraged farmers to give up cropping altogether and flee to the seashores and mountains to forage as of old.

Agriculture and Industry

Agricultural technology related to these population trends in complex ways. The government expressed in its law codes and various other statutes a desire to encourage the expansion of arable land, especially for paddy rice. After all, aristocrats preferred polished rice in their diets, and rice sheaves were a unit of administrative accounting. Yet records show time and again that cultivators not only struggled to open new lands, but also had trouble keeping fields productive. Laws stated that farmers had three years to bring wasteland into production, but most could manage to clear only about thirty to forty percent of their stake within the allotted time. Once converted to cultivated land, moreover, untended fields typically accounted for twenty to forty percent of all farmland; some have seen a fallow system in these figures, but no one knows how it would have operated. In sum, peasants struggled to open paddy fields and maintain them in continuous production. It was a cycle that mirrored the repeated demographic ebb and flow: rice farmers opened fields and cropped them for some years, and then paddies returned to wasteland.

The reasons for this agrarian cycle were manifold. Epidemics, famines, and erosion killed off or chased away cultivators. In the wake of the 735–737 epidemic, for instance, the government tried to return abandoned fields to cultivation by allowing peasants to hold in perpetuity any fields that they might bring into production, but the results seem to have been ephemeral. The new temple, Tōdaiji, took advantage of a 743 law to claim wilderness for conversion into paddies throughout

Japan, but even from the beginning of the projects in the 750s familiar problems troubled farmers. Along the Japan Sea littoral in Etchū Province, cultivators could not clear even half their stakes and untended fields accounted for a quarter of all arable land.

The primitive state of wet-rice technology also made farming difficult. There were many methods for growing rice, ordinarily using natural or artificial irrigation. Most fields were naturally watered—that is, they depended upon seasonal fluctuations in the water table to provide moisture for the crop. Typically, these fields were low-lying and swampy and had poor yields, or they were located in the small, flat stretches of Japan's innumerable mountain valleys. Because rainfall was the only means employed to water these fields, the hot, dry climate of the eighth century led to frequent crop failure; drought caused as many as two-thirds of the bad harvests between 676 and 800. Many rice paddies listed as abandoned or uncultivated probably became so when precipitation was inadequate and rice plants withered and died.

Those farmers watering their fields artificially struggled to master the engineering skills necessary to the task. Some ditches became clogged or were engineered incorrectly and failed to run downhill as they were intended to do. The ponds of this era were small and simple, constructed using a minimum of labor by damming up one end of a valley to catch the run-off. These "valley ponds" remained full all year round and mainly irrigated the same type of landform as naturally dampened fields—tiny, isolated parcels located in mountain basins or at the edges of larger plains. In essence, Japan's farmers had not yet learned how to exploit broad alluvial fans, river bottoms, or coastal plains, where the soil was most fertile and yields apt to be the highest. The importation of the waterwheel in 829 was evidently meant to encourage the irrigation of just such lands, but the device never caught on. Frustrated, some hungry commoners even tore holes in their "valley ponds" just to catch and eat the fish.

In addition to these engineering bottlenecks, there was at least one other technological problem. From the late Yayoi period, cultivators had fitted iron blades to their shovels, hoes, and sickles. Because Japan is iron poor and southern Korea had plentiful supplies, all of Japan's iron was imported from the peninsula until about 500 CE, and Korea probably continued to supply a great deal of the valuable ore to Japan thereafter. During the late seventh century, when Yamato's enemy Silla unified the peninsula, however, access to a major source of iron was reduced or severed. As a result, iron for farming tools became harder to acquire; by 800, as few as five percent of farmers possessed iron tools. Without iron tools, it was more difficult to cut and turn the earth and impossible to harvest rice stalks at the root with sickles. Despite the beginning of rice agriculture 1,600 years earlier, Japan was still a long way from becoming a rice-centered agrarian society.

Because paddy agriculture required hard labor, was the object of tax collectors, and depended upon the possession of iron tools and mastery of advanced irrigation techniques, it should come as no surprise that would-be rice farmers turned to other more familiar and easier livelihoods. Some persons preferred to remain cultivators, but instead of rice paddies they cropped dry grains such as millet, wheat, soybeans, barley, and buckwheat. Productivity of these unirrigated parcels was much lower than that of wet rice—only about a third as much. The great advantage of dry cropping, however, was that the government did not collect revenues on these fields, and so it would not be surprising if many resorted to this livelihood.

Slash-and-burn agriculture was also an effective means to elude the tax collector and support a family. In swidden farming, as it is also known, the cultivator went into the mountains, cleared away the forest and underbrush, and then burned the vegetation to produce ash for fertilizer. These farmers then planted beans, millet, or other crops for the few years that the mountain soil was productive, later moving on to another location, where they began again. Slash-and-burn cropping is associated around the world with low population densities; in Japan it was most common in northern Honshu, southern Kyushu, and other sparsely settled mountainous regions. The popularity of this occupation was undoubtedly one reason that the government found it so difficult to locate peasants and limit them to a fixed residence.

Finally, subsistence techniques that had started out as Jōmon livelihoods remained prominent. Hunting was still widely practiced, and the gathering of nuts, tubers, and berries must have been an important way to subsist. People undoubtedly employed these survival tactics even more readily when crops failed or other natural disasters struck.

Fishing was a major livelihood during the Jōmon period, but little is known about this occupation during later centuries. "Sea people" appear only occasionally in records. The list of local products sent from the provinces to the court as tribute items shows, however, thirty-one different kinds of fish, crustaceans, mollusks, and seaweed. Furthermore, day laborers building the cities and temples of the eighth century always partook heartily of fish, seaweed, and salt—"the riches of the sea." There is no doubt that fishing represented a major occupation, but, like so many aspects of life in eighth-century Japan, lawgivers gave it little attention.

The progress of industry during 600–800 was mixed, with most of the advances coming while the population was still expanding. One major accomplishment, for example, was the unification of land transportation. This occurred during the late seventh and early eighth centuries when the government was able to muster a large supply of day laborers. By the mid-700s, workers had completed a set of roads connecting every province and district to the Kinai. In western Japan, roads were either dirt or covered with sand, while in eastern Honshu they were gravel. Travel times from the capital were dramatically reduced to as little as fifteen days to northern Kyushu and twenty-four days to the northern tip of Honshu. The government also constructed post stations and provided officials with mounts and packhorses. Such a major improvement in transportation and communication helped promote commerce, the diffusion of microbes, and the movement of tribute items and corvée gangs.

By all accounts, the workers who ferried miscellaneous tax goods along these roadways faced harsh conditions. Often they did not carry enough food to return home and fled to new surroundings. Edict after edict complained of roads littered with the corpses of dead corvée laborers. To mitigate these hardships, workers carried prayer slips to donate to shrines along the way. Apparently, however, these were of little help, as these unfortunates were known as "tormented demons" in common parlance.[7]

Salt making and ceramics were industries remaining virtually unaffected by demographic trends. Just as in the Jōmon era, inhabitants of the archipelago manufactured salt by evaporating seawater in small clay pots over an open fire. By the eighth century, pots might also be made of stone. Enterprising salt makers hastened the process by draining the saline solution over seaweed to thicken it and aid in the formation of crystals. This process required intensive labor, but until 800 it remained the primary means to make salt. The spread of stoneware (Sue ware) to many households was another sign of technological progress in the 700s.

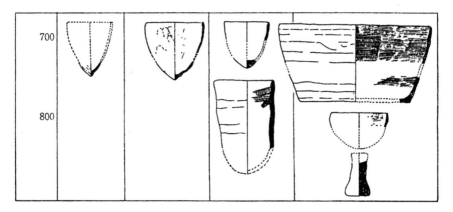

Salt-making was a major enterprise in eighth-century Japan and pots such as the ones sketched above were essential to the process of boiling seawater. *Source:* Kanō Hisashi and Kinoshita Masashi, "Shio tetsu no seisan to kōnō," *Kodai no chihōshi 2 San'in san'yō nankai hen.* (Asakura shoten, 1977), p. 176.

Not all sectors, however, exhibited continuous growth. Greater production of silk thread and cloth was a high priority in the early 700s, as the court eagerly adopted the latest Chinese technologies, including silk reeling. Silk manufacture spread to the provinces, but by 800 the experiment had apparently proved a failure, as the court protested bitterly and frequently about the tardiness and poor quality of silk products.

Construction is the most obvious example of industrial boom-and-bust during 690–800. The court undertook the construction of six capital cities, many temples and shrines, and lavish aristocratic mansions during these years. For instance, the capital at Nara, occupied almost continuously from 710 to 784, was a symmetrical city laid out along the points of the compass, measuring 5.5 kilometers east-west and 4.5 kilometers north-south. It contained dozens of roads and alleys measuring from 5 to 37 meters in width, most flanked by ditches, some spanned by bridges. Moving and leveling the earth and raising the buildings for a city of its size must have been an immense undertaking, requiring large inputs of labor and materials, and Nara represented only one such project.

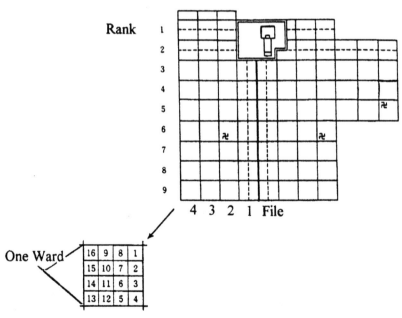

The layout for Nara, the most important capital city during the 700s, took its inspiration from Chinese models. *Source:* Kishi Toshio, "Nihon no tojō sei sōron," in Kishi, ed., *Nihon no kodai 9: Tojō no seitai* (Chūō kōron, 1987), p. 33.

As the eighth century progressed and disease, famine, and ecological devastation took their toll, however, healthy workers became more difficult to find and employ and construction projects ground to a halt. From 690 until 745, the court built four capital cities, as well as refurbishing Nara at least once. From 745 to 805, the government attempted two capitals—Nagaoka and Heian—and finished neither. The deforestation of the Kinai and environs was partially responsible, but so was the lack of healthy laborers. The court tried various means to assemble workers, including paying corvée gangs and impressing those not responsible for service. By the early 800s, the government complained that "emergency conscriptions [of workers] are many, while corvée adults are few" and that "people are few although deterioration [of government facilities] is increasingly widespread."[8] A rise in daily wages, from ten coins around 720 to fifteen or more by 800, also probably indicated that workers were becoming scarce, although inflation generated by coinage debasement may also be partly to blame. For the average laborer, ten coins could buy five melons or two and a half sheaves of soybeans.

Some artisans attempted to adapt to the demographic decline by shifting to labor-saving technologies. In the case of ironworking, smiths moved from a low, rectangular, box-shaped furnace complete with blowpipes and bellows, to a half-submerged vertical shaft furnace located on a slope. Instead of requiring the former devices to supply oxygen, the new furnace merely relied on up-drafting winds to fan the flames. Although simpler and more primitive than the older version, it needed no workers to operate bellows, thus saving on labor.

Domestic and Overseas Trade

With thousands of consumers located in cities, an improved network of travel arteries linking capital and province, and the constant movement of tax goods, it follows that a complex, three-part commercial system developed within Japan. First there was the most developed region (the Kinai), with official markets in the capitals and scattered throughout the region. Markets also opened for business in outlying provinces; those in western Japan were much busier than those in the Kanto and northern Honshu. Finally, medium- and long-distance trade connected buyers and sellers from the northern tip of Honshu to Kyushu.

The chief merchants were lower-ranking government officials, subject to some degree to the vagaries of the market. One bureaucrat, for example, made a whopping seventy percent profit shipping surplus lumber from a temple project. Another lost his shirt trading in cloth and was required to make up the deficit out of his own pocket. Even in the 700s, these merchant-officials almost always made attempts at comparison shopping, just as modern consumers do. Officials comprised the overwhelming majority of traders because they had access to tax goods to offer, government connections to wealthy courtiers, and numerous opportunities to cut a deal in all the construction projects ongoing at that time.

To facilitate commerce, the court minted copper cash beginning in 710. Greedy for revenues from the beginning, however, the government set the nominal value of a coin far above the actual value of copper. With copper so cheap and the coins priced so high, counterfeiting became common. Then the smallpox epidemic of 735–737 occurred, and the disarray in markets was so great that inflation ensued. In the 760s, the government minted a new issue of coppers, trying to offset the general decline in revenues by debasing its coins. As the supply of money expanded, inflation worsened and by 805 coins began to lose their value. Eventually, government-issued currency became all but worthless.

Overseas trade among the various states of East Asia operated behind the cover of official Chinese diplomacy. In this system, the Chinese court envisioned itself as the center of the world and allowed various "barbarian" governments to come to the Chinese capital at Chang-an and pay obeisance. One means of offering subservience to the grand Chinese monarch was to give him gifts. The Chinese especially prized spices, medicines, and horses, while Japanese envoys took home silk and books. The Chinese wrote of one eighth-century Japanese diplomat that "[e]verything given him by the court was used to purchase books."[9] Outside of the tributary system, the Tang court severely limited commercial opportunities, keeping foreigners in ghettos and requiring permits for nongovernmental trade.

These information-hungry Japanese embassies arrived in a new type of ship. Until about 650, boats had been made of hollowed logs with boards attached to the sides to make them more buoyant. Oars were the primary means of propulsion. The boats measured about two by fourteen meters and could hold as many as twenty-five people and two horses. These small vessels remained adequate for sailing in the waters around the archipelago and even to and from Korea.

Beginning in the 700s, however, the court assigned immigrant shipwrights to build Chinese junks for the dangerous crossing from northern Kyushu to the mouth of the Yang-tze River. Junks were superbly seaworthy vessels, because they had flat bottoms complete with transverse bulkheads and holds, woven bamboo sails, and huge masts. They held a complement of 120 passengers, along with provisions and trade items for the Tang court. Chinese technology made an impact on Japanese navigation and ship building, but it turned out to be short-lived.

Residents of the islands also participated in other overseas exchange networks. Despite sour relations, the Japanese court traded with Silla for spices, fragrances, medicines, cosmetics, pigments, gold, iron, and tableware and furnishings.[10] Parhae, a kingdom located in modern Manchuria, also engaged in commerce with Japan. Altogether, however, overseas trade was a tiny fraction of the increasingly diverse eighth-century economy.

Society: Class, Family, and Women

Class

During these two centuries, Japan's class structure became more elaborate than that of the Tomb age, resembling a pointed pyramid, with wellborn aristocrats at the top and commoners and slaves at the bottom. Aristocrats were defined as those holding one of the top five court ranks; in the 700s, they usually numbered about 150 individuals, an infinitesimal proportion of Japan's total population. Most occupied exalted offices and advised the sage-king, and enjoyed imported Chinese culture; for their labors, they were amply rewarded in lands and tax commodities. A highborn aristocrat essentially possessed resources equivalent to a small province. For example, Prince Nagaya (684–729), a grandson of Tenmu, held the Third Rank and was quite a political power in his day. His household included sixty attendants, twelve acres of rice paddies, and 200 or more "sustenance households" providing him with goods-in-kind. His estate contained thirty buildings, and he had four wives, eighteen children, and four wet nurses. The feeding and clothing of his family required a small army of cooks, rice-wine brewers, yogurt makers, firewood collectors, seamstresses, potters, dyers, tanners, movers, plasterers, weapons makers, bronze casters, sculptors, and many others. Nagaya also used people to care for his dogs, horses, and falcons, and employed doctors to look after the sick. He had an ice storage house, a charcoal-firing center, and a lumberyard. Moreover, household administrators assigned to him by the court operated Nagaya's system of interest-bearing rice loans and collected tribute items from thirty provinces.

The key to Nagaya's royal treatment was his ancestry reflected in his high rank, but it would be a mistake to assume that this sort of wealth and power were the birthright of men only. During 690–800, women occupied the throne more than half the time, and contrary to popular belief, they were not simply pawns for male politicians. Jitō and Shōtoku (r. 764–770) were particularly powerful, essentially dictating the formative policies of their respective reigns. Prince Nagaya took Princess Kibi as his wife, who had a brother and sister who became sovereigns. With such exalted bloodlines, Kibi held a rank higher than her husband and was permitted an even more elaborate household staff. Consort Kōmyō (701–760), the wife to Shōmu, held immense political and economic power in her day, spending lavishly on Buddhist temples such as Kōfukuji and numerous sutra-copying projects, as well as orphanages and medical clinics. Kōmyō provided the power base for her nephew, Fujiwara no Nakamaro (706–764), and once she died, Nakamaro fell from power and was beheaded. All these royal and aristocratic women came by their power through legal means, as the authors of the Taihō Code specifically granted such women court rank and all the emoluments going with it.

Male and female aristocrats occupied the apex of the social pyramid, but those who did not achieve promotion to the coveted Fifth Rank were much more numerous, did most of the actual paper-shuffling, and led dreary lives. Numbering several thousand, these low-ranking bureaucrats virtually lived in their offices. They did such work as sutra copying, paper making, and proofreading. They were required to present monthly reports when they received their meager stipends. A sutra copyist, for example, was paid five coins for every sheet he transcribed and worked at his job in shifts of twenty nights or days. They were fed twice a day— white rice, a bowl of soup, and side dishes of seaweed and vegetables, and this average diet deteriorated as the government fell into straitened circumstances after 750. The court knew that the lot of lower-ranking bureaucrats was demanding: it always allotted them numerous bottles of rice wine. They constantly requested vacation time and received it occasionally. One official asked for leave in 771 to nurse an ailing son, but the boy died while the father commuted from work to his home.

These lower-level bureaucrats suffered many hardships. Often their stipends were so low and the government so ravenous for revenue that their superiors

Sutra copyists led hard lives, but their work was considered essential to ensure the Buddha's protection of the realm. The Imperial Household Agency and the Shōsōin.

forced upon them loans at usurious rates—thirteen percent per month. Chances for advancement were nil. For instance, Takaya no Muraji Yakamaro was stuck at the lowest Initial Rank at age fifty; it would have taken him decades of consistently good evaluations to come even close to the Fifth Rank. In essence, Prince Nagaya and his ilk rode a "bullet train" straight to the top, while Takaya and his fellow functionaries were stuck in the lowest reaches of the bureaucracy for life.

The clergy comprised an important but unique adjunct to the ruling class. Buddhist monks and nuns were the most common religious figures. They were exempt from taxation, a perquisite carefully restricted by law, and their religious organizations received from the government tax revenues, large tracts of land, and other gifts. The reason for government support was that the Buddhist clergy was in charge of rituals designed to protect the realm as well as the body of the sovereign. Because conducting these ceremonies gave them special powers, the government clamped strict controls on Buddhist clerics. The court placed them in an official hierarchy, ordered them to study to receive state-sanctioned ordination, and prohibited them from interfering in politics or whipping up fervor by preaching or begging among the people without permit. Nor were Buddhist clerics allowed to marry. These ecclesiastics became more numerous as the eighth century unfolded, reaching at least 18,520 by 784.[11] More than 200 traveled to China for instruction between 668 and 882. A few headed powerful temples, monasteries, or nunneries, but most were lowly commoners following their faith (or seeking to avoid taxation). In particular, women took orders as nuns, becoming prominent in ceremonies and religious good works.

Dōji (?–744) and Gyōki (668–749) are two famous Buddhist monks.[12] Dōji studied in China and gained the support of Prince Nagaya. He advised the court on such matters as the compilation of court histories, the correct interpretation of *The Lotus Sutra,* and on the invitation of monks from China. Gyōki, by contrast, broke all the rules by going out among the populace to proselytize and beg. He conducted social work, overseeing the building of bridges, shelters, and irrigation ponds. Later, he redeemed himself in the eyes of the court by helping to raise funds for the erection of temples, most notably Tōdaiji. He was the subject of adulation as he traveled from town to town spreading Buddhist teachings. Women adored him.

The native cult (often mistakenly called Shinto) was charged by the court to carry out thirteen different types of rituals nineteen times a year. Its prelates—primarily Nakatomi, Imibe, and Kataribe—blessed the crops in the spring and celebrated good harvests in the fall. They also performed purification rituals to remove impurities responsible for natural disasters and plagues. The most important shrines were those at Ise, Izumo, and Usa in Kyushu.

Local notables, who usually served as district magistrates, encompassed a fourth class. Living in one of Japan's 550 districts, these men and women were the key to control of the provinces and the collection of sufficient revenues to keep the government going. The court treated them generously, granting them lifetime tenure, a sizable parcel of land, rank and office for their offspring, and appointments for their relatives as the district's military and religious officials. For example, district magistrate Hi no Kimi Ite lived in northern Kyushu in 702. Although he held lowly civilian and military rank, his household encompassed 124 members, including 4 spouses, 31 children and grandchildren, 26 dependents, and 37 slaves. He supported these persons with sixty acres of rice fields and extensive salt- and hemp-making operations. Or consider Ikue no Omi Azumabito, living along the Japan Sea littoral in 755. He held at least thirty acres of rice fields in addition to his official parcels and loaned out a total of about eight thousand rice sheaves at fifty percent interest to control the neighboring farmers renting his parcels. Most local notables, including Hi no Kimi and Ikue no Omi, were superb horsemen because they had the wealth and leisure to master the equestrian arts. In 792, when the court abolished the draft amid a declining population, it turned to this class of local magnates to provide them with mounted archers to keep the peace. At that time, the court was able to recruit about three thousand such fighters from this class.

Of course, the overwhelming majority of people were unranked commoners. Most lived in pit dwellings, just as their Jōmon-, Yayoi-, and Tomb-period ancestors had. They cooked with the boiler in western Japan but could manage campfires only in eastern Honshu. Beginning around 700, earthen floors were laid at ground level; residents led their daily lives in the center of the house and spread straw or grass at the edges to sleep. Such a house was probably cramped, drafty, dark, and prone to fire. Rural houses were scattered over the landscape, just as in the Tomb age. Typical villages included the solitary homestead, the small hamlet, or larger units of twenty to thirty dwellings, interspersed with wasteland, fields, and other topographical features. Little is known of the social organization of these rural settlements.

Besides living in a dispersed pattern, rural people changed residence frequently. Lawgivers sought to bind them to the land through various means, but in the course of the 700s, the court ran out of alternatives, changing its policy a bewildering seven times. Contrary to expectations, the typical migrant was female, traveled in groups, and was often wealthy. People moved for numerous reasons: to avoid the tax collector, clear or abandon fields, find jobs in an increasingly tight labor market, fish or practice slash-and-burn cropping, or to live with a partner. Mobility was part and parcel of commoner life, and the government could do little to stop it.

In other respects, commoner lives were much as they had been in the Tomb age. Clothing was woven of hemp or ramie. Diet was just adequate in the best of times, as revealed by the tiny size of armor for soldiers. People ate brown rice, wheat, barley, salt, seaweed, bean paste, vinegar, melons, and always consumed lots of rice wine. Some probably supplemented these foods with mushrooms, chestnuts, and local fish or game. The typical toilet was a hole in the ground spanned by two planks over which the user would squat. When the toilet became full, a new one was dug. In the cities, highborn aristocrats such as Prince Nagaya availed themselves of advanced toilets that washed away the droppings. Urban toilets reveal that intestinal parasites afflicted even the wealthiest defecators.

At the bottom of the pyramid was a small class of slaves. They accounted for about five percent of the population, and were owned by temples, officials, the government, and other wealthy individuals. Slaves had no surname and were essentially held in no higher regard than livestock. They could be bought or sold, with a good slave fetching about the same price as an ox. Masters could break up families through sale or inheritance, and the standing rule was that children always

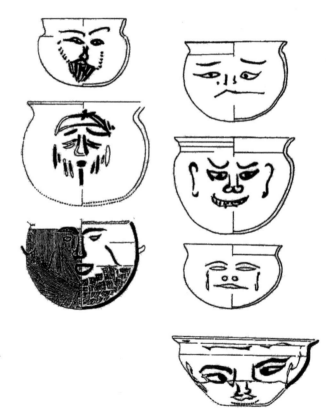

These "pots with human faces" depicted the epidemic demon and played a role in ridding the afflicted cities and villages of disease. *Source*: Kaneko Hiroyuki, ed. *Ritsuryō ki saishi ibutsu shūsei* (Nara: Nara kokuritsu bunkazai kenkyūjo, 1988), pp. 92–93.

accompanied their mother. As labor became scarce after 750, the enforcement costs for slavery rose, and masters began to manumit their slaves. Their numbers declined by 805.

As differentiated as the social pyramid was, people of all classes shared similarly practical religious beliefs. They petitioned for the safe delivery of a child, gave thanksgiving for a bountiful harvest, and prayed for long life and prosperity. These fundamental urges were just as much a part of the Buddhism of the time as the native cult. The hot, dry weather gave rise to numerous temples devoted to rain-making liturgies, such as those employing horses or straw dragons. Such cosmological creatures were thought to influence the forces of nature and were employed at temples such as Murōji in Nara. People also believed that a spirit dwelt in their bodies as long as they were alive, and even when the spirit departed, it floated about and might for a few days be recalled for resuscitation. The custom of cremation was imported into Japan in the early 700s, but most people were simply buried in a hole in the moors or mountains. Spirits of the dead, it was believed, ended up in the mountains, but some believers also envisioned the departed as going to the sky, islands, or even across the seas.

The fear of disease apparently haunted everyone. Archaeologists have excavated thousands of wooden figures, clay horses, miniature ovens, and "pots with human faces" attesting to this fact. They were part of a purification rite (*ōharae*) performed during epidemics and natural disasters. Perhaps most interesting are the "pots with human faces," many of them gruesome to behold. According to custom, the victim blew his or her breath into the open dish, which was thereupon given a lid. As the pestilence played out, persons collected the pots from the sick and dumped them into streams or sewers, apparently to wash the disease spirit away. These artifacts have been discovered all over Japan, but they are particularly common in cities. They began appearing in the late seventh century, just as plagues were becoming severe.

Family and Women

Despite the enormous gulf between aristocrat and slave, people of all classes shared similar kinship, marital arrangements, and even gender relations. Among people of all classes, kinship remained bilateral. This meant that a family could trace its lineage through either the mother's or the father's side; no distinction was made between one's father's and mother's relatives. Unlike patrilineal or matrilineal kinship, bilateral relations are highly flexible; sometimes the male would move to his current love's village, and sometimes the woman would change her residence. Or, if they lived close to each other, the man and woman might have maintained separate homes. Such a kinship system encouraged high mobility and a smoother distribution of people over farming units. Japan's bilateral kinship arrangements flew in the face of the Taihō Code, which tried to establish the Chinese patriarchal clan in high-sounding prose. It was another topic on which lawgivers expressed their desire to emulate China, to little effect.

There was considerable variety in the size and composition of the family. Of course, high-ranking aristocrats and local notables often had large, extended families, but doing so was not possible for most commoners. Their pit dwellings ranged from fifteen to fifty square meters, with the smaller ones probably holding two or three residents and the larger about eight. Most peasants lived in nuclear families consisting of one or both parents and their children. Some had enough wealth to build more spacious homes or even occupy more than one residence. Those families with property divided it equally among all heirs, both male and female, suggesting that there was little or no pressure on available land resources.

Relations between children and their fathers were distant or even nonexistent. A huge volume of eighth-century poetry portrays all sorts of human emotions, but fathers almost never expressed their feelings about their children. To the contrary, in bad times they sold their offspring for food; and if a person survived to old age, the government had to provide them with a means of support, probably because their children were unwilling or unable to do so.

Sex and marriage during these centuries were consistent with high fertility, because males and females were free to engage in virtually unrestricted intercourse. Among all classes, young people began to pair off after puberty, exchange love poems, and then have sex. Typically, the man made a nocturnal visit to his love's house, sometimes under the watchful eyes of her parents. The "marriage" continued for as long as the visits did. If the pair produced offspring, the man might move in with his spouse and children. To get a divorce, the man simply stopped visiting, either of his own or his partner's volition. Men might visit more than one woman and women might entertain more than one man. In other words, none of these relationships was exclusive or lifelong. Members of the same family could even "marry" as long as they had different mothers. A man could also inherit his brother's widow as a wife. In fact, sex was so free that villages engaged in orgies, condemned by the government in 797 because such behavior did not maintain "the [proper] distinction between men and women."[13]

When it came to marriage, the prospective "bride" had an advantage. Marriages are essentially arrangements about having children and controlling property, with gifts of land and other items frequently changing hands between newlyweds. In the Tokugawa period, the bride provided a dowry to her husband's family, but during the seventh and eighth centuries, men gave what is called *bridewealth* to women. Especially in the case of a rich family, males competed for the hand of the woman, and gave her (and not her family) property to secure the option to have children with her. There are actually cases in which duplicitous females accepted bridewealth from more than one suitor and refused any refunds.

Even though most of them also had multiple partners, married their kin, and raised their children in the mother's family, some members of the elite tried to formalize their unions through various customs. To symbolize a new marriage, they might have the prospective husband light a fire in his fiancée's family's boiler, or force him to eat rice cakes browned at her house. Aristocrats had considerable property and needed offspring to name as heirs and prospective rank-holders, engendering the need for the wellborn to make some nominal marital arrangements.

Equal inheritance rights, the custom of bridewealth, as well as the right to name and raise children suggests that women had high status and wielded considerable political and economic power at this time. We have already examined the cases of aristocratic females such as Princess Kibi and the Consort Kōmyō, but the same assertion can be made for women of all classes. In fact, commoner women may have been even freer than those in the aristocracy or local nobility. For example, when lawgivers established the system to allocate rice paddies to all persons for their support, women received their land not as wives—as in China—but as females. They raised silkworms and produced silk textiles, managed agricultural lands, and owned houses, cattle, and slaves, all of which they took with them when there was a "divorce." They managed loans, especially in rice or money, and made sake, sometimes carrying all these enterprises to excess: "[One woman] . . . made great profit by selling rice wine diluted with water. On the day when she made a loan, she used a small measuring cup, while on the day she collected, she used a big measuring cup. . . . She did not show any mercy in forcibly collecting interest, sometimes ten times and sometimes a hundred times as much as the original loan. . . . There has never been anybody so greedy."[14] Women served as soldiers and district magistrates, and were leading devotees of Buddhism.

Why did women have so much power and wealth? Of course, this question assumes that oppression has historically been the natural state of women. Nevertheless, several factors gave women of this age social, economic, and political advantages. Because most men and women had multiple sexual partners during their lives and paternity tests did not exist, the only sure way to trace an offspring's descent was through the mother's line. It is little wonder that the mother's family usually named and raised the children and that the husband might choose to live with his in-laws. This must have been especially important for the capital and local nobility, who needed heirs for their huge patrimony.

The law of supply and demand favored women, too. Because high-ranking aristocrats and local notables frequently chose to keep more than one wife, the supply of eligible women was reduced. Female mortality in childbirth had the same effect. Commoner men were left to compete among themselves for the remaining females, and as part of that competition, the custom of bridewealth undoubtedly arose. Finally, women's high status derived directly from a labor shortage that grew more acute as the eighth century wore on.[15] As noted above, females worked in the fields and at most other occupations, thereby gaining wealth and power. Taken together, these diverse factors help to explain the prominent status of eighth-century women.

Class, family, and gender placed countervailing pressures upon Japan's population during the era 600–800. Class was the most important of these three, as the social and economic gulf between a wellborn aristocrat and a commoner was enormous. Family was a fluid concept, having great variety and not much cohesion. And both men and women could and did hold considerable political power, high social status, and far-reaching economic power.

Toward a Society in Stasis: Who Wins and Who Loses?

Because modern people have lived during a capitalist age when growth is the watchword, it is hard for most members of the industrialized world to imagine a time in which the population or economy did not expand. In fact, through most of the human past, stasis has been the rule, and decline and decay have also occurred. The living conditions in which a sizable minority of the world's populace now lives—plenty to eat, long lives, and freedom from infectious disease—have developed only over the past century or so and may not last.

Even so, stasis should not be equated with stagnation or equally bad times for everyone. By the end of the eighth century, some were prospering while others suffered. Certainly victims of famine and epidemics lost out, but survivors often found themselves better off than otherwise could have been expected. The aristocrat who reached high office or greater wealth because his rival died of smallpox, the peasant who benefited from the labor shortage through higher wages and more opportunities, and the women who held high status in a society that needed their heirs and skills—they all prospered. It is axiomatic that growth never goes on forever and that stasis may bring prosperity to many.

3 State and Society in an Age of Depopulation, 800–1050

The Formation of an Aristocratic State

Decline of the Taihō System and Rise of the Provincial Headquarters

From the late eighth century, Japan's political system started to encounter problems. The most fundamental and far-reaching difficulty was that the government was not taking in nearly as much as it disbursed. Historians of the time portrayed the fiscal shortfall as the inability of a greedy elite to curb its desire to spend: on new capitals (Nagaoka and Heian), more temples and Buddhist ceremonies, the expeditions to subdue the *emishi*, and lavish aristocratic mansions and other fineries. In fact, the revenue shortfall resulting from sustained depopulation was at least as responsible for the government's financial woes. By the late 700s, the court complained repeatedly and bitterly about the nonpayment or tardiness of tribute items of all sorts.

Between 800 and 900, the court attempted to adhere to the system as outlined in the Taihō Code—register the populace in a census, allocate those persons a parcel of land to keep them alive and in one place, and collect poll taxes from adult males. It is doubtful that this system ever absorbed most of the human and material surplus of the islands, but between 690 and 800 it operated well enough to maintain a sizable bureaucracy and defend the elites' tax producers from attack. In the ninth century, however, abuses of the system multiplied.

One way to outwit the tax collector was to avoid the census, the first and most crucial step in collecting revenues. For example, a population register from 908 listed the household of Hatabito Hiromoto as containing forty-seven members, but only eight were men. In other words, local officials and the populace were conspiring to undercount taxable males. By the early 900s, census registers no longer reflected reality at all. In his famous Twelve-Article Opinion submitted to the court in 914, the aristocrat Miyoshi Kiyoyuki told the story of Shimotsumichi District in Bitchū Province. It had dispatched 20,000 soldiers to Korea in 660, but had only 1,900 taxable males in the 730s, and a pitiful seventy by 860.

By the time Kiyoyuki was writing in the early tenth century, Shimotsumichi purportedly boasted only two old men. This story reflected a sizable loss of population, especially in epidemic-riddled western Japan, but another reason for the lack of taxable males was that the census system had failed.

The district magistrate was the critical official for administering the census and collecting taxes. The Taihō Code in effect created an alliance between these local strongmen and the court, but, as the ninth century opened, it was clear that the old alliance was in disarray. One sign was a strange occurrence known as the "divine fires." District magistrates stole rice sheaves and other revenue items contained in local warehouses and then burned the structures. When the governor or other court official came to investigate, the responsible magistrate told him that "the gods had incinerated the storehouse." Incredibly, when this explanation was first tendered, the gullible investigators actually fell for it. Eventually, however, the central government learned the truth: their former lieutenants in the countryside were no longer reliable. The relationship between the district magistrates and the court continued to deteriorate thereafter.

In essence, incidents such as the "divine fires" amounted to a tug of war between district and court officials over a diminishing surplus of grain and other taxable assets. Many families of district magistrates suffered economic decline as a result of the continuous rounds of famines and epidemics and sought to make up the difference by stealing revenues. The central government, too, felt the decrease in revenues keenly and blamed the district magistrates. In trying to compel the cooperation of these magistrates, however, the court actually enacted policies resulting in the evisceration of that office. At first, the court sought to increase tax collection by creating competition among local families to serve the court. It broadened the pool of candidates for appointment, but the outcome was to create several aspirants for every position. Traditional officeholders often lost out. The long-term result was to demean and weaken the court's age-old supporters at a time when they were already facing economic challenges. During the 800s, the powers of the district magistrate fragmented irremediably as the court gave in and appointed everyone from a prominent family to a position. With no effective district magistrates to oversee the census, land allocation, and tax collection, all three institutions fell into abeyance. These systems no longer operated as a unit or throughout the entire realm; province-by-province attempts to enact elements of each eventually petered out in the early tenth century.

While this struggle was taking place between central and district officials, the court attempted to deal with the budgetary problem from the confines of the new capital at Heian (later Kyoto). It tried retrenchment, cutting offices and their perquisites. The court then cannibalized the revenue resources of the provincial governments, devouring most of the reserves by 900. It sent out representatives to oversee and scold provincial governors, to little avail. A few exemplary governors, such as Sugawara no Michizane, the court held up as "good functionaries" and rewarded them with praise and high office. Finally, some aristocrats and religious organizations decided to establish their own economic bases called estates *(shōen)*. Courtiers and Buddhist officials created personalized links to local figures who may have recently cleared some land and could guarantee them some tribute items or a portion of the harvest. These links multiplied over time and often became entangled with official lines of authority, leading to conflict and violence. Until 1050, however, these estates were generally taxable and not very extensive.

As these financial woes played out, other changes were underway in the countryside. A group of local power holders, known simply as the "rich," took advantage of the new social and economic realities. In its edicts, the court accused the "rich" of monopolizing fertile lands, lending grain at usurious rates during epidemics, and cheating starving peasants of their grain doles during famines. They hoarded cash and bribed officials to avoid tax assessment. The "rich" were a new class commanding considerable human and material resources, but the problem for the court was that they were not easily amenable to central control. By destroying the district magistracy, the central government had ceded away direct access to Japan's resources.

In line with declining revenues and the struggle to collect them, violence mounted everywhere. Throughout the 800s, there were repeated references to murder, assassination, and mayhem occurring between those trying to take in taxes and those avoiding payment. District magistrates fought provincial governors and bandits murdered governors and their families. One interesting group of brigands in the Kanto consisted of horse employers, who stole packhorses as they were carrying tax items. By 900, rural Japan was much less safe than it had been in the 700s, and the court neither had reliable representatives there nor could they put an end to the violence.

Disorder peaked in two well-known revolts, when local strongmen and other "rich" residents resisted taxation and hijacked provincial headquarters. The first occurred between 935 and 941 and was led by erstwhile royal Taira no Masakado in the Kanto and the pirate Fujiwara Sumitomo along the Inland Sea. The second took place under the direction of Taira no Tadatsune between 1028 and 1032, once again in the Kanto. In both cases, the court began to take the violence seriously only when the revolts threatened officials and regular tax payments. These rebellions are important for understanding the evolution of Japan's military power and the class known as the samurai and will be described in chapter 4.

By 900, the old Taihō system had come unraveled like a frayed rope and the court needed a new way to ensure its rights to part of Japan's produce. So it tried to make the best of a deteriorating situation by devising a new system to collect revenues and prevent the provinces from drifting into protracted violence. The first and most important reform was to allow the provincial governors to become tax farmers. As noted above, provincial governors numbered about sixty or so and were appointed from among the capital aristocracy for four-year terms. These governors-turned-tax farmers were assigned quotas of revenues to deliver to the capital, and as long as they met their quotas, no questions were asked. Tax farmers might use violence or any other means to gather grain, local products, and labor. Most important, any revenues collected above the quota were theirs to keep. In effect, now shorn of its lieutenants in the countryside, the court decided to make the provincial headquarters its island of authority.

For most of their terms, tax farmers lived in Kyoto and left the daily administration of their jurisdictions to their unsavory underlings and provincial officials. Once in his term, however, the tax farmer sojourned to his province from his residence in Kyoto to make a survey of the lands in his province, comparing the survey to prior maps and determining the legal status of the land (estate or provincial) and its cultivation conditions. All lands were given the title "name-field" (*myō*)—farmlands designated by the names of the most skilled among them—but name-fields varied considerably in size, cultivation conditions, and numbers of farmers. From the inhabitants of these name-fields the governor collected a grain tax, approximately equal to the various rice imposts of the Taihō Code, and a tax in tribute items such as silk or labor. While people were of course responsible for paying these taxes, the unit of collection now shifted from the individual to a measure of land.

Tax farming relies for its effectiveness on the ambition of the officeholder; these positions usually proved to be highly lucrative and competition for appointment was keen. Moreover, the court could forgive tax farmers if they were overzealous in doing their duties. Between 971 and 1041, provincial residents, sometimes led by long-suffering district magistrates, filed fourteen petitions of protest with the court against unscrupulous tax farmers. The most famous case comes from Owari in central Honshu, where the rapacious Governor Fujiwara no Motonaga angered his subjects in 988. The thirty-one-article protest accused Motonaga of bringing along various henchmen to expropriate peoples' goods; these hoodlums "scattered and filled the jurisdiction like clouds."[1] While mounted on horses, they wrecked residents' doorways and threw open the window shutters to look for and take various items. They falsified land records to claim taxes for unproductive or nonexistent fields and robbed people of their possessions. Many goods ended up in Motonaga's home in Kyoto. Motonaga and his cronies were "essentially no different from barbarians." The Owari protest succeeded in having Motonaga dismissed from his post, but he served again as a tax farmer in several other provinces later on.

In sum, beginning in 900 the elite took the position that, as long as it received its quota of revenues, most other matters in the provinces were not their concern. Having lost (or destroyed) its old allies in the countryside, the court made a strategic retreat, but it was a successful one. All manner of violence and mayhem might and did break loose in the provinces, but as long as the aristocracy received its quota of tax revenues, it paid only superficial attention. To ensure that tax resisters were punished, however, the court made the provincial headquarters into a more effective police agency. Previous restrictions against provincial officials' carrying weapons, conscripting large numbers of troops, and appointing and dispatching temporary arresting officers were lifted. The powers of the old provincial office had expanded greatly over the abstract authority granted to it in the Taihō Code.

Changes in Capital Politics

The critical transformation in court politics between 805 and 1050 was the rise of the Northern branch of the Fujiwara family to dominance. Between 645 and 805, monarchs had been vigorous enough to fend off any one family from overpowering them. Sovereigns such as Kanmu, for example, had appointed men of talent, but by the reign of Saga (r. 809–822), the ruler began turning to the Fujiwara for aid in political infighting. Between the early ninth and late tenth centuries, the Northern branch of the Fujiwara ascended to unprecedented power. Influential Fujiwara no Fuyutsugu (775–826) and his daughter Nobuko (809–871), who managed the consorts' office, started the Fujiwara on their march to power when Nobuko gave birth to the future monarch in 827. He ascended the throne at the age of thirteen, in 850. Under Yoshifusa (804–872), the Fujiwara hatched a political plot to exile their rivals, enthrone a Fujiwara grandchild, and have Yoshifusa serve as his prime minister and regent. Yoshifusa became the center of court politics for as long as he lived and his heir succeeded him.

For a brief time under the sovereign Daigo (r. 897–930), there was an attempt to balance rule between the new scion of the Fujiwara house (Tokihira) and the brilliant scholar-governor Sugawara no Michizane. Eventually, however, Tokihira succeeded in a plot against Michizane, banishing him to northern Kyushu, where he died. In the process, however, Tokihira's high-handed actions created one of the tragic figures of Japanese history and gave rise to a cult devoted especially to Michizane. Despite bad omens indicating the gods' displeasure at Michizane's fate, Tokihira managed to pass the regency intact to his brother Tadahira (880–949). He ruled unencumbered by combining control of the throne with his domination of the Council of State and the consorts' office. Following Tadahira's passing in 949, there was no single regent, but his sons succeeded in placing their daughters as royal consorts and having their infants made sovereign.

Between 960 and 1050, Fujiwara power reached its apex. Once again, it opened with the exile in 969 of a rival engaged in a supposed plot against the monarch. After 970, Fujiwara leaders served as regent and prime minister and were granted the special privilege of inspecting royal documents almost as a matter of course. During the years 967–1068, there were eight rulers, but only two were more than twenty when they came to the throne, and only one was older than thirty. They often vacated the palace and their mothers—Fujiwara consorts all—took control at court as "Mother of the Realm."

In essence, the Fujiwara became a new imperial mating line, reviving an old custom dating back to the fifth century. They achieved their amazing dominance, however, through a variety of methods. Famously, the Fujiwara used their daughters to manipulate the consort's office and court, and through that office they wielded power over the occupant of the throne, usually an under-aged Fujiwara scion. Yet they also relied on control of the highest offices in the Council of State, the advisory board to the monarch. For example, the Fujiwara went from holding only four of nineteen positions in 852, to seven of eighteen in 872, to eleven of nineteen in 972, to all twenty-five high councilor positions by 1028. The Fujiwara were also not shy about employing force to eliminate rivals in plots, real or imagined. Of course, with this unprecedented power came wealth in the form of numerous estates, sizable stipends, the sale of office, and outright bribes.[2]

The apogee of Fujiwara power came during the age of Michinaga, who began his rise to power during an epidemic that killed off many rivals. From the time of the plague in 995, Michinaga assumed the prerogative to inspect royal documents, and when his nephew challenged him, Michinaga quietly had him banished. He also eliminated the nephew's brothers for presumably practicing black magic. Between 995 and his death in 1028, Michinaga's power was unchallenged. He placed his daughters as royal consorts, manipulated the Council of State, and appointed his favorites to positions ranging from court councilor to tax farmers in the richest provinces. His sobriquet, the "Sacred Hall Regent," sums up the aura surrounding him. He was lionized after his death in two rather fanciful historical tales entitled *A Tale of Flowering Fortunes* and *The Great Mirror*. During an illness in 1019, Michinaga reportedly said, "I have nothing to be embarrassed about if I die; no one in the future is going to equal what I have done."[3]

Despite Fujiwara power, the family could not and did not rule as dictators. Throughout the period, the Council of State that had weighed issues and formulated policy in the 700s was the real aristocratic decision-making body. Deliberations of high rank holders became even more critical after the 940s, when discussions were held at palace guard posts and produced judgments submitted for approval to the throne by the regent or prime minister. With few exceptions, all policies came out of these conferences. It has been said that Fujiwara ascendancy saw a "return to familial authority," but aristocratic rule had always been familial, and there was nothing more "private" than "public" about the new system.[4] Instead, the reformed political system during 900–1050 is best thought of as the first phase of an "aristocratic" or "dynastic" state *(ōchō kokka)*. It was a collegial body of rule, led by the Fujiwara, but not dictated to by them, even under Michinaga. Unfortunately, the college was becoming increasingly rent by factionalism and violence as a growing number of rank holders struggled to support themselves in an age of depopulation.

The Economy in an Age of Depopulation

Population

Although the number of rank holders expanded between 800 and 1050 and the government continued to spend, the other side of the budgetary problem was that the resource base was static, or more likely, shrinking. The most reliable estimates for the archipelago's population around 950 range from 4.4 to 5.6 million. At its acme, around 730, there had been between six and seven million residents, and so the contraction amounted to more than a million, or about sixteen to twenty percent of the population. Between 820 and 930, almost all parts of Japan lost inhabitants, except for the Japan Sea littoral north of Kyoto; decline was particularly striking in western Honshu. The depopulation of that same region continued at a slower pace between 930 and 1050. Under these conditions, vital statistics worsened, as infant mortality became even more devastating and life expectancy may have sometimes slipped below the age of twenty.

The decline in cities clearly reflected the trend toward a decreasing population. During the eighth century, there had been three major urban centers: Nara, Naniwa, and Dazaifu, with an estimated total of perhaps two hundred thousand residents. Between 800 and 1050, the number of large cities included only Heian, at about one hundred thousand. Naniwa shrank because of both a flood and its abolition as co-capital. Fujiwara Sumitomo burned Dazaifu in 941, and although it was rebuilt along simpler lines, in 1019 Jurchen nomads invaded northern Kyushu and the port suffered again. Many provincial headquarters, formerly the home to as many as six hundred officials, decayed and even were moved during this epoch.[5]

Reasons for the continued depopulation during 800–1050 included the factors responsible for reversing the growth trend in the first place: the recurrence of deadly epidemics and famine and continued ecological degradation in central Japan. To these variables must be added a fourth: devastation from the occasional war or revolt. For most of history, disease contributed most heavily to extraordinary mortality, followed by famine. War was a distant third. One of the great ironies of history is that until recently invisible microbes and chronic malnutrition were more lethal to humans than their own species was.

Precise mortality statistics for the epidemics of this time are occasionally available. During 865–866, for instance, the island province of Oki suffered a staggering loss of thirty-four percent of its residents from some unknown pathogen. Between 993 and 995, an outbreak of smallpox coming from abroad killed twenty to twenty-five percent of the aristocratic class in Kyoto. These figures help bolster the contention that this epoch constituted Japan's "age of microparasitism."

A Tale of Flowering Fortunes, that paean to Fujiwara rule, is no less a record of lethal disease. In 974, its author wrote, "a smallpox epidemic raged among all classes of the populace, striking terror into every heart and killing gently born men and women in appalling numbers."[6] This same historical tale also describes the "terrible" pestilence of 995, so crucial to Michinaga's drive to power. During 1019–1022, *A Tale* relates a textbook example of how foreign-borne pestilence wreaked havoc and death: "According to reports from Tsukushi [Kyushu], everyone in that region had been sick since the preceding year. Because more than two decades had elapsed since the [prior] epidemic, most people had acquired no immunity to the disease, and there was great alarm and agitation at Court and elsewhere."[7] Eventually the smallpox virus reached the capital, causing many highborn to die, creating a great uproar. In addition to these cases, *A Tale* records epidemics in 998, 1000, and 1025, and usually the short depictions state that the pathogen entered from Kyushu—a sure sign of the foreign origin—and that most residents had no immunities because the last outbreak had occurred before they were born. Between 800 and 1050, a smallpox epidemic swept the islands on average every thirty years.

With a population of one hundred thousand, Kyoto was gigantic, and its poor sanitation contributed to these outbreaks. Residents of Kyoto produced about 18,250 kiloliters of waste annually. Toilets, at least for many aristocrats, may have been remarkably good, constantly flushing away the droppings. Even some of these toilets, however, apparently overflowed and frequently backed up into nearby streets. The city had some seven hundred kilometers of roadside ditches, which the government mandated should be cleaned out regularly, yet some byways were so filthy that they had names like "excrement alley." To make matters worse, the city had its share of corpses lying around—not only during plagues—as beggars, abandoned children, and dying servants succumbed. Japan's only major city was a cesspool of killer microbes and a fitting symbol of mid-Heian depopulation.

Descriptive sources reveal the effects of pestilence and the resulting depopulation in the countryside, too. In 951, officials from Tōdaiji surveyed their estates in Echizen, concluding that "even though the outlines of the fields still exist, the

An archaeologist demonstrates the use of an eleventh-century toilet. The Kizugawa City PTA. *Source:* Ōta kuritsu kyōdo hakubutsukan, ed., *Toire no kōkogaku* (Tokyo bijutsu, 1997), p. 47.

area is all wilds and swamps, and the cultivators are gone."[8] In 1017, for example, a record states that at one sizable estate in Ise province, "the amount of land currently under cultivation is even less than [one-third of the total]. This is because of frequent epidemics; officials and cultivators have mostly died."[9] In 1023, an especially deadly outbreak took place at one estate in Mino and a functionary wrote, "Last year during the great plague, estate officials and cultivators all died. Most land went out of cultivation." Again in 1041 in Iga: "The long-time residents of this district have died or fled. Thereafter, there has not been even one person here for several decades." Fewer producers meant that less grain and other commodities were funneled to the court. From this basic shortfall arose the government's budgetary tribulations and much of the political infighting.

Material and cultural evidence also reflects the major impact of microbes on the mentality of the populace. As described above, archaeologists have recovered artifacts associated with the rite of purification *(ōharae)* during the 700s. These wooden figures representing afflicted individuals, pots painted with the face of the epidemic god, shattered clay horses, and smashed miniature ovens also appear in ninth-century excavations. Beginning in the late ninth century, however, a different magico-religious approach to plagues gained credence. Called "vengeful spirit" rites, these ceremonies were based on the belief that a divine curse was responsible for disease outbreaks and other disasters.

When the move to Heian took place, Gion Shrine became the chief religious establishment for allaying epidemics through the "vengeful spirit" rite. The first performance at Gion occurred in 863, but, when Sugawara no Michizane died in exile in 903, his angry ghost presumably returned to inflict untoward weather events, pestilence, famine, and other catastrophes on the populace at large and his enemies in particular. Eventually, Gion Shrine developed its own mythology, imported from India, to explain the efficacy of its ceremonies. According to this story, a deity called the bull-headed king of the *deva*s had tired during a long journey and sought lodgings with each of two brothers. One refused and the other acceded to the deity's request. When the *deva* left the agreeable brother's house, he granted him life-long immunity from disease but destroyed the other. On the basis of this Indian myth, Gion and other religious centers presented people with wooden tablets stating that they were descendants of the good brother and should be spared from disease outbreaks.

The Gion "vengeful spirit" rites help us understand the origin and geographical and chronological extent of these epidemics. In other words, popular belief ascribed to a foreign deity the power to loose epidemic visitations, just as the plagues themselves came from abroad. These ceremonies took place throughout the archipelago. Although Gion was located in Kyoto, it soon had branches nearly everywhere. When the rites were invoked in the countryside, rural folk played musical instruments, blew whistles, and danced "with no end to the insanity."[10] And Gion's "vengeful spirit" rites acted exclusively as ceremonies to chase away disease until about 1100. This timing suggests that plagues afflicted Kyoto, Japan's only real population center, until at least the early twelfth century.

Famine and chronic malnutrition also boosted mortality and lowered fertility, helping to diminish the population. During the ninth century, hunger was common, as famines occurred more than once every three years. After 900, however, the court lost interest in most events in the hinterlands and information about starvation almost disappears. Only seven widespread famines were noted between 900 and 1050. It is possible that agriculture improved, that the tax collector took less, or that the smaller population placed less pressure on food resources. In light of the prominence of famine during later periods, however, hunger was undoubtedly still widespread but went unrecorded.

The carnival atmosphere of the modern Gion Festival belies its origin as a ritual to cast out the demons that caused epidemics. *Source*: Wakita Haruko, *Chūsei Kyoto to Gion matsuri* (Chūō kōron sha shinsha, 1999), frontispiece.

Of the thirty-five famines recorded during the ninth century when the evidence is more complete, drought caused nineteen of them and cold, rainy summers sixteen. Drought predominated through 860, after which the weather seems to have turned colder and wetter. The early spate of drought may have reflected the inadequate irrigation technology of that time, while the later appearance of a wet,

cold climate may have been related to volcanic activity or the continued deforestation of the Kinai and widespread erosion.

Unlike the eighth century, there are no reliable mortality statistics on famine
between 800 and 1050, but there are a few indirect indications that malnutrition
was a significant cause of death. In 841, for example, about twenty-seven thousand
farmers in northern Honshu were dropped from the tax rolls "on account of crop
failure."[11] During the 860s, when the climate appears to have become colder and
wetter, the price of polished rice jumped thirty-five percent and that of brown rice
forty percent. Official policies during the ninth century, when the elite was still
concerned with such matters, indicate that they took famine seriously. One tactic
was to encourage the planting of other grains, such as wheat, soybeans, barley, or
buckwheat to tide over the hungry populace after the first crop had failed. Elites
tried prayers to the gods and then grain relief, at least while it had any to dispense.
The central government also implored the "rich" and others with reserves to help
the needy. After 850, as the district magistracy declined steeply, the court began to
blame corrupt officials and press farmers to work harder, drink less rice wine, and
refrain from gambling. In sum, malnutrition was undoubtedly a chronic condition for many people between 800 and 1050.

Even though the building boom was over by the 800s, deforestation and ecological damage continued to beset the Kinai and surrounding provinces. In 821,
for example, the Council of State condemned peasants who "stripped groves on
mountains near rivers as they pleased. When a drought comes, run-off is scarce
and the crop withers."[12] Both archaeological and written evidence support the notion that the Kinai and environs had become deforested, and when a new building
project was approved, lumbermen were forced to go even farther afield to harvest
timber.

War and the occasional revolt constituted a more sensational cause of mortality. War first beset the archipelago during the Yayoi period, and, although there was
violence between 250 and 800 CE, conflicts seem to have been so few and short
that only a few died. The wars against the *emishi* in northeastern Japan changed all
that, however, because they were protracted and the court assembled huge armies
to fight. Between 774 and 812, the court sent five expeditions to subdue the hapless
residents of the northeast, and its armies numbered in the tens of thousands. In-
decision and poor leadership plagued the campaigns at first, but eventually the famous General Sakanoue Tamuramaro subdued the *emishi*. When he won his first
great victory during 792–793, he reported that his men had "beheaded 467, captured 150, collected 85 horses, and burned 75 villages."[13] The casualties may seem
few, but the razing of the villages must have resulted in great hardship. In other
words, many noncombatants lost their homes and fields because of Sakanoue's
campaigns.

Later, when Taira no Masakado attacked his relatives in 935, he "set fire to everything," incinerating at least 500 residences.[14] Arson committed against potential enemy bases continued to be a favorite tactic throughout his rebellion. He also destroyed the seasonal harvest and robbed, pillaged, and raped when he began his revolt in earnest by capturing various provincial headquarters in 939. In 941, Masakado's contemporary in rebellion, Fujiwara Sumitomo, burned Dazaifu, the official port to the Asian mainland. When Taira no Tadatsune rebelled in 1028, the court conducted a campaign of scorched-earth tactics against him. By late 1031, Tadatsune was dead, but the new governor of a province that was the scene of much fighting reported that immediately after Tadatsune's capture only eighteen of almost twenty-three thousand units of cultivated land could be farmed. Three years later, a mere five percent of the fields had returned to production. Even two hundred years later, the province had not fully recovered.

To be sure, lengthy fighting was rare and most violence in this period involved only a few people. Yet war now included so-called collateral damage, a new aspect of campaigning. Warfare combined with disease and famine to make the populace even more vulnerable. Pillage and arson would serve as important weapons of war for the next millennium, and would expand as a cause of extraordinary mortality as the age progressed.

Agriculture and Industry

It should come as no surprise that as depopulation took place, fewer acres produced less grain. Several examples cited above state that farmers were dead or had abandoned their fields and large tracts had become wasteland. In fact, untended fields were so common after 900 that, when tax farmers made their reports to the court in preparation for sending in their quotas, the central government automatically assumed that at least ten percent of arable land was not being cultivated. Any greater proportion required special dispensation and might bring down the wrath of the court on the tax farmer. Officials became so mindful of the problem of vacant fields that their legislation used at least two different legal terms for land permanently and temporarily untilled.

Estate lands located along the Yoshino River in Yamato Province and belonging to the Buddhist temple Eizanji provide the classic example of how the number of fields under cultivation fluctuated from year to year. Eizanji divided its estate into thirty-five equal parcels and made fifteen surveys from 990 to 1059. Cultivation of almost half the arable land (seventeen plots) shifted dramatically over this seventy-year period; in some years they were planted and in others they were not. Thirteen units were farmed somewhat more regularly, but only four parcels— eleven percent—were fully cropped in each survey. Apparently, the era from 990 to 1060 was an especially harsh time for agriculture in Japan, because recently archaeologists have uncovered numerous barren fields dating to this epoch, as both estate and provincial lands disappeared from maps across the archipelago.

Under conditions of depopulation, labor was in short supply and estate managers and provincial officials developed a system to "encourage agriculture." Highly ritualized, this procedure included a ceremonial offering of rice wine on the first day of the year, "playing in the fields" to soothe the spirit of the lands with dance and song, and a petition to family gods to protect the household from disaster. Village women also performed in the early summer for "the bird who promoted fruitful agriculture."[15] This magico-religious system was popular until about 1300.

"Encouraging agriculture" also had more functional elements. One was the breaking up of soil with hoes and shovels, a practice beginning as early as the late winter and continuing until the early summer. This back-wrenching labor was essential because each parcel was not cropped regularly and therefore required a thorough sod busting, raking, and grading each season. Toward the end of the process, tillers might apply fertilizer (usually grasses and leaves) and clean irrigation channels. Of course, in many paddies transplanting was carried out in the late spring, and weeding and shooing away insects and birds were constant tasks.

Another element was the annual spring visit by "officials who encouraged agriculture." Their main purpose was to attempt to capture an adequate labor force and assign cultivators to name-fields. Full cultivation was their goal, but it was rarely achieved. Officials might conduct a land survey, help to decide which crops to plant, and try to determine which plots might be the most exposed to drought or flooding. They also estimated a reasonable amount for rent. To attract peasants, these officials came prepared to dole out grain and food to potential sharecroppers, who paid a portion of their output in return for the rest of the harvest and the use of common lands. In the fall when the harvest was due, these officials returned to assess yields. If the harvest was damaged, as it seems often to have been, they would either have to reduce the proposed rent or watch their scarce labor force leave for better prospects next season. Life was certainly hard during these centuries, but if cultivators survived the various threats to their existence, they commanded more opportunities than ever before in a labor-short economy.

The scarcity of labor also gave rise to innovation. The development and diffusion of a new type of dual harness helped to promote the wider use of oxen for plowing. This harness, placed over the neck and shoulders of the animal, became popular with the "rich" and other leading peasants precisely as the amount of human labor was decreasing. Not only did demand for workers outrun supply, but there were also more wide-open spaces for the oxen to be housed in and graze

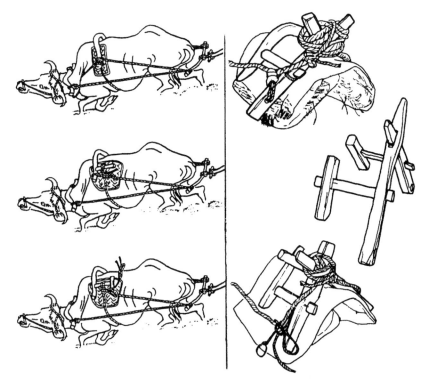

New plow harnesses like the one sketched above allowed more widespread use of oxen for breaking Japan's stubborn soils. *Source*: Kōno Michiaki, *Nihon nōkō gu shi no kisoteki kenkyū* (Osaka: Izumi shoin, 1994), p. 265.

on. Although livestock never became as important for Japanese agriculture as for European or American, the small role that it did have began during this age.

Other aspects of rural life changed very little. The plethora of livelihoods evident during the prehistoric age continued; peasants survived by dry cropping, slash-and-burn agriculture, hunting, fishing, and gathering tubers, nuts, and berries. Many rural people took up these occupations according to the conditions of the moment: when the harvest failed, many took to the mountains, moors, and seashores to survive. In fact, although the government officially counted only paddy fields (862,000 units) among its assets, it would not be surprising if these other livelihoods were greatly popular during this era of depopulation. Settlement patterns remained the same, too, as rural folks lived dispersed over the landscape. Boundaries were malleable and with a smaller population, migration was more common than ever. In essence, Japan's peasants were an elusive class for an elite that survived by collecting annual rent from them.

In industry, too, the labor shortage led to important changes. After Heian was left half finished in 819, the court attempted no more capitals until the late 1100s, and the repair agency for the city was abolished for about a century. Temple-building, at least that supported by the government, also fell on hard times, as even construction on the headquarters of the new Shingon sect at Tōji and Mount Kōya dragged on for decades. The government fired and hired directors for the construction of Tōji almost annually, and the entrance to Heian where Tōji was located became "unsightly."[16] Kūkai, the monk who transmitted Shingon Buddhism to Japan, died before the lagging building at Mount Kōya could be finished. When its central structures went up in flames in the late tenth century, the reconstruction proceeded so slowly that the monks left in protest.

The same fate also befell the main temple complex for the other new Buddhist sect, Tendai, brought to Japan by Saichō. He had laid plans for a massive set of first nine, and then sixteen, halls on Mount Hiei, but he lived to see the completion of only one or two. Long after Saichō's day, in 966, there was a conflagration on the mountain, and thirty-one structures were destroyed. It took at least seventeen years to rebuild the main halls, despite the able leadership of the monk Ryōgen.

Even the all-powerful Michinaga could not have his Tsuchimikado Mansion reconstructed within the allotted time after a fire in 1019. When he became ill and commanded the erection of an Amida (a Buddha) hall for his salvation, workers ended up using recycled foundation stones and tiles. Although completed in 1021, after it burned in 1058 it was not reconstructed.

Between 900 and 1050, tax farmers in the provinces contributed toward construction projects. The behavior of these officials also suggests difficulties in raising sufficient labor because they frequently resisted levies or tried to shift their duties onto others. Lacking an adequate supply of workers, the government apparently neither refurbished the sovereign's residence between 800 and 960 nor reconstructed the great wall around the palace grounds for two hundred years. There are no records for the rebuilding of Ise Shrine between 900 and 1050, even though customarily it was to be reconstructed every twenty years. Systematic rebuilding for Izumo Shrine did not even begin until the late tenth century.

Another sign of the scarcity of labor was the transformation of widely differing industrial sectors. Some, like the manufacture of silk products, suffered outright decline. As noted earlier, the government attempted to encourage the silk industry in the early 700s, but these efforts apparently produced mixed results. The amount and quality of silk thread and cloth degenerated rapidly during the ninth century. The damasks and brocades donned by Prince Genji were imported from China or produced within his household.

Transportation became less efficient, too. During the early 700s, the court built a system of roads and provided packhorses, lodgings, and mounts for officials. Beginning in the ninth century, however, the court no longer had the resources to construct roads and the system of post stations had neither the manpower nor the financial support to continue. The efficiency of land transportation fell off sharply; the journey from the Kinai to northern Kyushu took five or six days in the 700s, but by the Heian era it had doubled to twelve days. Travel to northeastern Japan was impeded even more. No wonder Heian aristocrats enjoyed their leisurely outings into the country.

Other sectors turned to labor-saving devices and technology. The transformation in ironworking, from a box-shaped furnace using blowpipes and bellows to a half-submerged vertical shaft furnace relying on up-drafting winds, embodies just one such effort to save on labor. Salt making reveals another example of the development of labor-saving techniques. The traditional method required boiling down the brine in pots and cauldrons and used seaweed to thicken the solution and accelerate the formation of salt crystals. It was labor intensive, as workers made the containers, collected seawater, seaweed, and firewood, and continuously poured the brine over the outstretched seaweed.

From the late ninth century, however, salt makers employed a much simpler, more labor-efficient method. They carved "salt fields" on the beach to trap ocean waves and let the sun evaporate the water and produce crystals. The industry moved from "salt making" to salt collection. The new method required less labor and equipment and was faster and could produce more salt. These salt fields became widespread just as the population declined.

Domestic and Overseas Commerce

Depopulation and the changes ongoing in agriculture and industry had a debilitating effect on mercantile activity, too. The construction boom of the period 700–750, the large consumer class residing in the capitals, and the constant movement of tax commodities made for a robust commercial sector, at least in the Kinai and adjacent provinces. The government minted copper cash and officials accumulated tidy profits in various transactions.

Between 770 and 850, trade became a crucial aspect of court finance, because the government prevailed upon provincial officials to exchange their reserves of loan rice and other commodities for aristocratic necessities. As the provinces frittered away their financial reserves for these items, though, this policy had to be replaced by 900 by the system of tax farming described earlier.

Government handling of the mint exacerbated a downward spiral in domestic trade between 850 and 1050. The court struck twelve issues of cash between 708 and 958, and each time it debased the currency. By the late 900s, the coins were worthless and the central government complained that no one was using them. In

984, one official wrote that "the world has never avoided the use of cash more than it does now." Three years later, the police ordered "people of all ranks" to use coins in their transactions.[17] Barter became more prevalent, while high-ranking officials relied upon their estates and tax farmers to provide the mix of commodities they required for consumption. Once centers of local commerce, provincial headquarters declined drastically in population. Some disappeared completely.

At the same time, overseas commerce and travel—at least for the elite—seems to have begun to grow, despite the political hibernation of the court after the collapse of the Tang and Silla around 900. Heian elites were reluctant to become involved politically on the continent as numerous Central Asian nomads caused turmoil there. Then, too, there was a technological reason for the posture of the Japanese court: its abandonment of sophisticated Chinese junk technology at home. Instead of continuing to follow the Chinese example as they had done earlier, Japanese boat builders returned to their traditional ways, merely hollowing out logs, attaching boards to the sides to enhance seaworthiness, and using oars or sails for propulsion. Because these ships could cross the East China Sea directly only with the greatest difficulty, there was little chance that Japanese merchantmen were going to be able to sail to China directly to trade or travel.

Making use of their more advanced vessels, the Chinese came to Japan in ever-increasing numbers, providing the essential link to East Asian commerce and tourism. Having begun one of the world's most remarkable demographic and economic expansions by at least 900, China of the Sung dynasty (947–1279) regularly sent its traders to Japan to supply the elite there with Chinese fineries, such as elegant damasks and brocades. In return, the Japanese court shipped gold, hides, and other goods from northeastern Honshu. Giant junks from China carrying crews of a hundred or more docked in Japan during the tenth century. By the end of the eleventh century, Sung merchants were so common in northern Kyushu that they married Japanese women and adopted mixed surnames. The government in Kyoto tried to reserve for itself the top priority in purchasing Sung goods, but the repetition of laws against smuggling surely indicates that the laws were ineffectual. It would be a mistake to exaggerate the extent of overseas trade before 1050, but it would later grow and help "jump start" the Japanese economy.

Society: Class, Kinship, and Gender Relations

Class

During the mid-eighth century, Japan's class system resembled a sharply pointed pyramid, with an infinitesimal number of aristocrats at the top and the rest of the populace occupying the lower reaches. As the population slowly declined, however, the pyramid became misshapen, with more and more nobles at the top and too few commoners at the bottom to support them. The most significant classes during 800–1050 were similar to those discussed in the previous chapter, which suggests that the static economy resulted in glacial social change. These major classes comprised the high- and mid-level aristocracy, the Buddhist clergy, local power holders exemplified by the "rich," and commoners practicing diverse occupations. The most important social change was that almost all slaves surviving from the preceding age received or took their freedom because owners could not enforce control in a labor-short economy. The remaining classes became more rigid, with each family having its own function and status. In essence, Heian society had become "frozen."

About 150 aristocrats held the Fifth Rank and above in the 700s. The highest rungs—the Third Rank and above—were usually left empty. From the 800s onward, however, many more persons achieved high rank; by the year 1000 there may have been three hundred or more men at the Fifth Rank or higher. Furthermore, nobles were not as reticent about assuming the First, Second, and Third Ranks as they had been before, which led to a decline in the relative status value of the lower grades, a phenomenon known as "rank inflation." Though disease decimated the aristocracy, the court always seemed to find more highborn people to promote. In the end, those low-ranking, paper-pushing bureaucrats described earlier left their unattractive positions, which were not refilled. The "court" now meant those holding one of the first six ranks, with the bottom, where most bureaucrats had formerly resided, disappearing.

For those aristocrats at the top, mostly the Northern branch of the Fujiwara, life was elegant and luxurious. Consider the household of Fujiwara no Sanesuke (957–1046), a contemporary of Michinaga.[18] His residence, called Ononomiya, spread over about three acres and was only a few minutes walk from the imperial palace or Michinaga's Tsuchimikado Mansion. Although he had originally lived in the homes of his first two wives, when he was widowed the second time he had Ononomiya built and never married again. The main residence had four dwelling places, connected by roofed hallways. Smaller wings were attached to each building. Altogether, Sanesuke had access to more than 19,000 square feet of living space. This massive domicile faced south to an open garden where he held parties. His garden was expansive, containing three ponds and two hills. Nearby were horse stables, storage bins, and a large and a small Buddhist chapel. A wall with three gates surrounded this stately mansion.

Inside Ononomiya lived Sanesuke's staff, including ladies-in-waiting, servants, wet nurses, workers, and various lackeys. Sanesuke's household staff was at least as elaborate as that of Prince Nagaya; it had offices for attendants, escorts,

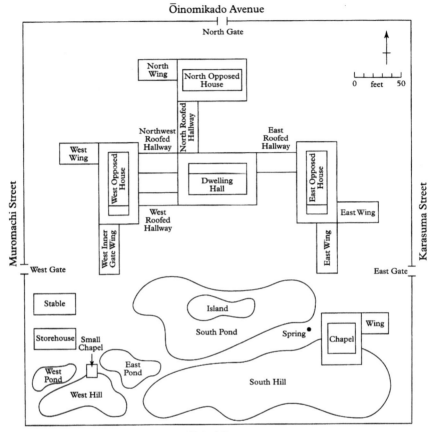

Ōinomikado Avenue

Onononomiya Mansion. Heian aristocrats like the powerful Fujiwara lived in magnificent mansions, such as Onononomiya, with facilities for storage, parties, and Buddhist rites. *Source*: William McCullough, "The Capital and Its Society," in Donald H. Shively and William McCullough, eds., *The Cambridge History of Japan: Heian Japan* (Cambridge: Cambridge University, 1998), p. 145.

administrators, repairmen and women, servants, pages, and the kitchen and pantry help. Workers included seamstresses, artists, lacquer painters, carpenters, and metallurgists. The storehouses contained not only daily necessities, but also paper, dyestuffs, aromatics, precious metals, religious icons, scriptures, medicines, and heirlooms. Sanesuke's stipends, the rents from his estates and official lands, and, most important, the gifts, bribes, and his portion of the fruits of tax farming, paid for this elaborate mansion and its residents.

As during the eighth century, Sanesuke's luxurious mansion and his various incomes were a function of his rank or status. Women also held high rank and therefore had separate residences, often every bit as elaborate as Sanesuke's. Rinshi, principal wife of Michinaga, conducted their courtship in her own domicile. Eventually, she had Michinaga moved into her house, and in the end Rinshi deeded what was to become Tsuchimikado Mansion to Michinaga. Heian literature also supports the proposition that powerful, high-ranking women possessed stately mansions with sizable staffs; for example, Fujiwara no Kaneie, the villain of *Kagerō nikki*, kept his own home apart from his wealthy main wife Tokihime. The Shining Prince Genji lived separately from Lady Aoi, and Tō no Chūjō had a similar arrangement with his high-ranking wife. The Third Princess in the *Tale of Genji* had such an expansive estate that nobles played kickball on her land. All of these ladies had high status, large mansions, and considerable household staffs of their own.

Because of the extensive literature of this period, almost every detail of aristocratic material life is known. Interiors of the great mansions were sparsely furnished with blinds and screens. Only darkness and curtains gave a copulating couple privacy. Aristocrats wore silk almost exclusively and sported fans. Their diet was surprisingly poor, mostly polished rice, various vegetables, fish and shellfish, and lots of rice wine; nobles ate little protein. Because of their unhealthful diet and lack of activity, the highborn were susceptible to all sorts of chronic diseases. Genji, for example, suffered from malaria, and Michinaga had diabetes, apparently hereditary in the Fujiwara line, which eventually made him blind and impotent. Beriberi was another common illness.

Highborn aristocrats, primarily concerned with ceremonial duties, occupied one of the top three ranks. Those listed at the Fourth, Fifth, and Sixth Ranks had much lower status and spent most of their careers serving the privileged. They might do so through special skills that they had acquired, such as the ability to compose official documents, write poetry, make paintings, interpret laws, or perform as wet nurses. Sugawara no Michizane, one of the few ever to take a degree at the state university, belonged to such a family. These men and women were not poor, but their economic resources and households could not compare to the highborn. In one case, the owner's main hall was twenty-one by sixteen meters, with two smaller buildings nearby, crowded onto a modest lot.

Military men formed another group fitting into this category of skilled lower-ranking nobles, known for their expertise in "the way of the bow and the horse." Men such as Taira no Masakado and Minamoto no Mitsunaka alternated between living in the capital and the provinces and therefore might just as easily be considered local notables. These masters of violence frequently pledged loyalty to more than one lord and were well known as the "hired assassins" of the highborn. Mitsunaka helped Michinaga in a plot in 969; Minamoto no Yorichika was such a skillful murderer that in 1017 when he cut down a rival, Michinaga made a note in his diary that "this Yorichika is good at killing people."[19] Of course, men like these made excellent tax farmers. The full story of the samurai will be addressed in chapter 4.

The pool of officials appointed as tax farmers also held similar status as lower-ranking nobles. These men hungered to be named the governor of rich provinces. Fujiwara no Motonaga, known from the Owari Protest, collected taxes of all kinds at exorbitant rates; withheld aid from the poor, transport workers, and ditch and pond repair; and spent so much time in the capital that people could never air their grievances. The violent Taira no Korehira was another lower aristocrat who aimed first for the wealthy province of Ise. When his patron Michinaga objected to Korehira's brutality, he quietly sent the Fujiwara leader ten horses and eventually assumed governorships in seven provinces, including his coveted Ise. His greed was so all-consuming that whole provinces reportedly became deserted.

The Buddhist clergy continued to serve as an adjunct to the aristocracy, not only performing state rituals but also helping the privileged gain salvation. During these centuries, however, several changes overtook this class and Japanese religion in general. Buddhism and the native cult, already starting to meld in the 600s, became amalgamated and local gods and goddesses turned into protectors of the Buddhist law and then manifestations of Buddhist deities. Buddhist temples and shrines combined into powerful religious complexes, such as Kasuga Shrine and Kōfukuji, and helped the religious class acquire even more wealth and power.

The gender and class composition of Buddhist devotees also began to change. The state all but stopped ordaining women and banned them from some sacred sites because they might be a temptation to sin. Still, some women, especially of aristocratic birth, continued to accept unofficial ordination. The class origins of powerful monks began to shift as rank holders with many sons and no other outlets for them started to place them in high positions at famous temples. For example, between 782 and 990, ninety-seven percent of these powerful monks were of commoner background, studying for and attaining ordination. Between 990 and 1069, however, that proportion slipped to fifty-two percent.[20] In other words, the crowded aristocratic class began to seek religious appointment as a way to produce an income for their children. Temples no longer followed rules of seniority but instead rewarded their aristocratic patrons, despite loud protests from well-qualified ordinands.

The increased role of aristocratic offspring in administering the daily affairs and extensive estate lands of these temple complexes helped to politicize these institutions and increase factionalism. By the mid-tenth century, violence occasionally broke out among factions within and between religious complexes. These confrontations could cause considerable damage, as when more than forty buildings were destroyed on Mount Hiei in a factional dispute in 993. Many monks of minimal education were there merely for the tax exemption—and readily took part in scuffles. These same clerics engaged in all sorts of behavior once banned by monastic rules, including eating meat, drinking rice wine, and engaging in homosexual and heterosexual liaisons. Some abbots such as Ennin (794–864) condemned these violations of religious conduct, but until 1050 the anticlericalism implied in terms like "evil monk" (*akusō*) was not yet widespread.

Ryōgen (912–985) was a powerful monk of this time.[21] Born to a poor commoner family, he ascended Mount Hiei at the age of eleven, found a suitable teacher, and was ordained in the Tendai sect at sixteen. Lacking a powerful sponsor and ambitious for a career that included more than just performing everyday ceremonies, Ryōgen succeeded in attaching himself to more powerful monks and showing off his knowledge in a series of religious debates. This attracted the attention of court aristocrats, especially members of the northern branch of the Fujiwara. In exchange for his expertise at various esoteric rituals employed when Regent Fujiwara no Tadahira died, Ryōgen became a protégé of Tadahira's son Morosuke. Morosuke obtained a series of important appointments for Ryōgen and cemented his alliance with the monk. Eventually, Ryōgen was appointed to the headship of the Tendai sect. In that post, he strengthened monastic discipline and helped rebuild many structures on Mount Hiei after the disastrous fire of 966. He also expanded Tendai power into the provinces and aided in the ordination of women. He remained the head of the Tendai sect until his death.

Missing from Ryōgen's career was travel to China. Some Buddhist monks sojourned to the continent in search of Buddhist law, usually aboard Chinese junks. For example, Ennin took passage on a Chinese junk in 853 and stayed in the country until 858, visiting temples, living in Chang-an, and studying the Buddhist canon. Jōjin (1011–1081) had similar experiences during 1072–1073. When they returned, these monks brought news about the luxurious Sung court as well as Buddhist sutras, mandalas, relics, and ritual texts. They also sent home calendars and books on Chinese philosophy and history. Eventually these clerics would become a major conduit for diverse Chinese ideas, institutions, and materials influencing many aspects of Japanese life.

Out in the provinces a new group of local power holders took the place of the district magistrate. Most were lower-ranking men like Masakado and Tadatsune, possessing moated, fortified residences and controlling the surrounding cultivators through interest-bearing rice loans and the dispersal of tools and seed. Their dwellings had iron furnaces and charcoal makers, probably for producing weapons. They also headed ephemeral military forces composed of a few close followers and many peasant foot soldiers. Several formed ties with the high aristocracy in Kyoto, sending grain and other items to their absentee lords in return for honorary rank and office or governmental designation of their fields as estates. Tax farmers cultivated alliances with these local magnates to enroll them in provincial police forces by honoring them with temporary appointments and participation in religious rites, archery contests, wrestling matches, and legally sanctioned hunts.

Unlike the former district magistrates, however, most of these people were outside the government structure and often proved intractable foes. Fujiwara no Haruaki was one such "rich" man. A resident of Hitachi province unrelated to the Fujiwara at court, he was infamous for never granting famine relief to his cultivators. He robbed the poor and refused audiences to official messengers. When the tax farmer in Hitachi tried to arrest him, Haruaki incinerated several storehouses. He eventually sought shelter with Masakado and presumably died a rebel.

Commoners, often farmers when conditions were right, comprised the overwhelming majority of the populace. Among cultivators, a few were rich enough to afford oxen and plow more extensive lands, serving among the peasantry as leaders and heads of name-fields. Other than more references to these wealthier farmers, however, very little seems to have changed for rural folk. Material life—housing, clothing, diet, and sanitation—remained the same as in the eighth century. Beliefs emphasized rites for the ancestors and benefits during this lifetime.

Ōyama Estate, established near the capital around 850, provides more specific insight into the life of the average peasant. Composed of about thirty acres of rice fields scattered in the numerous small valleys formed by the Ōyama River, the estate was watered by two ponds, one enclosed by a 212-meter dam. Even today, the waters at Ōyama receive little sun and are cold, making rice cultivation risky. For this reason, the villagers turned to other livelihoods, as shown by the tillage of dry fields and the remnants of many large stoneware kilns (Sue ware) dotting the landscape. Then, too, Ōyama Estate included 105 acres of grasslands and forests, where residents gathered lumber, firewood, fertilizer, and chestnuts. High up in the hills, people tended a graveyard and there was a shrine for various seasonal festivals. Because the land was situated on a major roadway, peasants found it easy to deliver their grain, lumber, and pottery to the proprietor in Kyoto.

Legally speaking, the peasants rented their parcels annually and belonged to one of two groups, depending on the nature of their tax burden. It is unclear how many name-fields there were at Ōyama, but relations between the farmers and the tax collector were apparently testy. In 932, the provincial governor entered the home of a leading peasant and stole two hundred sheaves of rice, claiming them as taxes. To protest this behavior, all the residents at Ōyama went into hiding in the surrounding woods. Farmers incurred the wrath of officials by trying to avoid paying rents and taxes on newly cleared paddies, too. To improve their access to warmer waters, the peasants at Ōyama traded their woodland resources to the cultivators of a nearby estate that possessed much of the precious liquid. Nevertheless, the number of fields at Ōyama grew only slowly until the twelfth century.

Rural life at Kuroda Estate, situated on the all-important route from Kyoto to the Kanto, repeats similar themes. Kuroda began as a timber forest supplying the building needs of Tōdaiji during the 700s. Around 950, a local notable donated more forestland to enhance the chances of salvation for his ancestors. Eventually, the fifty or so lumbermen working at Kuroda cleared a small area for rice paddies to supplement their incomes. Gradually so much land was given over to the temple as forest and fields that the local tax farmer was unable to meet his quota. In 1053, the official tried to retake the lands by removing the boundary stakes and forcibly collecting all overdue tax items. To enforce his demands, the tax farmer sent in his henchmen, who burned down residents' homes and harvested all their crops. Some peasants fought back, but many fled. In the end, however, the tax farmer was forced to yield back all the land he had taken from Tōdaiji. Like Ōyama Estate, the story from Kuroda illustrates the variety of livelihoods in rural Japan, the slow progress of rice farming, and the often violent clash of interests between villagers and officialdom.

About merchants even less is known. As the population declined and Japanese cities shrank, money went out of use and commerce lessened. In Kyoto, markets disappeared, yet some mercantile activity apparently survived in the capital. For instance, officials controlling tax items and other commodities still acted as traders. One story relates how the wife of a sutra copyist was a famous dealer in second-hand goods. In fact, buying and selling may have been a chief occupation for commoner women. And in southern Kyoto, blacksmiths, metal casters, and experts in gilding and inlaying plied their trades.

As noted above, products of Japan's lakes, rivers, and seas comprised a large portion of the tax items sent to the court in the eighth century. During 800-1050, the number of people making their living by such means increased and the court gave them special prerogatives. Instead of limiting their activities by province, the court opened up the entire archipelago to these fishers, salt makers, and seaweed collectors. One regulation counted more than 3,000 sea people residing in the Inland Sea just beyond Kyoto; they gathered like clouds but then disappeared like mist, hampering the livelihoods of local farmers. Many were attached directly to the imperial house, such as 204 fishing people residing around Lake Biwa. Soon aristocratic houses, temples, and shrines joined in the competition for control of these groups. For example, Michinaga had his fish sent to him from sea people living in Kii Province near the Kinai, and these same people acted as helms operators, carrying products and travelers around the archipelago and to Korea.

Kinship and Gender Relations

Kinship, family, and marriage among all classes were fundamentally unchanged from conditions of the eighth century. Bilateral kinship and partible inheritance still obtained. "Marriage" remained a vague arrangement, with the man
visiting his love nocturnally until either he took up living with his in-laws or the
relationship waned into a nebulous form of divorce. The concept of incest was
nearly nonexistent. It is unclear whether the custom of bridewealth continued,
but women of all classes had considerable power over property, child rearing, and
household and farming tasks.

The only difference among commoners was growth in the average size of the
family due to the increasing popularity of uxorilocal marriage. Because most rural
settlements were small and scattered and there was a lack of farmhands, it was
sensible for the husband to move in with his in-laws. The family became bigger,
numbering eight to ten members, and this larger unit helped offset the dearth of
workers. Even within these more stable peasant families, however, birthing and
menstruation took place in parturition huts under the most primitive conditions.
The corpses of dead babies were abandoned in the wilds.

More is known about family life among the high aristocracy. Conditions at
their stately mansions placed countervailing pressures on interpersonal relations.
On the one hand, strong bonds formed between the highborn and their servants.
For instance, because the "good people" did not suckle their infants, as many as
two to four wet nurses, holding rank and receiving modest incomes, breast-fed offspring for a year or two. They maintained lifelong relationships with their charges
and the parents. On the other hand, the close bonds with servants stood in stark
contrast with the loose familial ties. Early mortality, the practice of multiple sex
partners, and the frequent moving of residences reinforced this tendency. Nevertheless, affective ties did bind members of aristocratic families, especially fathers
and daughters. Male homosexuality was known, even though there was no such
concept per se and men were not so defined.

Romances began as they had previously, with males and females exchanging
poetry. Michinaga, for example, wrote,

> Since we all have cooked you up
> As "that relish,"
> No man who caught a glimpse
> Would pass on you—
> Of that I am certain.

To which Lady Murasaki, authoress of the *Tale of Genji,* replied:

Who could possibly
Have gone about repeating
How he savored me,
A thing
Yet to know a lover's pass?[22]

During the courtship, the gazes of each sex were direct expressions of desire. Men most often peeked at an aristocratic woman through the openings in a fence or home, but women, too, fixed men intently with their erotic gazes. For instance, "A man who was a great gallant once built himself a house at Nagaoka and took up residence there. Several very attractive ladies were in service at a neighboring imperial establishment, and one day some of them caught sight of the man as he was superintending the rice harvest in the fields. . . . The assembled ladies bore down on him, calling, 'Isn't this a rather odd occupation for a famous lover?' The man fled in confusion to the privacy of an inside room." In this case, the sexual aggression of the women had put the man at a loss.[23]

Ordinarily, however, wealthy noblemen had the upper hand because they desired multiple progeny and thus practiced polygyny. The designation of one woman as the "principal wife" was normally done after the fact. Other wives lived on their own; sometimes their lovers provided residences for second or third wives of lowly status. When the couple was of equal rank, however, the woman or her family almost always provided the dwelling and the marriage was uxorilocal. Even Fujiwara no Sanesuke conveyed Ononomiya to his daughter when she married. Aristocratic women also held many other types of property, and their wealth, in the form of clothing and other assets, supported their husbands and offspring in their quest for office.

To be sure, Heian literary masterpieces such as the *Tale of Genji* and the various pieces of diary literature contain numerous examples of high-ranking men taking advantage of, and perhaps even raping, women with lesser pedigrees. Prince Genji's behavior with Yugao, Kaneie's heart-rending treatment of "Michitsuna's mother," or Izumi Shikibu's melancholy during her affair with a prince showed the emotional dependency of these women on their men. It is interesting to note, however, that the women who authored and appeared in these stories were all from the lower aristocracy, often the daughters of tax farmers. No doubt, their fathers wanted literate, attractive daughters to help them secure an appointment to a wealthy province. Striking up a liaison with a highborn man and writing a paean to his abilities was one means to that end.

Ultimately, class trumped gender in sexual relations.[24] High-ranking men who took lower status women as lovers were often abusive, but, as the *Tales of Ise* demonstrates, low-ranking men really had no chance with highborn women. Lady

Rokujō, a minister's daughter and the widow of an heir apparent, haunted Genji whose mother was a mere commoner. A man's freedom of movement as compared to the cloistered existence of his women gave him certain advantages. Then, too, primary and secondary aristocratic wives could never "marry" more than one male. Only lesser ladies-in-waiting and concubines at court, such as Izumi Shikibu, could take more than one lover at a time; yet within aristocratic uxorilocal households, women such as Michinaga's primary wife Rinshi held high status and great power. They provided invaluable support for their husbands and bore male heirs who became the next generation of rank holders. In the "frozen society" that was Heian Japan, a person's class was his or her most important defining characteristic.

Aristocratic Culture and the Plight of Commoners

The early and mid-Heian period is renowned for some of the world's greatest art and literature produced at the courtly salon. Many people admire the elegance of the aristocratic class and the devotion of its members to traditions of beauty, summed up by such phrases as *miyabi* (refinement) and *mono no aware* (the sadness of passing beauty). The clergy was responsible for elaborate ceremonies and the construction of beautiful temple complexes. It is important to remember, however, that these great achievements came at the expense of considerable suffering for the mass of the populace, particularly at the hands of the agents of the elite: the "rich," tax farmers, and warriors. Most people received little or nothing in return; indeed commoners were objects of scorn and ridicule as "basket worms" in Sei Shōnagon's *Pillow Book.*[25]

Were the achievements worth the sacrifice? Various people will answer that query differently, but in defense of the Heian elite, at least they produced world-class art, religious ceremonies, and great literature. They may have lived off others' labor and produce and done nothing or, worse yet, created mayhem. All ruling elites prosper at the expense of the great mass of rent and tax producers, but few have left such a brilliant legacy as the Heian court.

4 Rising Social and Political Tensions in an Epoch of Minimal Growth, 1050–1180

The Establishment of a Trifunctional Elite

The Evolution of the Samurai

Since the Tomb era, an aristocracy had ruled Japan. It grew and became more elaborate over the centuries, but the essential idea of a hereditary class of noblemen and women administering the islands had remained unchanged. Beginning about 1050, however, the aristocracy—now exclusively civilian in function—was joined by two other elites: the clergy and the military. Each class had its own function, clientele, geographical base, and relation to the sovereign, which in conjunction provided legitimacy for the system. Further, members of each branch formed alliances with the others, and joined together in political factions. These three functionally distinct but politically and socially intertwined elites held sway in Japan until about 1300.

The military was the newest group to attain elite status, but the roots of the samurai lay in the Tomb age. Around 450, the horse had been introduced to Japan from Korea, and when men combined riding the animal with the Jōmon technology of archery, a deadly new form of combat was born: mounted archery. Even the small, unneutered horses of early Japan (about one hundred thirty centimeters at the shoulder) made armies more mobile; equestrians could annihilate lightly armored foot soldiers. The two major drawbacks to this form of battle were the great expense of buying and feeding a horse and the large block of time required to learn to ride and shoot from a galloping animal. Typically, a horse cost five times the annual income of a peasant, and would-be mounted archers had to have time to practice. They needed to learn to release the bridle, and guide the on-rushing beast with their legs or voice, all while taking aim and firing arrows. The cost and time invested in mounted warfare meant that it was an occupation limited to local notables and certain members of the service nobility.

Under the Yamato monarch, around 600, armies fighting in Korea or Japan included forces supplied by approximately one hundred twenty local magnates allied to the sovereign, as well as smaller contingents led by the service nobility or from the royal guards. Altogether, these armies may have numbered ten to twenty thousand fighters. The first riders wore iron helmets and slat armor, in which iron pieces were sewn together with leather into flexible sheets. Wielding straight swords, these elite warriors fought alongside foot soldiers employing spears or swords and protected by a cuirass or other armor. During battles, infantry formed lines behind walls of wooden shields.

Beginning in the early 600s, the court feared invasion from either Tang China or Silla and hurriedly adopted a version of the impressive Chinese military system. The main element was a draft of common soldiers, determined through the census and then posted to the local militia. During the winter, these commoner draftees were to drill as units to engage the enemy in the same coordinated way that Tang forces did. Because fighters were responsible for supplying their own weapons, the new system was inexpensive for the government but burdensome for the draftee. Nearly a quarter of adult males were called for service, and the duty was so onerous that there was a saying that "if one man is drafted, the whole household will consequently be destroyed."[1]

Despite the adoption of the draft from China, the Japanese court retained two crucial elements originating before 650. They designated local notables, at that time usually district magistrates or their kin, to lead armies as cavalry. Even in the late seventh century, the Kanto region was home to the largest number of daring and skillful mounted archers. In addition, certain court families—the Ōtomo, Saeki, and Sakanoue among them—gained reputations as military aristocrats, holding high rank and office.

As described in chapter 3, the Chinese-style army met its stiffest challenge during the wars against the *emishi* between 774 and 812. The residents of northeastern Honshu were expert mounted archers fighting as guerillas. During the long conflict, the court discovered how inadequate peasant conscript foot soldiers were against the *emishi* cavalry; there was a dictum that "ten of our commoners cannot rival one of the enemy."[2]

These long wars helped lay the foundation for the classical samurai way of doing battle. From these small bands of *emishi* riders, the court learned that leather armor was better suited to mounted warfare and soon abandoned iron. The *emishi* also wielded a curved sword, instead of the straight one employed by government soldiers. The *emishi* curved sword was probably the predecessor of the vaunted samurai slashing weapon. Because most engagements involved mounted archers, there were many opportunities for the government's equestrian elite to hone its skills. In other words, these long wars constituted "practice for becoming samurai." With the cessation of hostilities in 812, the technology of the samurai had come together: they were lightly armored mounted archers wielding curved swords.

The wars against the *emishi* had other important consequences. First, because most supplies and many fighters came from the nearby Kanto region, that area became economically exhausted and even more highly militarized. Moreover, based on the peasant infantry's poor performance in the wars, the court cancelled the draft, noting that many commoner draftees had become too sick, weak, or hungry to be useful troops. From the late 700s, the court turned exclusively to cavalry for internal peacekeeping, and to experts in the crossbow, borrowed from China, for external defense. Neither required large bodies of troops, which saved on labor as the population first leveled off and then began to shrink.

Earlier it was suggested that the ninth and tenth centuries witnessed increased competition for a decreasing surplus, leading to murder and violence. The court initiated several policies to counter that trend, including the growing militarization of the provincial headquarters. Then, too, it sent certain members of the royal family, such as the Kanmu Taira and Seiwa Minamoto, to the provinces as peacekeepers. This meant that these families lost their rights to government support, in the ongoing effort to solve the budgetary crunch.

The provinces quieted for a few decades thereafter, but then three rebellions exploded. The *emishi* rose up in northeastern Japan, while the revolts of Taira no Masakado and Fujiwara Sumitomo took place between 935 and 941 in the Kanto and western Japan, respectively. Masakado's uprising began as a quarrel with his relatives, but when he captured nine provincial headquarters in the Kanto and refused to send in revenues, the court had no choice but to deal with him. Before he was beheaded early in 940, during the rebellion he declared himself "the new sovereign" and challenged the court's right to rule. He was the first leader of what would later become a Kanto independence movement.

Both Masakado and Sumitomo, whose specialty was naval warfare, were destroyed not by official forces, but by "setting a thief to catch a thief." The man who executed the critical maneuver against Masakado was himself a criminal, and others joined as bounty hunters to kill or capture the rebels. The court rewarded all these men with governorships and rank, thereby making them tax farmers and members of the lower aristocracy. As described above, the Heian class system was "frozen" into a familial status hierarchy; descendants of the men who had crushed these revolts gained recognition as the exclusive practitioners of the "way of the bow and horse." These houses encompassed not merely several branches of the Taira and Minamoto, but also the Ōkura, the Tachibana, and the Hidesato line of the Fujiwara (not to be confused with the Fujiwara at court). In the capital they were the "hired assassins" of the highborn, while in the provinces they controlled from their fortified compounds small forces of peasant foot soldiers. They especially coveted appointment as tax farmers. By the tenth century, military men had added a social dimension, as the practitioners of mounted archery belonged to certain exclusive lineages, often ranked among the lower aristocracy.

The period between 990 and 1060 was a bad time for population and agriculture as fields disappeared from cultivation all over Japan. The reasons for the increase in abandoned lands most likely lay in a spate of epidemics wracking western Japan between 995 and 1030, and due to the devastation from Taira no Tadatsune's revolt (1028–1032) in the Kanto. To reverse the downward spiral, in 1045 the court announced a new policy on estates (*shōen*). Whereas previous laws had tried to abolish or limit estate lands, the new law legalized and encouraged their development to revive the agrarian sector. Moreover, the new estates gained the privileges of tax exemption and freedom from entry by the provincial governor/tax farmer or his staff.

The new policy, combined with a revival in population, seems to have had the desired effect. Abandoned fields came back into production and some new lands were opened, especially in eastern Japan. Soon about half the acreage in Japan was held as estates, with the rest still falling under the control of the provincial government (*kokugaryō*). In estates, there developed a system of layered rights to the produce. No one "owned" the land; instead, the absentee landlords in Kyoto, local managers, and the farmers each had rights to a certain percentage of the harvest or whatever commodity the estate produced. In essence, a new dual system of land tenure coupling estate lands with areas still administered by the provincial government came into existence. In addition, the court created an all-new tax system consisting of a set grain impost, a levy on special regional products such as silk, fish, or salt, and a corvée system run by tax farmers.

One of the two main components of the system to "encourage agriculture" described earlier was a visit by local officials who assigned name-fields and eventually collected rent from sharecroppers. Even from the beginning of this system around 900, local warriors likely served as the developers of new lands and organizers of peasant labor. Beginning with the institutionalization of the estate system in 1045, more warriors became on-site landlords, acting as the crucial link between farmers and the rent-collecting absentee proprietors living in Kyoto or Nara. In return for their management of the *shōen* labor force and dispatch of rents to the cities, warriors obtained a small slice of the harvest for themselves. They increased their share by bringing some parcels—old and new—into cultivation. To be sure, not all warriors served in this capacity; religious establishments generally preferred monks as landlords. Yet many local warriors—now rightly called samurai—added this economic dimension to their lives. Warriors made good on-site landlords because, in an era of labor shortage, they had a monopoly over the means of violence to "convince" the populace to settle down and farm wet rice.

Boasting deadly technology, established social status, and an economic base, warriors still needed the political skills to compete with wily civil aristocrats and scheming monks. After all, Masakado had been beheaded when he antagonized the court by naively declaring himself the "new sovereign" in 939. In a series of wars taking place in the late eleventh and early twelfth century, certain samurai began to gain a considerable following and high political rank, emblematic of growing political savvy. During 1051–1062, Minamoto no Yoriyoshi triumphed over descendants of the old *emishi* stock, using the wars to build his clientele and ascend to the Fourth Rank, making him a military aristocrat. His son Yoshiie suffered politically and economically after waging an unwarranted campaign of personal revenge against another family in northeastern Japan (the Latter Three Years' War, 1083–1087), but he redeemed himself and was eventually granted court privileges restricted to all but a few. By the early twelfth century, Yoshiie became known as the "chief of all warriors," holding the Fourth Rank. With the rise of Yoshiie, the military leg of the trifunctional elite was more firmly entrenched than ever, having its base in the Kanto, boasting many samurai followers, and forming factions with religious complexes and the civil aristocracy.

The High Aristocracy and Clergy in Capital Politics

Changes were not nearly so dramatic for the other two elites. At court, the numbers of civil aristocrats grew while rank inflation continued. The critical transformation for the nobility was the end of the Fujiwara stranglehold and the appearance of wealthy and powerful retired emperors as the new leaders in policy making. In 1068, Go-Sanjō came to the throne as the first sovereign in one hundred seventy years without a Fujiwara mother. At thirty-four, he was to conduct a "short, active, and exemplary rule."[3] He began to break the Fujiwara monopoly over court offices, appointing scholars and scions of the royal family to at least a third of the positions in the Council of State. He took estates away from the Fujiwara and established a new category of lands just for the imperial family.

In 1073, Go-Sanjō abdicated in favor of his son Shirakawa. He named another son as crown prince, thereby assuring the succession for his offspring. Both ignored the Fujiwara, exercising direct personal rule. Other royal lineages also continued to gain power at the expense of the Fujiwara. When Shirakawa resigned in 1087, he retained power in retirement and began a trend that was to last for the next two hundred years. Retired emperors served as the leaders at court, legitimizing policy-making decisions at the collegial Council of State. They developed their own offices and staffs, issued their own edicts, struck up alliances with pliable tax farmers, and accumulated an ever-growing portfolio of estate holdings, totaling two hundred twenty by 1280. Abdicated sovereigns also organized their own group of military men and made alliances with powerful samurai like Yoshiie. Finally, the ex-emperors confirmed their status as Buddhist kings through religious pilgrimages and served as the cultural leaders at court, raising funds for temples and poetry compilations. Of ex-emperor Shirakawa it was said that there were only three things that he could not control: the floods of the unruly Kamo River, the throw of the dice, and the riotous monks of Mount Hiei.

The religious complexes making up the third leg of the trifunctional elite also saw relatively little change, although more so than the civil aristocracy. Shrine-temples based in Nara and Kyoto accumulated the rights to many estates and served in their traditional capacity leading grand ceremonies for the body politic. Lofty civil aristocrats and ex-emperors served as their patrons, sponsoring buildings, sutra transcription, and works of sculpture. They sent devout monks to Sung China in ever-growing numbers. At the same time, the "aristocratization" of high clerical posts continued from the previous period. Between 1070 and 1190, ninety percent of the heads of major temples were from aristocratic families, all but shutting out commoners.

The rise of apocalyptic thought articulated by the clergy was a crucial development for all three elites. According to one Buddhist reckoning, the year 1052 officially witnessed the beginning of the "Latter Day of the Buddhist Law" (*mappō*), when no believer could achieve salvation. Members of the elites began to think that they saw signs of corruption and the end of the world everywhere. Many monks ignored the strictures of devout conduct, eating meat, drinking wine, and engaging in sexual relations with women and young boys. Then, too, the aristocratization of high clerical offices led to growing factionalism and more violent incidents among Buddhist temples and the government. Between 1050 and 1180, there were at least fifty-one disputes, protests, riots, and battles of this type. Most were caused by disagreements with provincial governors over lands and revenues, opposition to court appointments to high clerical office, and conflicts between institutions over the right to perform certain court ceremonies. A new term, "evil monks," reflected the reaction of many courtiers to the growing involvement of the religious establishment in politics. It is unclear whether living conditions during the "Latter Day of the Buddhist Law" were really worse than before 1052, but many in the elite shared that perception.

The main political issues confronting the trifunctional elite during this age had at their core increasingly bitter and violent factional strife. This infighting surfaced in the competition between the Fujiwara regents' house and the ex-emperors. It was also apparent in the growing number of demonstrations and battles between religious complexes and the government, and it appeared among the samurai as well: Yoshiie's Minamoto descendants struggled to retain the title of "chief of all warriors" against another family, the upstart Ise Taira.

The struggle for power became so intense that in 1156 the Hōgen Insurrection erupted in Kyoto. The Fujiwara house took the head of the Minamoto family as an ally against ex-emperor Go-Shirakawa and the Ise Taira. In the outcome, the winners were Go-Shirakawa and the Ise Taira, who gained control of the military system as the "teeth and claws" of the court. The Fujiwara regents lost out badly, and police executed the head of the Minamoto house, the grandson of Yoshiie, following his ignoble defeat. In 1159, Taira leader Kiyomori engineered further humiliation for his Minamoto foes, killing his rival Yoshitomo and having his children Yoritomo and Yoshitsune banished and placed under house arrest. Between 1159 and 1180, things were quiet, as Kiyomori developed the military, political, and economic power of his family under Go-Shirakawa. Yet the potential for protracted conflict remained. The trifunctional elite sat atop a teetering social pyramid that still basically could not meet its needs.

A Modest Revival in Population and the Economy

Population

During 800–1050, Japan became depopulated, but by 1150 a minor recovery was underway. From a low of 4.4–5.6 million around 950, the number of inhabitants of the archipelago rose to 5.5–6.3 million, a growth of about fifteen to twenty percent. Japan's population was still basically standing still, however, when compared to the mid-eighth-century high of six to seven million. A recovery in vital statistics to the levels of the 700s—life expectancy of twenty-five and infant mortality at about fifty percent—was probably the main reason for the modest demographic recovery.

The distribution of population changed from the previous period, too. It showed continued decline in western Honshu, albeit at a slower pace, while the Kinai and northern Kyushu gained modestly. Eastern Honshu, however, grew by twenty-five to thirty-three percent. These regional trends suggest that western Japan, the traditional tax base for the civil aristocracy and Buddhist clergy, was losing out to central and eastern Japan, where many samurai had their homes. These regional trends were certainly a portent of things to come.

A rebound in the number and size of cities supports the notion of a modest revival in population. Kyoto remained by far the largest municipality at about one hundred thousand, but the area around Dazaifu once again became a sizable urban center. Eventually nearby Hakata replaced Dazaifu, reaching a population of several thousand by 1180. There were also numerous small towns, such as Ōtsu, Yodo, and Hyōgo near Kyoto, Wakasa in western Honshu, and Hiraizumi in north-

Hiraizumi, the city of gold, housed a Golden Hall complete with gilt status of Amida and his entourage. Chūsonji. *Source*: Mimi Yiengpruksawan, *Hiraizumi: Buddhist Art and Regional Politics in Twelfth-Century Japan* (Cambridge, Mass.: Harvard University, 1998), p. 48.

ern Honshu. Urban dwellers probably numbered at least two hundred thousand, or just more than three percent of the total population.

Hiraizumi is a famous example of the urban splendor achieved during this epoch. The rulers of northeastern Honshu, the northern Fujiwara (not to be confused with the northern branch of the Fujiwara at court), started construction in the late eleventh century. Leader Kiyohira chose the marshy land near the Kitakami River for his capital. Like Kyoto, it was laid out along the points of the compass. Kiyohira's mansion had a moat five meters deep and at least seven meters across. Nearby stood a pagoda, with representations of the Buddha Amida drawn in gold. Eventually, Kiyohira and his descendants constructed more than forty halls on the site. The city had dozens of blocks of shops, storehouses, and residences. Archaeologists have recovered a great store of Chinese porcelain shards, testifying to the city's participation in overseas trade. When Kiyohira and his descendants died, their bodies were mummified and encased in a house of gold replete with sculptures of Amida and his entourage. Probably no city in Japan could rival Hiraizumi for its wealth and beauty, but it was destroyed in a conflagration in 1189.[4]

Better lighting during the evening added to the lure of cities for migrants. Urban centers had oil-lamp stands made of stone or occasionally metal. During the night, lamp-lighters poured sesame, hemp, or bean oil into dried rushes arranged in a bronze or unglazed earthenware holder. Mainly temples, shrines, offices, and aristocratic mansions used such lighting, so large areas of the cities may still have been dark. Inside these upscale buildings clay or bronze dishes supplied with different oils helped to illuminate the darkness somewhat, yet the average urban and rural house apparently had no lighting either inside or out.

The demographic rebound reflected in both the illuminated towns and the dark countryside derived primarily from a rising level of disease immunities among the general populace. By 1180 residents of the archipelago had more than five hundred years of experience with pathogens like smallpox, measles, influenza, the mumps, and dysentery. Moreover, the East Asian pandemic that had started in China around 160 CE had already drawn to a close there. By 1150 at the latest, major killers such as smallpox had probably found a permanent home among the archipelago's residents, no longer acting as the foreign-borne killers of yore. Epidemics became more frequent and killed fewer people when they did strike. Finally, because they had often been immunized by a plague occurring in their lifetime, fewer adults succumbed to disease, lessening the broader social, political, and economic consequences of epidemics.

Between 1100 and 1150, for example, there were sixteen epidemics, including three of smallpox in 1113, 1125–1126, and 1143. This was a greater frequency than in previous centuries, when the poxvirus had visited about every thirty years. The level of immunities rose more quickly and made it less likely that adults would succumb, but they carried away infants, children, and youth in countless numbers. In sum, disease was still a significant but declining drain on the population between 1050 and 1180.

Alone among the various pathogens, influenza became more deadly, with about half such outbreaks for the Heian period (784–1185) coming after 1080. The influenza virus thrives in cold, damp weather. Between 1108 and 1110, Mount Asama and Mount Fuji erupted several times in eastern and central Honshu. These volcanoes spewed ash, smoke, and other debris high into the atmosphere in such quantities that the earth's surface cooled for decades. The climate for the first half of the twelfth century was unusually wintery, probably affected by more volcanic activity. During 1134–1135, an influenza plague induced by this cold, wet weather struck. As the outbreak attacked "all under heaven," the harvest failed in 1134. Increased social stress caused by the combination of disease, crop failure, and the harsh climate was apparent in the government's condemnation of violent "evil monks" using the crisis to create mayhem. Piracy was rampant along the Inland Sea, as the failure of agriculture there encouraged former peasants and legitimate maritime traders to turn to thievery.[5] Influenza was an exception to the reduced impact of most pathogens.

Elite culture, however, still reflected a terrible fear of disease. Although after 1100 the "vengeful spirit" rites at Gion became less focused on epidemics and more concerned with Kyotoites' general prosperity, other aspects of cultural output showed the hold that physical maladies still had over the imaginations of the civil aristocracy. About this time the court commissioned *The Book of Illnesses*, compiled from a Tang list of 404 sicknesses afflicting humanity. Furthermore, wealthy nobles paid for thousands of elegant Buddhist sculptures during these years, perhaps as a reaction to the disfigurement of disease.[6] The horrors of everyday life heightened the appeal of aesthetic concepts such as *miyabi* as a form of escapism.

Although the East Asian pandemic that had killed so many was drawing to a close by 1150, deadly famines were becoming more frequent. Even during the eleventh century, the government noted six widespread famines and several limited to specific regions, a marked increase over the tenth century. Conditions apparently grew worse during the period 1100–1150, when a severe famine was recorded once every eight years, in addition to a few local crop failures. The cause for most of these food crises was cold, rainy weather that ruined the harvest in the summer.

One particularly harsh famine occurred during 1118–1119. At first, hunger was limited to Kyoto, but by 1119 it had spread throughout the realm. Hungry peasants tried planting wheat to tide them over, but that crop failed also. Then early in 1119, an epidemic purportedly broke out, but it was more likely diarrhea and the general digestive failure that occurs in the last throes of starvation. One

This illustration from the *Book of Illnesses* pictures a doctor peering down the throat of a patient with sores in his throat, possibly from influenza. Kyoto National Museum.

aristocrat wrote of the famine that "the realm has many dead, and there are starving folk, too. In the capital those who commit arson and robbery are numerous every night. Superiors ask no questions and inferiors pretend as though nothing has happened. It is truly frightening."[7] The same author later complained of the frequency of violent crimes, especially murder, during the famine years. Combined with the frequent epidemics, starvation served to raise mortality and lower fertility in selected years.

The long-standing ecological degradation of the Kinai region continued to contribute to crop failure and chronic malnutrition. Most deleterious during the building boom of the 700s, deforestation slowed between 800 and 1050 because of depopulation and the resulting labor shortage. Even so, lumbermen were forced to go farther outside the Kinai to find old-growth stands of cypress and cedar, the preferred lumber stock. As the population recovered somewhat by 1150, the pressure on timber reserves increased again. By 1180, contractors were going all the way to the western tip of Honshu to find the best lumber for pillars and boards.

War occasionally added to the death rate. Two conflicts in northeastern Honshu—the Former Nine Years' War and the Latter Three Years' War—each inflicted significant local devastation and depopulation. For instance, in 1062, half of Minamoto no Yoriyoshi's men deserted because of crop failure and the resulting lack of grain. In 1086, commander Minamoto no Yoshiie lost many men to exposure and starvation during a winter campaign. The Hōgen Insurrection of 1156 resulted in arson within Kyoto, and frequent religious demonstrations during this period contributed to intermittent death and destruction in the Kinai. In sum, though, war probably had even less effect on the death rate between 1050 and 1180 than it had during the ninth and tenth centuries.

Agriculture and Industry

Agriculture also underwent a slight recovery. Around 930, Japan's total area under wet-rice cultivation amounted to 862,000 units. By 1150, that acreage had grown about eleven percent to 956,000 units. Both figures undoubtedly included fields that were not cropped annually, and much of the acreage listed for 1150 recorded lands that had gone to waste and then later been successfully brought back under tillage. Most redevelopment of once-abandoned fields took place in western and central Japan, while in eastern Honshu farmers converted more wilderness to productive agriculture. A warmer and wetter climate was once thought to have been responsible for the expansion of arable land in eastern Japan, but the evidence of significant volcanic activity and the cold, wet climate noted previously for the period 1100–1150 undermines this view.

The modest increase in acreage masks great changes in how the land was settled, administered, and taxed. As noted previously, the times between 990 and 1060 were particularly harsh—when the population declined markedly and fields and villages disappeared from maps. Eventually, revival took place under the dual-land system of estate and provincial control; new, more permanent settlements replaced the ones that had been deserted. To deal with changes in village location and size, the court reorganized its local administration, often subdividing or reducing in size the old district units from the eighth century. The court invented new designations for these smaller and more numerous official territories. The political geography of rural Japan was transformed almost completely between 950 and 1150, but the net gain in settlements and cultivated lands was minor.

Cultivators still faced the same problems of maintaining their fields in continuous production. "Pig-and-deer preserves" was a common term employed to describe fields that had returned to wasteland.[8] During the early 1100s, almost fifty percent of all fields in Sanuki in Shikoku and of rice paddies at Ōyama Estate in western Honshu were barren. Along the eastern shore of Lake Biwa, human occupation had just begun to recover to earlier levels by 1150. In the Kanto, archaeologists have uncovered early twelfth-century paddies and ditches buried in volcanic ash from the eruptions of Mount Asama. It is not surprising that on-site landlords who assigned name-fields and "encouraged agriculture" were essential for getting in a crop.

Rice yields seemingly improved very little. At Ōba Estate in Sagami, farmers tilled about ninety-five units of paddy fields in 1144, and the harvest amounted to approximately 48,000 sheaves of rice. Simple division suggests that the average yield of one unit was around 505 sheaves, just above the harvest from a single good unit 450 years earlier. Though we do not know the grade of these lands or the comparative richness of the harvest in 1144, this one case—the only quantifiable example from this period—implies that there was not much expansion in the supply of rice between 700 and 1150. No wonder the population grew little over these centuries.

There were, however, small, gradual improvements. Dry cropping in particular advanced, as the cultivation of wheat, buckwheat, soybeans, millet, and barley became more common. Prior to 1050, officials ignored lands planted in these grains, but by 1150 they tried to tax them, presumably because the lands were more productive. In particular, the Kanto was the scene of widespread expansion in tillage of these unirrigated crops. Most significantly, by 1160 peasants at Yugeshima Estate in western Japan began double-cropping their dry fields. This development was important because it required little extra effort and the reward was big. By applying more fertilizer to their dry fields, peasants could harvest a second winter crop to tide them over the spring and summer, when hunger was most acute.

Other advances also took place. With the collapse of Silla in the early tenth century and the establishment of friendly relations between the Japanese government and the ascendant Koryŏ court in Korea, the iron of the peninsula once again became readily available in trade. The price of a unit of iron dropped from seven to between two and four sheaves of rice by 1100, and much of that iron probably went for tools. This encouraged the transplantation of rice seedlings to more lands, as did the employment of draft animals for plowing. In some areas, farmers converted dry fields to more productive rice paddies, and reclaimed lands from the sea. The acreage under wet-rice cultivation and average yield may have grown only slightly from 950, but farmers were beginning to use their lands in a more labor-intensive form of cultivation. The gradual intensification of land use combined with the small increase in overall acreage to supply the grain needed for a slight population recovery.

The labor market was still tight and industry continued to rely on labor-saving methods, in step with demographic and economic trends. After 1050, when the court adopted a new revenue system, tax farmers raised labor gangs in what was called "equal corvée by province." The intent was to spread the burden around to outlying regions, but the financial condition of the court had declined to such an extent that the sale of office and rank became the primary means of collecting materials and raising wages and provisions for workers. Under these conditions, government construction stalled. For example, the sovereign's palace was rebuilt only once, in 1100, and the official residence eventually became so run down that the court used it only when it had to—for the accession ceremony. Most emperors lived their daily lives in temporary lodgings. In 1142, repair of dams controlling the badly behaved Kamo River stopped. In that same year, one chronicler lamented that "the provinces responsible for constructing Government Ministries exist in name only. The palaces and halls of previous sovereigns have all become grass. Oh, what a scar!"[9]

The shift to labor-saving methods in industry is especially evident in ceramics and lacquerware. In ceramics, the volume and variety of dishes, jars, and other containers decreased notably, showing a greater simplification and efficiency. This transformation in pot making reflected the shortages of both workers and firewood. A similar change overtook the lacquerware industry, as producers began to apply persimmon juice instead of the more expensive sap from the sumac tree. The utilization of persimmon juice was both simpler and less labor-intensive than collecting and applying lacquer. The new preference may also have been related to changes in the composition of forests in central Japan. Soon wooden plates and saucers covered in persimmon juice became common everyday items.

Domestic and Overseas Trade

Commerce grew to become a vibrant sector, primarily because Japan was located next to the most dynamic economy on earth: that of Sung China. Sung Chinese invented gunpowder, the compass, and mass printing. The country also had advanced carbon-stoked iron furnaces producing high-grade ferrous products and a cotton industry producing everything from ships' sails to military uniforms. The population grew by leaps and bounds during the Sung period, as the "rice bowl" of southern China was more intensively cultivated and regional craft and trade specialization took place as never before.

Trade between China and Japan, exclusively for the archipelago's elite, was already underway in the tenth century. By the late eleventh and twelfth centuries huge Chinese junks called even more regularly at Hakata, Kamizaki, and other Kyushu ports. By 1100, a community of overseas Chinese took up residence in northern Kyushu cities such as Hakata. They held rank at the Japanese court and some even attended the funeral of an important official in northern Kyushu in 1097. In 1151, two samurai attacked the overseas Chinese there, and the fleeing merchant families numbered more than sixteen hundred. Archaeological evidence also points to a dramatic increase in commerce with China during the twelfth century, as the number of sites in Japan containing shards of Chinese porcelains grew exponentially. Besides Kyushu, Chinese traders also called on ports along the northwestern coast of Honshu. By 1180, some daring Japanese captains attempted the passage to southern China as well.

The Chinese merchants traded their silk, spices, and porcelain for northeastern Japan's furs and gold. The Chinese especially coveted gold; a Chinese trader wrote in 1118 "the country of Japan . . . in its earth has a wealth of precious products."[10] Perhaps for this reason, the dynamic Sung state, populated by wealthy consumers, ran a balance of trade deficit with Japan. Piles of Sung cash were soon helping to remonetize the Japanese economy. By 1150 there were signs that the outflow of Sung cash was causing the economic giant problems. In 1199, the Chinese government tried to ban the use of its coins in trade with Korea and Japan. A significant increase in the amount of Sung coins in Japanese sites took place beginning in the 1170s. People wrote of a "cash sickness" in 1179, and then the court banned the counterfeiting of Sung coppers.[11] These proscriptions were apparently ineffective, because the court repeated them in 1187, 1189, and 1192. Along with the cash came an inflationary price spiral, beginning in the 1170s, helping to further destabilize an already teetering social pyramid.

The Ise Taira built a trading empire in western Japan during their tenure as the military arm of the court from 1159 to 1180. They controlled bases such as Fukuhara in modern Kobe, Itsukushima along the Inland Sea, and Kamizaki in northern Kyushu. The Taira made allies of the seafaring families in western Japan. They were so involved in the Sung trade that in 1180 ex-emperor Takakura, born of a Taira mother, was induced by Kiyomori to sail from Fukuhara to Itsukushima aboard a Sung junk.

In addition, the Koryŏ dynasty (918–1258) exchanged goods frequently with Japanese merchants. Following the collapse of the Silla kingdom, relations between the Japanese court and Korea improved. Between 1050 and 1090, Japanese merchants visited Korea in sixteen trade missions, bearing weapons, screens, and precious metals for the Koryŏ court.

This strong external stimulus, combined with the modest demographic recovery, led to a rebound in Japanese domestic commerce between 1050 and 1180. As had occurred during the eighth century, the capital and Kinai constituted

the core of commercial activity, because that region had a large number of consumers and the remnants of an advanced transportation system. Commerce was
more dynamic in western Japan and probably less important in eastern Honshu.
Long-distance exchange, however, enabled the elite to acquire the marvelous
products of northern Japan, such as gold and wild horses. The elites also still
received most commodities in kind from their on-site landlords and tax farmers, and peasants bought and sold at markets only occasionally, yet demographic
and economic recovery supported and was assisted by the return of a more vital
market system.

Late Heian Society: Class, Family, and Gender

Class

Society during the period 1050–1180 differed somewhat from that of the preceding era, in tandem with the modest recovery in population and the economy.
At the top, things were more precarious than in the past because of the addition
of Buddhist clerics and warrior nobles as essential members of the trifunctional
elite, described above in its political aspect. Below them was the commoner class,
which comprised well over ninety percent of the population and included artisans, traders, farmers, and diverse other occupations. The slight demographic and
economic improvement helped to enhance stability for the average person and
encouraged class differentiation. Still, though, the commoner class was too small
to supply the needs of the expanded elite. The reappearance of a servile class after
a near absence of two hundred years, and the formation of a group of beggars and
social outcasts as a new group of rootless people, were other harbingers of social
change.

The highborn civil aristocracy cleaved to their elegant and luxurious lifestyles
even while decline was beginning. They continued to dwell in expansive mansions
staffed by numerous personnel, such as that described for Fujiwara no Sanesuke.
Their material life, leisure activities, and even illnesses changed very little. "Rank
inflation" continued to swell their numbers, although more often than not new
appointees bought their status and received no stipends.

The growing apocalyptic belief in the "Latter Day of the Buddhist Law" had
important social repercussions for noble lay believers. By the late tenth century
some civil aristocrats had formed groups seeking a simple form of salvation more
attuned to the corrupt world they believed they were living in. They hoped to attain rebirth in paradise by reciting the name of the all-merciful Amida Buddha.
They relied upon such texts as the monk Genshin's *The Essentials of Pure Land*

Rebirth, the Pure Land being Amida's paradise, and took turns caring for sick and dying members, helping them envision their coming blissful state.

Pilgrimages also became popular for the highborn. These sacred journeys to revered temples or shrines constituted another facet of the concern for rebirth in paradise. At miracle temples such as the Shingon center at Mount Kōya, aristocrats sought aid from the Buddhas of the future, as well as mercy and healing. Usually the religious center was located on a mountain, and the best travel seasons were spring or autumn. Before setting off, the pilgrim observed a period of abstinence in diet and performed select rituals. The journey for these devout aristocrats included a small retinue and was undertaken in either a carriage or on foot. Pilgrims wore special clothing including a hood and veil. Most pilgrimages were made to nearby temples, such as Ishiyamadera on Lake Biwa, just a few hours from the capital. The sacred shrines at Mount Kumano were more remote but popular among aristocrats, monks, and the imperial family.

Having arrived at the destination, the pilgrim spent several days or nights in retreat, reciting sutras and hoping to receive this-worldly benefits such as wealth, good health, or the safe birth of a child. The pilgrim might also undertake a funereal or memorial journey in which the bereaved buried sutras or other sacred objects. In return for giving lodging and food to their visitors, temples and shrines received ample compensation in the form of clothing, food, and cash. After the retreat, the pilgrims returned home, sightseeing along the way. Although civil aristocrats and even the imperial family initiated and participated in almost all pilgrimages at this time, a few wealthier commoners gradually joined in the practice. Once at the temple, this handful of lesser pilgrims had the opportunity to encounter those of widely differing social status, opening the possibility for greater contact among various classes.

Below the privileged few, middle-level officials holding the Fourth, Fifth, and Sixth Ranks continued to do their duties, based on distinctive skills or abilities. For example, wet nurses at court, such as the Rokujō during Shirakawa's reign, gained considerable political influence.[12] As already noted, these various jobs were hereditary, and the families of these bureaucrats lived in modest homes with small incomes.

The clergy underwent more marked change during 1050–1180, primarily because of the near-complete domination of the high ranks by the offspring of civil aristocrats and the rise of apocalyptic thought. Both these factors increased the number of demonstrations and violent confrontations involving members of the clergy. After 1080, the term "evil monk" entered common parlance, amid a feeling that clerics were either violating Buddhist behavioral precepts or becoming too involved in politics. Despite being almost completely shut out from advancement within the established Buddhist hierarchy, many commoners remained serious students of religious doctrine, especially the *Lotus Sutra*. Eventually most received ordination enabling them to carry out religious ceremonies.

At the same time, however, persons interested in a religious career turned to one of two alternatives outside of the establishment. Many served in the monk armies that battled the court, warriors, tax farmers, and other clergy, using the judicial immunity granted to temple-shrine complexes to their advantage. In their daily lives, they were a heterogeneous lot, some being little more than menials, cooking, cleaning, and gathering firewood. Monastic workers such as carpenters

Beginning in the eleventh century, so-called evil monks like the ones pictured here fought the government over various political and economic issues. Konkōji, Kyoto.

and metal workers often joined, also. Lowly attendants at affiliated shrines filled the ranks of monk armies, as did wandering ascetics and even untutored temple residents.

Most seeking to join a temple had undergone some religious training, but usually very little. They might eventually reach the status of full-fledged monks, but others were mere novices who could hardly read and write. They often even married and retained their secular names. Because the commanders for these monk armies all came from the highest levels of the civil aristocracy or warrior class, there were occasions when the people composing the monk armies and their leaders clashed, too.[13]

Another alternative for the person of religious bent was to become an itinerant beggar, leading an ascetic life in seclusion, circumambulating the mountains or spreading simple Buddhist doctrines by preaching. Such figures had existed since the 700s, as the example of Gyōki cited in chapter 2 shows.

From the year 950 or so the perception that religious complexes were corrupt institutions grew in society at large, and especially among the elites. This incipient anticlericalism gave rise to greater numbers of hermits, holy persons, and lay preachers wandering the countryside and revealing their own supernatural truths. These people found excellent opportunities among the poor and commoners to spread sermons weaving disparate elements of Buddhist teachings with magic and folk beliefs. For example, the priest Chingen assembled his sermons about miracles and great religious devotion in *Miraculous Tales of the Lotus Sutra*. Holy men such as Kūya (903–972) lived off the donations they received in marketplaces for spreading the "good news" about Amida's Pure Land. Some performed faith healing, exorcism, divination, and soothsaying for the crowds; others focused on themselves by carrying out self-mutilation or ritual suicide to reach paradise. Combining evangelism with this-worldliness, these various ascetic preachers were popular in a world where disease, famine, inclement weather, natural disasters, and political strife prevailed.

Warriors were the newest partner in the trifunctional elite, and like the civil aristocracy and the clergy, a few held high status while most ranked lower in society. Military aristocrats had been members of the court since its formation, but the new lineages such as the Kawachi Minamoto (a branch of the Seiwa Minamoto) or Ise Taira had large followings that their predecessors lacked. Some, such as Minamoto no Yoshitomo, commandeered rights to estate produce and badgered beleaguered local samurai families into becoming their followers. Others, like Taira no Kiyomori, combined old and new methods to build their wealth and a fragile system of vassals at the local level. Between 1160 and 1180, Kiyomori captured high office and rank for himself and his close relatives. He also married his daughters into the imperial family, attempting to form a new marital line. He oversaw Taira participation in the lucrative Sung trade and exploited positions in the provincial headquarters. Kiyomori developed a sizable following throughout Japan, especially in western Honshu. By 1180, the Ise Taira claimed adherents in fifty-seven of Japan's sixty-six provinces. At court, they participated in cultural activities such as poetry writing and government ceremonies.

Numbering between two and three thousand, samurai who dwelt in the provinces signed on to fill the ranks of Yoshitomo and Kiyomori's bands, as well as serving civil aristocrats and the clergy. Even though not all local notables were warriors, they usually worked as officers in the provincial headquarters or as on-site landlords in estates, thereby achieving a modest income. Local samurai had their own small band of loyal followers, most of whom resided with their lords in fortified compounds complete with their own lands and facilities for making clothing and weapons. They also controlled nearby peasants through loans of rice seed, food, and tools and sometimes impressed them to serve as porters and horse grooms.

Although there were vast disparities between the status of military aristocrats and local samurai, they held both values and a fighting style in common. Like the

National Museum of Japanese History

Warriors residing in the countryside constructed compounds surrounded by ditches and walls. These fortifications provided storage for weapons and offered sanctuary for the warriors' closest followers. *Source: Kokuritsu rekishi minzoku hakubutsukan tenji annai* (Kokuritsu rekishi minzoku hakubutsukan, 1984), p. 4.

civil aristocracy, samurai were known for their arrogance and pride in lineage but added a reputation for courage and guile in battle. They often engaged in blood feuds, and they developed a unique style of combat that told as much about their class as any aspect of their lives. Essentially, they were lightly armored, mounted archers carrying curved swords, but by 1100 combat was almost always one-on-one. Battles took no planning and usually turned into groups of riders skirmishing with each other. Donning colorful armor sewn together with brightly tinted thread, these warriors were always careful to choose a foe worthy of their own status and prowess. Before engaging in combat, a rider would frequently announce his pedigree—his name and lineage, his home, and his battle experience—to his opponent. Then the two fought an archery battle from horseback, jousting for the advantage (maneuvering one's opponent to the left, or bow, side). When one warrior had succeeded in wounding or unseating his enemy, his attendants would decapitate the rival and the head would become a trophy and the basis for reward. In this form of combat, the identity of the enemy was all important, a deadly dance aiming to establish hierarchy and dominance among males.

With the recovery of urban centers and the rejuvenation of commerce, the general populace became more specialized into distinct occupations. The formation of separate organizations (*za*) for traders and artisans by 1092 suggests a noticeable growth of these classes. Members of these organizations essentially made a bargain with a major temple or aristocratic household to produce or market a product exclusively for that consumer in return for monopoly status. The artisans and traders gained a new source of revenue while the temple or aristocratic house received valuable goods. During 1050–1180, these groups were loosely bound together, but all merchants and artisans shared a special place in society. They were considered to be practitioners of the "fine arts," much like artists and musicians are today.[14] Their links to wealthy patrons reinforced a status at the top of the commoner class.

A "merchant-prince," for example, dealt in finished goods and regional specialties for markets in Kyoto.[15] Many of his commodities undoubtedly found their way into the households of wealthy civil aristocrats. Residents at Yugeshima Estate in western Japan produced salt that was then sold to merchants. In turn, these salt entrepreneurs shipped their precious cargo up the Inland Sea to ports just outside their consumers' homes in Kyoto. Throughout western Japan, independent salt producers plied local waters to sell their products from boats. Paper makers and ironworkers were increasingly notable practitioners of the "fine arts," too.

Fishermen faced growing restrictions from the government during 1050–1180, but they found ways around them. The two major reasons for the crackdown were governmental attempts to return more people to farming and to enforce the Buddhist ban against the killing of all living things. Apparently, however, these various policies failed. Traders still hawked fresh fish in front of Gion Shrine in the old capital; they were organized into groups with a boss possessing links to fishing communities throughout western and central Japan. Other major shrines joined in the competition for products of Japan's rivers, lakes, and seas as well. Even as late as 1147 the members of *only one* of these fishing units numbered "several thousand households."[16]

Women played the predominant role in the production and sale of silk. To illustrate, one story describes a local notable with two wives. Although charged with overseeing the complex procedures of silk manufacture, these women unhappily allowed most of their silkworms to die, and the family dog ate a lone remaining mulberry leaf. When the women fed and nursed the dog, it spewed forth a great amount of silk thread from its nose and then passed away. After the women buried the animal, a mulberry tree sprang up from its grave and the women became famous as the finest producers of silk floss and cloth in the region. When silk was marketed in Kyoto, most of the merchants were female, too.

The life of the vast majority of the commoner population—the peasants— repeats a story of slow change. Most settlements were spread all over the landscape, and those rural folk who survived the numerous epidemics and famines were frequently on the move in a mobile society. Cultivators continued to rely on the nonagricultural pursuits that had stood them in good stead since prehistoric times: hunting, fishing, and the gathering of roots, nuts, and tubers. The foods from these activities supplemented their diets in good times and kept them alive when the harvest was inadequate. Slash-and-burn farming remained popular in mountainous regions. Farmers' material life saw little improvement, as the basic dwelling unit, clothing, diet, and sanitation were nearly the same as in the eighth century. Only dry cropping was producing more consistent yields and helping occasionally to relieve the threat posed by the "spring hungers."

Yet change was afoot. The settlements and estates established during the late eleventh and twelfth centuries proved to be more permanent than ever before. Many lasted well into the fourteenth century and beyond, as attested to by excavations. At one site near Osaka, residences and storehouses first appeared during the ninth century; their number even increased somewhat for the next one hundred years. These scattered buildings, however, were never rebuilt and the village eventually disappeared. Beginning in the latter half of the eleventh century, though, pit dwellings and warehouses reappeared in a more clustered formation. More important, residents rebuilt their homes repeatedly and lived there until the 1300s. This story of greater stability in residential patterns occurs repeatedly throughout the Kinai during this era.

As described in chapter 3, Kuroda Estate adds interesting details to the picture of rural life during the late eleventh and twelfth centuries. By this time, Kuroda had grown considerably, stretching across a fan-shaped delta created by the Tama River. Numerous villages, each housing a dozen to about fifty people dotted the landscape and their boundaries overlapped throughout the estate. Many cultivators planted small gardens near their pit dwellings. From the Tama River, cultivators drew water for their rice paddies, but apparently the supply was insufficient because they frequently fought over irrigation rights. A major reason for these battles was the increase in land under tillage; in one village, farmers under the guidance of a local warrior built a large pond and trebled the area of their fields. It would be a mistake, however, to assume that rice was all that residents of Kuroda produced. They continued to practice logging in the nearby woods and, most impressively, cleared some higher ground for abundant dry fields. The mountain forests also provided residents with firewood, leaves and roots for fertilizer, and foods such as nuts, berries, and game.

Kuroda was divided for tax purposes into sixty-six name-fields. Each one covered from thirty to ninety acres and a wealthy peasant represented the other farmers in the unit to the authorities. No one knows how many people made up each name-field, but in the mountains where peasants lumbered and farmed, each unit spread across the valley and came closest to being a village unto itself. Even those cultivators, however, did not possess property rights over their individual plots of land until near the end of the period. Only then could they buy, sell, or transfer their fields.

To judge from the history of Kuroda Estate, it must have been a productive land coveted by many. In the early 1000s, for instance, a local warrior owning high-grade fields and numerous storehouses managed one of the richest villages. In 1161, however, an "evil monk" organized three hundred peasant-soldiers on behalf of Tōdaiji and expelled the warrior, taking the village for himself and reducing the tillers' rents. Later, recalcitrant residents commended the lands of another village to a major shrine to gain its protection against warrior encroachment. Fighting as guerillas, the peasants won victory and significantly reduced their tax burden. In all of these conflicts, the residents of Kuroda played a critical role, often tipping the balance in their favor. At least in some instances, the peasantry was gaining a sense of its own power.

The lowest rungs in society belonged to two newly created classes: servants or slaves (*ge'nin*) and social outcasts (*hi'nin*). Acting as laborers for temples, attendants for warriors, or menials within the households of the wealthy, the unfree reappeared as the population recovered and the severe labor shortage of the period 800–1050 subsided, thereby reducing enforcement costs for owners. More important, when crops failed, some people chose to sell their kin or themselves into bondage. Convicted criminals and debtors also fell into slavery. This class was still relatively small in 1180, but the court was sufficiently concerned about the plight of these persons to issue prohibitions against kidnapping or otherwise enslaving unsuspecting commoners.

Social outcasts included all those discriminated against because of their supposed pollution, revealing the purity fetish of the society at large. Beggars, criminals, and those with debilitating maladies, such as Hansen's disease (leprosy), were all shuffled into this class. Often homeless, they meandered along the banks of rivers or in the streets. When they were employed, they conducted funeral tasks or other presumably "polluting" jobs such as producing leather or handling animal carcasses. This class was small but growing in the 1100s.

Although the class hierarchy described above was sharply defined, during the twelfth century people of diverse backgrounds began to mix more readily. As indicated previously, pilgrimages could play this role. Another opportunity came during cherry blossom time, when men and women donned festive costumes sporting pink flowers, and danced and sang to encourage a long flowering season. For example, during the spring of 1154, "men and women from Kyoto and its surroundings gathered at [a local] shrine and enjoyed themselves by performing elegant dances. They sang songs accompanied by flutes, drums, and gongs, claiming that they were entertaining the gods."[17] Organized by itinerant Pure Land preachers, peoples of all class backgrounds participated in these mass spectacles designed to calm the angry spirits who were thought to be causing disasters. Open and egalitarian, these festivals offered a temporary chance for men and women ranging from the aristocracy to outcasts to come into contact.

Family and Gender

Trends in family and gender relations changed in important but subtle ways from the mid-Heian period. Attempting desperately to cling to the elegant lives that they had known for centuries, civil aristocrats maintained the basic family arrangements described above. Women of lofty status maintained their own mansions where spouses might dwell on a temporary or permanent basis, and her family provided substantial wealth to the couple. They helped the man in his quest for high rank and office and raised the children. Sex continued to be free and easy for polygynous males, concubines, and ladies-in-waiting. Highborn men who kept several wives named one as the principal mate, but in fact all were treated as equals. These primary wives were restricted to a single partner and had little freedom of movement.

As always, aristocratic households encompassed numerous kin, including the brothers and sisters of the mother's line and their offspring and the aunts' and uncles' families of both the husband and wife. Kinship remained bilateral and inheritance partible, with portions usually given to both male and female children.

Considerable wealth was necessary to sustain such large groups of kindred in the luxurious mansions of the age. Estate managers or tax farmers eager to curry favor delivered such riches as they could, including grain, salt, fish, lamp oil, woven goods, and other processed food products.

In some respects, however, the patrilineal bias of late Heian noble society became stronger in reaction to the strain upon the resource base. For example, the practice of having young sovereigns vacate the palace so that their mothers might take control as "mothers of the realm" fell into desuetude. Instead, the authority of consorts began to derive exclusively from their relationship to their husband, the emperor or ex-emperor. The retired ruler usually exerted total authority over his son, the reigning emperor, and the connection between the mother and her aristocratic children grew weaker. Although inheritance was still partible, the custom of handing down the family's most important possession—political rank and office—from the father to a single most-favored son took root. In later centuries, this patrilineal bias would expand and have immense repercussions for the civil elite and its numerous offspring, especially females. The trend toward male empowerment is also observed in families of mid-level officials, as fathers passed on their skills, often teachings secret to their various lineages, to a son or sons.

Within the clerical class, more women seemed to have turned to Buddhism. After numerous prohibitions against female ordination during the previous age, devout women anxious to become nuns began to cut their hair to a set length, taking a partial tonsure. Aristocratic women were even more eager participants in pilgrimages than men.

Samurai of all statuses practiced bilateral kinship, like the civil aristocracy. Because inheritance was partible, there was little cohesion in warrior families. Parents, children, aunts, and uncles all held their property individually, and any household might have a combination of all these relatives dwelling therein. Even among samurai, where masculine values supposedly held sway, women possessed high status and females had as much right to property as males.

Little is known of the familial relations of commoners, but the patterns of previous ages probably held sway. Families were highly unstable aggregates of kin disintegrating through hardship or personal preference. "Marriage" was ill defined, and each gender was available for multiple partners and short liaisons. The status of commoner women remained high, higher than their counterparts in the civil aristocracy where men were gaining ascendancy. As always, these women engaged in the hard work of farming, salt making, ceramic manufacture, and trade, right along with men.

Commoner women even created their own specialized occupation: the sex trade. Organized into matrilineal units, these women sang, danced, and had sex with their patrons, usually wealthy aristocrats. They plied their vocation most often from boats, especially along the Yodo River. They are described as covering their faces with rouge and powder and as being fully knowledgeable of a variety of sexual positions. They might also cross-dress, titillating members of both genders. Noble women apparently also enjoyed their songs.

Mature women oversaw the operations of these sex workers, because there were no male pimps. Unlike Europe, there was no government policy on the practice of receiving payment for sex, and it was not considered either immoral or transgressive (except for Buddhist monks). Although authors during this era sometimes grouped them with beggars and other lowly classes, female sex workers were considered neither unclean nor undesirable. In fact, some were even thought to have become Buddhist saints (bodhisattvas); early Heian poet Ono no Komachi was eventually included in their ranks. In a society where sex was relatively free and easy and marriage ill defined, these women felt no special opprobrium. Sometimes they were criticized for quarreling over their payments or for luring men to financial ruin, but for most "a tryst on a boat on the waves equaled a lifetime of delightful encounters."[18]

In sum, late Heian society was subtly different from the preceding two centuries. The creation of a trifunctional elite, the patrilineal bias apparent among civil aristocrats, and a more diverse clergy were three major changes. The creation of a small group of social outcasts and the reappearance of slavery were also new. Most noticeable was the rising prominence of the samurai at court. The changes were subtle, but they helped define society for the next one hundred fifty years.

Japan on the Eve of Civil War

Since the late 700s, Japanese society had been struggling with a fundamental problem: how to support an expanding elite while the general population was either shrinking or static. During the ninth and tenth centuries, rulers had been able to stave off major conflict by applying various policies, such as converting provincial governors into tax farmers or trying to reduce expenditures. The modest demographic recovery between 1050 and 1180 helped to give the Heian court some breathing room, too, but not much. As new groups joined the elite, political strife and factionalism increased markedly. Eventually, the infighting would become so intractable that a major civil war erupted, the worst in Japan's history to that point. The war would have both its revolutionary and conservative aspects, and would be accompanied by significant changes in both the economy and society.

5 Economy and Society in an Age of Want, 1180–1280

Elite Politics

The War of 1180–1185

Throughout the period 1160–1180, the Ise Taira under the able leadership of Kiyomori built their political and economic power, acting as the "teeth and claws" of the court. For most of that time, Kiyomori's relations with the wily ex-emperor Go-Shirakawa were amicable, but in 1177 the Taira uncovered a plot against them in which Go-Shirakawa's allies were implicated. After the conspirators were banished, Go-Shirakawa continued to operate behind the scenes to undermine the Taira. Finally, in 1179, Kiyomori had thirty-nine of Go-Shirakawa's clients dismissed from office and placed the retired sovereign under confinement.

Kiyomori then enacted policies having the effect of alienating the other two branches of the trifunctional elite. He assumed wide powers to enforce order by dealing with bandits and "evil monks." Kiyomori expanded the number of provinces from which he collected taxes, lessening dividends for others. Men once enrolled as Taira followers began to have second thoughts about the wisdom of throwing in their lot with Kiyomori. So when Prince Mochihito, the third son of Go-Shirakawa, was passed over and the infant Antoku was made emperor in the fourth month of 1180, Mochihito raised the standard of revolt against Kiyomori and the Taira. Antoku was not only younger than Mochihito, but also of Taira blood.

This conflict over imperial succession might seem like an elite affair, but it triggered the most protracted, damaging, and significant war in Japanese history to that point. It was more than merely a battle between two imperial princes, resonating deep within the major fissures in Japanese society. It pitted numerous warrior houses against each other, particularly against the Ise Taira. The war, more importantly, also set temple complexes against each other and the Taira, and involved the court in political maneuvers first on the side of Kiyomori's army and later in negotiations with the Minamoto under their brilliant leader Yoritomo.

At the heart of the war was the question of the proper role and reward for the military leg of the trifunctional elite. Prior to 1180, warriors had served as officials in the provincial headquarters or as on-site landlords in estates. They organized and disciplined the farmers while being asked to deliver rents and other emoluments in a timely way to the Kyoto and Nara elites. Despite these demands, their incomes were paltry in comparison to high-ranking aristocrats or members of the clergy and they had no security of tenure, often being dismissed from office by their urban betters for the slightest of infractions. In essence, the War of 1180–1185 was really about solidifying and expanding warrior control over their incomes and jobs and making them more secure members of the trifunctional elite.

The war may be divided into three phases: the year 1180, when Yoritomo consolidated control of the Kanto; the period from 1181 to the middle of 1183, when the war settled into a stalemate; and from mid-1183 through 1185, when Yoritomo vanquished all his rivals and annihilated the Taira. During the first stage, the Taira easily destroyed Prince Mochihito and his chief Minamoto supporter. In the autumn of 1180, however, Yoritomo escaped from house arrest in Izu and began a campaign to capture the provincial headquarters in the Kanto, enrolling men and confirming them in their lands as he made them his followers. Other Minamoto kinsmen such as Kiso Yoshinaka also rebelled, claiming to act in the name of Prince Mochihito. Late in 1180, the Taira sent an army to the Kanto to destroy Yoritomo, but the army panicked and retired without doing battle. In the confusion, Taira horsemen discarded their armor and mounted the first horses they could find to return to Kyoto.

Soon the Taira faced rebellions all over Japan, much as the court had during the revolts of Masakado and Sumitomo between 935 and 941. A supposedly firm Taira ally in Kyushu rebelled. Militant monks in the capital region and the pirate-priests of Kumano lined up their forces against the Taira. To counter the clerical hostility, Taira no Shigehira made the grave mistake of incinerating numerous temples, including Kōfukuji and Tōdaiji. Presumably, the Taira were acting in the name of the court when they attacked Yoritomo, but the burning of these symbols of courtly authority deeply antagonized many aristocrats.

During the second phase, Kiyomori died, and the war became a three-ring circus, with Yoritomo in control of the Kanto, his kinsman Kiso Yoshinaka in command of the northern Japan Sea littoral, and the Taira struggling to cling to western Japan. Each side had its victories and defeats, but the pace of warfare slowed to a standstill because of a severe famine afflicting central and western Japan. Without provisions, the Taira forces could not move. Yoritomo was so content to remain at his base in Kamakura in the Kanto that he even proposed carving Japan into a Minamoto sphere in eastern Honshu and a Taira one in western Japan. Kiyomori rejected the plan on his deathbed.

Later in 1183, as the third stage of the war commenced, Kiso Yoshinaka succeeded in ousting the Taira from the capital and became the general designated to fight the court's enemies. All of his battles against the Taira in western Japan ended in defeat, however, and he also ran afoul of Go-Shirakawa. Soon Yoritomo's troops under the command of his brother Yoshitsune rushed to Kyoto, crushed Yoshinaka's forces, and had him beheaded. The court then named Yoritomo to head the armies sent to destroy the Taira. Several hotly contested skirmishes took place, including the famous Battle of Ichinotani, where Yoshitsune led his horsemen to victory by circling around behind Taira mountain fortifications and then attacking down steep slopes. In the spring of 1185, Yoritomo's men prevailed in a naval engagement at Dannoura. Almost all the Ise Taira, along with their boy sovereign Antoku, perished. Yoritomo assumed the Second Rank and was now truly the "chief of all warriors."

More important, Yoritomo's enrollment of numerous followers during the conflict and his confirmation of their lands gradually gave birth to a military government based in Kamakura. From the start of his rebellion, Yoritomo had issued orders to the provincial headquarters under his control. In 1183, when the court was struggling with Yoshinaka, Yoritomo negotiated an accord with Go-Shirakawa that gave a solid foundation to the evolving government in Kamakura. In effect, the court granted the Kamakura regime—later to be known as a "tent government," or *bakufu*—the supreme police and tax-collecting powers for all Japan. During the war, samurai throughout Japan had taken advantage of the conflict to withhold rents and use grain reserves for provisions. Yoritomo devised a brilliant solution to the conflict between warrior provisioning and the other elites' rights to their rents—Yoritomo placed his followers in diverse estates, guaranteed them modest but secure incomes, and simultaneously made them responsible for shipping the lion's share of the rent to civil aristocrats and religious complexes in the Kinai. Yoritomo thereby assured support and provisions for his men while satisfying the other two members of the trifunctional elite. His actions were both revolutionary and conservative.

Despite the creation of a regime solely for warriors by the late 1180s, it is important to realize that the Kyoto court did not disappear and the religious complexes throughout the Kinai still had enormous clout. The War of 1180–1185 created a dyarchy, with a civilian branch in Kyoto and a military one in Kamakura. The jurisdictions of these two branches overlapped considerably, as Yoritomo appointed military governors to oversee the provinces along with the court's provincial staff. Each government also employed personnel from the other, as some civil aristocrats went to Kamakura to assist in the administration there and many warriors chose to avoid designation as one of Yoritomo's housemen and so served independently as clients of the civilian aristocracy or religious institutions.

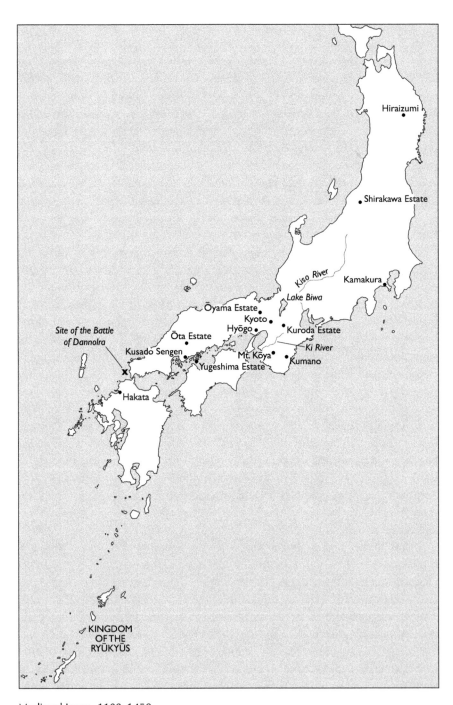

Hiraizumi

Shirakawa Estate

Kamakura

Kiso River

Lake Biwa

Ōyama Estate

Kyoto

Hyōgo

Ōta Estate

Kuroda Estate

Ki River

Site of the Battle
of Dannoïra

Kusado Sengen

Mt. Kōya

Kumano

Yugeshima Estate

Hakata

X

KINGDOM
OF THE
RYŪKYŪS

Medieval Japan, 1180–1450

In the aftermath of the war, events solidified Yoritomo's hold on his men and power. Fearful of the court's manipulation of Yoshitsune, Yoritomo had a falling out with his brother and spent much of the immediate postwar years hunting him down. In 1189, Yoshitsune fled to Hiraizumi, the capital of the kingdom of the northern Fujiwara, but he was soon captured and beheaded. Yoritomo received the head of his brother in a jar of rice wine as a gift from the northern Fujiwara leader. This provided a pretext for Yoritomo to attack Hiraizumi, and his army annihilated that enemy in a month. The court issued an attack order to Yoritomo only after his victory, revealing its reluctance to authorize the war and thereby strengthen Yoritomo's hand. The War of 1189 enabled Yoritomo to take control of northeastern Honshu, to enroll more followers, and at the same time to pose as the preserver of temple and aristocratic lands in the area. In 1192, Yoritomo led a procession to Kyoto, where he received the official title of *sei-i-taishōgun*, or "Great Barbarian-quelling Generalissimo," and although he later resigned the post, the leader of the Kamakura regime thereafter became known as the *shōgun*. What had begun as a quarrel about imperial succession led to the formation of a military government with firm control in eastern and northern Honshu.

East Is East, and West Is West, 1190–1281

For the next thirty years, relations between the two partners in the dyarchy were uneasy. Go-Shirakawa tried to embarrass Yoritomo at court through various ma-neuvers. Yoritomo then tried his hand at playing politics in Kyoto but failed in his quest to place his daughter as an imperial consort and to use his wet nurses as spies. When he died in 1199, Yoritomo left two sons, who served briefly as shogun but were rather incompetent. By 1219, both were dead, and Kamakura was left without a shogun, as Yoritomo's line came to an end.

Even while Yoritomo's sons were alive, the true power of the shogunate fell to a group of his followers, led by his in-laws, the Hōjō. These families oversaw the *bakufu* and dominated Yoritomo's sons by surrounding them with their own wet nurses. Then, in 1219, Yoritomo's last son was assassinated. In that year, the Hōjō took the title of regent to the regime and became the real leaders of the shogunate. Because Yoritomo's lineage was moribund, the Hōjō soon sought a suitable candi-date for shogun from the court, now under the sway of ex-emperor Go-Toba. Go-Toba was hostile to Kamakura and wanted to see the new government destroyed. He refused to allow his infant son to be named the next shogun.

In 1221, during the so-called Jōkyū War, Go-Toba attempted to overthrow the shogunate by assembling a motley crew of warriors, many of whom had earlier fought for the Ise Taira. Go-Toba tried to entice other samurai families loyal to the shogunate to desert to his side. This temptation was considerable, as the position of ex-emperor was powerful and Go-Toba a charismatic leader. Most warriors, however, rejected the retired sovereign's entreaties.

In Kamakura, Hōjō Masako, Yoritomo's widow, made a stirring speech rallying Kamakura's troops. Within a month the samurai army was occupying Kyoto and had banished Go-Toba. What had begun as an attempt to eliminate the *bakufu* had had the unintended consequence of strengthening its hand immeasurably. From 1221, the Kamakura regime was on much firmer footing, as it had an aristocratic youth to serve as the titular shogun. It placed its own office in Kyoto and assumed the right to tinker with appointments at court. Kamakura was also able to replace disloyal warriors acting as on-site landlords in western Japan with its own lieutenants, giving it a measure of parity with the court in that region.

From 1221 until 1281, Kyoto and Kamakura functioned as equals in an interlocking dyarchy, with the court overseeing western Japan and the shogunate eastern Honshu. There were innumerable conflicts over rents and other issues between urban proprietors and warriors living on the land, usually adjudicated by Kamakura courts. There was also the usual quota of protests from religious complexes. The most significant events during these sixty years were the dyarchy's attempts to deal with two harsh famines during 1229–1232 and 1257–1260 and its thwarting of the Mongol invasions in 1274 and 1281. The famines will be described below; here follows a brief discussion of the Mongol attacks.

The Mongols were central Asian nomads rising to power in the 1200s. Temujin, also known as Genghis Khan, united the Mongol tribes and conquered first central Asia and then northern China by 1234. The Mongols next overran Russia and the Middle East and reached their peak under Kublai Khan (r. 1260–1294), when they conquered the rich Sung Empire in 1279. They administered the greatest land empire in world history, stretching from Poland to the Pacific Ocean.

Ever since they had crushed the Koryŏ dynasty in Korea in 1258, the Mongols had sent emissaries to Japan demanding friendly relations. Kyoto remained paralyzed while Kamakura made preparations for war. Early in 1274, the Mongols could wait no longer and launched a major invasion of the archipelago. After several initial victories, the Mongols met the Japanese samurai for the first time. As was their wont, the samurai attempted to engage the Mongols in single mounted combat, but when a samurai fired a whistling arrow to announce the beginning of hostilities, "the Mongols down to the last man started laughing."[1] Despite the small size of the samurai force, it managed to slow the Mongol advance, and then, just as suddenly as they had come, the Mongols departed, for reasons unknown.

Not to be halted in their imperial designs, the Mongols tried again in 1281. In the interval between strikes, the *bakufu* called on warriors in eastern Japan to go to Kyushu to face the impending invasion, but since they had no land there, only a few

During the Mongol Invasion of 1281, Japanese warriors destroyed the remnants of their enemy from traditional boats made of logs and a few boards. The Imperial Household Agency.

heeded the call. Kamakura also had a large wall built across northern Kyushu to repel the invaders. When the Mongols attacked again in 1281, their complex battle plan called for two armies numbering more than 100,000 to strike Kyushu from the north and west. By contrast, samurai defenders totaled 1,500 horsemen with about 3,000 infantry. No matter how well the samurai fought, the outcome was a foregone conclusion. While the Mongol armies were preparing to disembark, however, a gigantic typhoon struck and destroyed most of the nomad's fleet. Later dubbed the "divine wind," the *kamikaze* preserved the hold of the trifunctional elite on the lands and human resources of Japan as nothing else could have. These invasions and their aftermath eventually had profound repercussions for Japan's polity and society.

Population and Economy in an Age of Deprivation

Population

Japan's population stood still between 1150 and 1280, numbering about 5.7–6.2 million in 1280. By the late thirteenth century, however, the distribution of the islands' inhabitants had changed dramatically. Prior to 1150, western Japan had been depleted while eastern and northern Honshu showed substantial growth. By 1280, these trends had been reversed, with sizable increase taking place in Kyushu, little or no expansion in western Honshu and the Kinai, and demographic contraction in the northern archipelago. The drastic change in the distribution of Japan's inhabitants indicates that new factors were affecting population trends.

Despite some commercial growth and the founding of a second political center in Kamakura, the landscape remained overwhelmingly rural. Kyoto was home to about 100,000, and Kamakura had around 60,000 residents. Hakata, Ōtsu, Yodo, and Hyōgo—all ports—added to the size of the urban population. Even including such small towns as Obama along the Japan Sea littoral and Kusado Sengen and Anotsu in western Honshu, urbanites comprised no more than 250,000 people, or about four percent of the total population. In other words, the number of Japan's city dwellers expanded only marginally. Most cities and towns lacked segregated cemeteries and had concentrations of beggars, the sick, and abandoned children, making them cesspools of disease and requiring constant in-migration to maintain their populations.

As during the twelfth century, pestilence continued to recede as a major cause of mortality. By 1150 the most dangerous pathogens, such as smallpox and measles, had become endemic to Japan. No new microorganisms were introduced to the archipelago or carried away large numbers of victims during 1180–1280. Because there were no major improvements in land or water transportation, the probability of contact between a host and susceptible members of the population was about the same as before, but simultaneously immunities continued to rise. For example, there were twelve outbreaks of smallpox between 1150 and 1280, but only one outbreak was severe. Most killed infants and small children. Measles also had little demographic impact, having become a disease of childhood.

Only influenza struck with continued lethality. Forty percent of the influenza epidemics ravaging Japan before 1600 occurred between 1143 and 1365, perhaps indicating that the virus had mutated into a new, more deadly strain. Influenza epidemics erupted more frequently during this age for another reason. Several protracted and violent volcanic eruptions, global in scope, are known to have affected Japan's climate in the thirteenth century. Catapulting ash and debris high into the atmosphere, they blocked out the sun and caused the climate to become markedly colder and wetter.

The sharp drop-off in the number of inhabitants in eastern and northern Japan may have been another result of the wintry climate. The prevalence of Hansen's disease was yet a third. Spread by close contact, Hansen's disease took root during the cold, wet weather that encouraged hosts to huddle together with susceptible friends and relatives.

Disease was an important but declining cause of mortality during 1180–1280, still an impediment to population growth, but insufficient by itself to explain the continuing demographic stasis. Rather, the rise in immunities and consequent survival of more people made for a new problem: how to feed a potentially grow-

The famine and chronic malnutrition stalking most Japanese before 1600 gave rise to frightening depictions of "hungry ghosts" haunting the afterlife. Tokyo National Museum.

ing population. Apparently, society made little progress in solving this problem, because famine came to the fore as the chief brake on population growth. During the years from 1150 to 1280, there were at least twenty-one years of widespread starvation, and another six of local crop failure. These figures represent a considerable increase from the preceding century. As if to symbolize the dire effects of famine, Go-Shirakawa commissioned both *The Hungry Ghosts Scroll* and *The Scroll of Hell*, which contained horrible images of people tormented by starvation and death.

The famines during 1180–1280 were particularly deadly because they extended over multiple years, giving commoners and others reliant on agriculture no chance to recover. The Yōwa famine of 1180–1182, already mentioned in connection with the War of 1180–1185, was caused by drought. It afflicted central and western Japan most harshly, helping to prevent the Ise Taira from mounting effective resistance to Yoshinaka and Yoritomo. The war exacerbated the famine in Kyoto, as hostile armies surrounded the capital and denied urbanites food and supplies. One elite resident of Kyoto wrote that the famine was "a terrible thing," with neighboring farmers abandoning their fields and desperate Kyotoites selling their possessions for food.[2] By 1182, so many city dwellers had left the capital to find food in the mountains and on seashores that Kyoto became a ghost town, eerily silent and vacant.

Between 1229 and 1232, the Kangi famine struck. Possibly the worst famine in Japanese history, it was caused by unusually cold, damp weather related to world-wide volcanic activity. The weather was so severe that snow fell in central Japan in the summer of 1230, while aristocrats noted days when the sun did not shine and complained because they had to wear heavy clothing even in the spring and summer. The death toll was high—in 1231, in one estate in central Japan about twenty percent of cultivators died in less than a month.

Both governments attempted to ameliorate the harsh conditions but to little avail. Law and order broke down; countermeasures against nocturnal marauders and "evil monks" were largely ineffectual. Outlawry even affected relations with the Korean kingdom of Koryŏ when hungry residents of Kyushu raided the neighboring peninsula for food. The famine also led to numerous quarrels between on-site warrior landlords and urban proprietors, with many estates unable to pay taxes or organize labor gangs. When harvests were inadequate, warriors also pressured and abused hapless cultivators, driving them from their fields. Both Kyoto and Kamakura took steps to make more grain available to commoners, but the results of their actions were only modest.

The most important countermeasure taken to try to reduce the impact of the lengthy crop failure was the legalization of the sale of human beings. When a family was faced with starvation, members might choose to sell children or other kin in return for grain, at the same time ensuring enough to eat for the sellers and the person to be sold. This behavior had been going on illegally for centuries, but its official authorization from 1231 to 1239 showed just how severe the Kangi famine was. The policy helped to spread starving victims around to people who could take care of them, but it also ripped more families asunder.

In addition, all those sold became members of a servile class, dwelling in small lean-tos or perhaps even in a room of their master's house. These conditions did not encourage large, stable families. The new policy may have saved some lives, but the creation of so many dependent, broken, and poor families helped lower fertility, making recovery from the famine even more difficult. After the famine in 1239, the *bakufu* tried to abrogate the more lenient laws, without success. The famine expanded the size of the servile class considerably; it was to remain a significant proportion of Japanese society for the next four hundred years,

The third devastating famine, the Shōga crisis of 1257–1260, was also caused by cold, wet weather, again tied to worldwide volcanism. During this time, starvation was so common that people took to lampooning the government: "In the land there are disasters, while in the provinces there is famine. On the riverbanks, there are bleached bones."[3] Statements like these suggest that many died.

As during the Kangi disaster, the nonpayment of taxes, the inability to enlist labor gangs, and conflicts between warriors and higher-level proprietors for grain and other items routinely occurred. On-site warriors trying to collect rents abused cultivators. In 1259, the *bakufu* issued an order allowing farmers whose harvest had failed to leave their lands and head for the mountains, moors, rivers, and seas to take advantage of old forager livelihoods. This command shows that the peasantry shifted back and forth from paddy rice or some other form of agriculture in good times to hunting, fishing, and gathering in bad.

The Shōga famine also marked a turning point in the maintenance of law and order. As during the Kangi crisis, residents of northern Kyushu once again assaulted nearby Korea and stole food. The years 1257–1260 marked the sustained appearance of what the government termed "evil bands" (*akutō*). Many were indeed bandits, thugs, and outlaws who robbed and murdered freely, but others were law-abiding commoners resisting official trampling of their legitimate rights. In the face of such outlawry, Kamakura found its jails so full that it could not feed the inmates and simply released them.

Along with the demise of infants and youths from disease and the high mortality and lowered fertility due to starvation, more familiar factors made for a static population at this time. Ecological damage to western Japan spread and became more pronounced. The clearest indication of this problem was the means by which the court gathered lumber to rebuild Tōdaiji and Kōfukuji after the Taira had incinerated both in 1180. Having stripped cypress and cedars from nearby Nara centuries before, the court now relied upon distant Suō Province at the western tip of Honshu to supply timbers. Even there the desired logs were apparently in short supply, because wooden posts supporting the new temples were much smaller and shorter than their grand predecessors. As the area of deforested land expanded, landslides, flooding, and topsoil erosion occurred more frequently.

War and political instability helped raise the death rate, too. The nature of combat—usually single-mounted archery—limited the number of combatants dying in battle to just a few dozen at most. For instance, even when Kamakura fell in 1333, only about four hundred thirty determined Hōjō succumbed defending the shogunate. Like combat today, however, wars spawned what we have euphemistically come to term "collateral damage." For example, at Shirakawa Estate located along the Japan Sea littoral, the amount of land yielding a harvest during the war years of 1180–1185 fell to about ten percent of an average crop. Throughout the war, Taira, Yoshinaka, and Yoritomo's men also appropriated peasant grain for provisions. In 1184, Yoritomo, undoubtedly referring to the toll his own provisioning had taken, wrote that "the eastern and northern provinces are just as if there are no residents. . . . [W]e ought to have the floating population come back and settle in their old villages."[4] Similar provisioning activities during the Jōkyū rebellion of 1221 and the Mongol invasions of 1274 and 1281 also took food away from peasants.

Throughout this period, soldiers usually operated on the principle that "might made right" and took what they needed to feed themselves. This idea was even enshrined in Kamakura law, making the robbery of a peasant's harvest a property, not a criminal, matter. Yoritomo had indeed solved the problem of how to feed his warriors and guarantee rents to the civil aristocracy and religious complexes in Kyoto and Nara, but at a cost. During war and peace, samurai serving as on-site landlords regularly abused their cultivators, resulting in peasant deaths or their flight from agriculture. For instance, at Ategawa Estate in 1275, the on-site samurai bound up the wives and children of farmers who refused to sow wheat. The men having fled to the mountains, the samurai proceeded to slice off the ears, cut off the noses, and shave the heads of the remaining family members. This case was eventually adjudicated, but the warrior won. This sort of behavior was common and resulted in peasant death and dislocation, hindering the steady work necessary to bring in a good yield.

For all these reasons, population grew very little between 1150 and 1280. Vital statistics remained virtually unchanged for the mass of the population, with low life expectancy and high rates of death and infant mortality even in relatively good years. There was now a class differential in mortality, because the two major causes of death—famine and military depredations—affected only the great mass of commoners. Warriors and civil aristocrats probably could expect to live somewhat longer. Until conditions improved for the vast majority of the populace, however, a deep-seated transformation of Japanese society was unlikely.

Agriculture and Industry

Agriculture revealed a steady continuation of the trends evident during 1050–1180. On the one hand, the annual agrarian cycle was the same, including the highly ritualized breaking of the soil and the encouragement of farming through assigning peasants to till name-fields as sharecroppers. On-site landlords and others often had trouble finding enough peasants to cultivate the land, even with gifts of food, seed, and rice wine. And of course, untended fields still bulked large in most estates—at least twenty-five to thirty-three percent even in the advanced Kinai.

On the other hand, there were signs that peasants were learning to work their fields more effectively than before. Iron tools came into the hands of more farmers. This change was helped along by improvements in iron making, as furnaces became sturdier and blowpipes and bellows were used as they had been in the 700s. Itinerant artisans and merchants offered their ironware for sale around the islands. More peasants used draft animals, as indicated by scroll paintings and police records describing thefts of the beasts. Animal manure increasingly supplemented grasses, roots, and fibrils as fertilizer.

These innovations spurred more efficient land use and better yields—perhaps as much as twenty percent above those of the eighth century. One method of making more productive use of the land was to divide a parcel with poor access to water into two parts, digging down one side and piling the extra earth on top of the other. The result was a rice paddy more likely to absorb water in the lower section and a good dry field yielding wheat or barley on the higher portion. Because of their appearance, these lands were called "island dry fields."

Double-cropping also became somewhat more common. Already by 1160, some peasants were harvesting two crops from dry fields, where all they needed to do was add more fertilizer. Double-cropping rice paddies was much more difficult because it meant closing off intake valves or terracing around the paddy. Still, peasants were beginning to engage in double-cropping paddies by 1280, harvesting rice in the fall and wheat or buckwheat in the spring. This practice was still hit-or-miss during this era, and most farmers turned to it only when the initial rice crop had failed. Most important, because the paddy needed to dry out completely before planting a second crop, Japan's swampy topography dictated that the area of farmland where double-cropping was viable was only about twenty to thirty percent of all acreage. Still, double-cropping rice paddies potentially helped alleviate the effect of "spring hungers."

Other, less noticeable, advances occurred. Cultivators built more irrigation works and took better care of them, and farmers were more careful to leave the remaining hills and mountains lush with vegetation to retain moisture. More strains of various grains may also have been available. Certainly there was some conversion of wilderness into fields. Like its predecessor in Nara in the eighth century, the Kamakura shogunate tried to encourage major land-clearance projects, but usually these orders appeared after war or famine had left fields vacant and unproductive. Such commands probably had little or no effect. It is best to think of agriculture during this century as making more intensive use of tillage rather than expanding the area of cropped fields.

The gradual move toward more intensive farming continued to affect settlement patterns. Previously, most rural folk had been spread over the countryside in small hamlets or large, dispersed villages. By 1280, in a few places in the Kinai, clustered settlements came into being with houses in the village separated from fields and common lands. This trend, however, was only barely underway by 1250. As always, peasants continued to migrate frequently, in the process spreading microbes, evading taxes, and separating from mates during the woman's child-bearing years. Physical mobility was ingrained in the very fabric of rural society.

The labor market reflected a long-term shortage of workers. The first warrior legal code compiled by the *bakufu,* in 1232 after the Kangi famine, allowed commoners to move from parcel to parcel as they pleased. In other words, the ruling class could not bind them to the land because the elite was too fragmented. Different lords competed for the few hands and had no choice except to permit peasants who had paid their rent on time to migrate freely. When badly treated, farmers went on strike, declaring a collective oath and going into hiding, leaving their families behind in their homes. The women would then draw down the blinds and take care of the children and other relatives.

Yet the labor market was only half free. Beginning in the late twelfth century, the servile class expanded rapidly, as slaves could be found all over the islands and were particularly common in isolated hinterlands. Usually, a household held only a few, but one warrior family living in western Japan, for example, possessed fifty-six male servants cultivating seventy-two plots of land. Most slaves had lost their freedom by falling into debt and had been in that state for at least a generation. They were often passed on to the master's kin through inheritance. The legal status of servants varied considerably, but owners frequently listed them with their livestock. The creation of this sizable servile class helped to supplement the labor of free commoners, probably making for more flexibility and control in a tight market.

Because of the lack of workers and materials, monumental construction took decades. For example, after the fire in 1180, Tōdaiji was reconstructed at a snail's pace. Although a much inferior statue of the Great Buddha had been recast as early as 1185, primarily because of the leadership of Go-Shirakawa and the monk Chōgen, the new Tōdaiji was incomplete when each died, in 1192 and 1206, respectively. Hundreds of wandering ascetics scoured the countryside, soliciting funds for reconstruction, taking even a "half a copper or a scrap of wood."[5] In fact, it was not until 1289, after many civil aristocrats had complained, that a much less impressive Tōdaiji was finished. And Tōdaiji was the symbol of the realm and had the highest priority for rebuilding.

Other industries still relied on labor-saving techniques. Iron production became more sophisticated and employed more workers to operate bellows and other devices. Most other industries, however, remained the same, emphasizing techniques to conserve labor. Salt making continued to rely on "fields" cut out of the beach, where the mineral was collected. Silk production declined further, as fewer regions in Japan specialized in the material and Chinese merchants took over production almost completely. Ceramics remained unglazed, simple in form and variety. There was no additional investment in the transportation infrastructure, as both water and land travel remained unchanged from the 1100s. Thus, most important industries represented a continuation of past technologies.

Domestic and Overseas Commerce

Trade was the brightest spot in the economy. Although estate lords relied on their properties to provide them with the appropriate mix of commodities before 1250, thereafter monetization and commerce spread more widely. From 1251 to 1300, for instance, records show six times the commutation of tribute items into cash than in the half century before. Land sales conducted in cash doubled between 1220 and 1283. More local markets opened and more trade specialists and moneylenders used bills of exchange. Much of the commerce was in luxury goods for the richest members of the trifunctional elite, as had been true since 900. Peasants could not rely continuously on good harvests and rarely traded their produce for tools or other goods. Local markets were still few and often closed for many days.

Increased trade with Sung China and the Koryŏ dynasty was a major reason that commerce was more vibrant. Sung merchants resided in large numbers in northern Kyushu cities like Hakata and Kamizaki from around 1150 on and gathered considerable political and economic clout in Japan. Their porcelain wares arrived at towns and villages all over the islands during the 1100s, in exchange for Japanese swords, screens, sulfur, precious metals, and lumber. The volume of trade and traffic with China and Korea grew in the 1200s, and despite the best efforts of Sung officials to forbid the practice Chinese coppers flowed into the archipelago in ever-greater quantities. Japanese traders began making the trip to China, so that by 1250 there was a colony of Japanese merchants in the southern port of Ningpo.

When the shogunate was founded in the late twelfth century, Kamakura established a fine port at nearby Yuigahama. Soon the warrior government became alarmed because many of its best samurai were spending so much on Chinese fineries such as silk and medicines that they were falling into severe debt. In 1254, the *bakufu* limited the number of ships trading with the Chinese to five per merchant, perhaps to control this problem. The Mongol invasions further stymied trade between Japan and the continent in the latter part of the thirteenth century.

The century from 1180 through 1280 witnessed change within a basic continuity. The population remained static, but its distribution and the reasons behind the stability shifted. The urban population was still only a tiny percentage of Japan's total, but new ports like Hyōgo joined the upstart warrior capital at Kamakura to present a new urban landscape. Agriculture continued to rely on ritualized practices dating back to the tenth century, but there were signs of improvement, especially through more intensive and efficient use of the soil. The labor market was tight, combining the free movement of commoner tillers with the toil of a sizable servant class. Although most industries were little changed, commerce showed continuing growth in the number of markets and merchants and the use of money. Exchange with the dynamic Chinese and Korean economies increased. These demographic and economic trends also affected social life.

Society during the Latter Age of the Buddhist Law: Class, Family, and Gender

Class

Although the population and economy remained virtually static, this century witnessed some social change and much turmoil. There was still a trifunctional elite at the top supported by commoners and the servile and outcast classes at the bottom. The social pyramid remained unbalanced, with too many rulers and too few producers. Society, however, began to move toward new solutions to this problem by redistributing tribute items and labor among members of the ruling class. As might be expected, warriors began to take a greater share, while civil aristocrats lost out. Both groups also moved away from partible inheritance and toward unigeniture, meaning that a designated child inherited the family's patrimony. The clergy held its own economically. Social specialization advanced little, but commoners, especially peasants, gained more rights and security.

The civil aristocracy witnessed several subtle changes in their lives as the political power of Kamakura waxed stronger. The northern branch of the Fujiwara split into five lineages, competing for land rights, service as the regent at court, and liaison to Kamakura. Moreover, the imperial family fragmented into two lines in 1243. This only made factional strife at court worse and weakened Kyoto in its dealings with Kamakura.

It should not be assumed, however, that civil aristocrats were poor, especially relative to many members of the warrior class. In western Japan, where the court was stronger, the privileged had well over twice the income of on-site samurai landlords. In eastern Japan, where the *bakufu* held sway, the proportions were reversed—warriors received the lion's share of tribute items and civil aristocrats unlucky enough to hold rights there took whatever the warriors deemed a fair share. Eventually, the civil aristocracy would lose all control in eastern Honshu.

Inheritance also commenced a swing toward male unigeniture as a way of making do with less. While many women still inherited their own homes and sources of wealth, some aristocrats wrote wills assigning their main properties to a son, often the eldest. Of course, only one male could ascend in the court hierarchy and assume the powers of his father. With more offspring than wealth, the civil aristocracy was adapting to meet the challenge in a new way.

Faced with a rival government in Kamakura and dwindling economic power, the prevailing sentiment at court was pessimistic. It truly was the end of the world that the highborn had known for half a millennium. This pessimism is apparent in the diaries kept by literate aristocrats, who frequently referred to the "Latter Day of the Buddhist Law," reinforcing a general feeling of unease and decline.

The samurai class consisted of a few nobles at the top and a large number of followers residing on the land. With the death of Yoritomo in 1199, the Hōjō regents became the most prominent and wealthy warriors. They had considerable lands and received large amounts of grain and tribute items, as indicated by Hōjō Yasutoki's grand gesture donating grain and food to starving peasants during the Kangi famine. They eventually took wet nurses to suckle their children, as had civil aristocrats and even the Minamoto. The Hōjō also acquired a taste for Zen Buddhism, sponsoring Chinese prelates and ordering the erection of temples in Kamakura. Eventually, the Hōjō established five Zen monasteries as rivals to the older sects in Kyoto. The Hōjō also dabbled in Confucianism and collected Chinese art objects as signs of conspicuous consumption.

The House Regulations of Hōjō Shigetoki (1198–1261) convey much about the values of his high-ranking family.[6] He stressed the absolute power of the lord's will as handed down hereditarily. The father of each household was supreme and could be promiscuous or take more than one wife. By contrast, female adultery was punishable by the confiscation of half the lands of both parties. The spousal residence was neolocal, established by the husband. He was responsible for training his children (both boys and girls) in the martial arts and for teaching them to read and write. Gift giving, even in cash, was the glue that held warrior society together. To ensure succession and the proper transmission of property, the patriarch resorted to a period of retirement. Shigetoki stressed frugality and decorum, in line with an outward devotion to Confucianism. For Shigetoki and the other Hōjō leaders, warriors needed to be gallant fighters, who should also know the civil arts of administration so necessary to their new position as regents to the shogun.

The overwhelming majority of the nearly three thousand warriors were either administrators in the provincial headquarters or on-site landlords at estates. Their incomes were modest, especially in western Japan, even though they held their own lands from which they received the full harvest. From their compounds, these local samurai controlled and organized the cultivator class. Despite the settlement terms of the War of 1180–1185, material welfare for this group improved only gradually.

The clergy constituted the most dynamic group in the trifunctional elite, primarily because of the apocalyptic implications of the "Latter Day of the Buddhist Law." Confrontations over appointments and revenues among religious complexes, and between them and court or local officials, continued unabated. Monk armies carried out these demonstrations, and those of a religious bent not drawn to fight became hermits and itinerant preachers in ever-growing numbers. Clergy also received lay believers of all classes as pilgrims seeking escape from the corrupt world and communion with the divine. Wandering hermits concocted magical cures and their devotees placed votive tablets at temples. Faith in the "Buddha of the Future" flourished. "Evil monks" who would dabble in politics or violate precepts of proper monkish behavior seemed to be everywhere.

The century from 1180 through 1280 is widely recognized as a period of religious ferment; both anticlericalism and heterodoxy were rampant. Recall that chapter 3 described the career of the exemplary monk Ryōgen. He led the Tendai school through political factionalism and a disastrous fire that destroyed most of the buildings on Mount Hiei in 966. By the thirteenth century, however, Ryōgen had, in the popular consciousness, become a demon, known for his worldly desires.[7] Because they could not assure salvation, other priests of several major temples were depicted in narrative scrolls as devils, too. By 1300, Ryōgen was usually described as the chief of them all. Even the sun goddess, now reconceived in Buddhist terms, became a wrathful deity judging the dead in hell and threatening violence at a whim.[8]

The Tachikawa Skull Ritual, a new belief later deemed to be heterodox, held that fornication and meat eating formed the main elements of its version of Shingon Buddhism.[9] Believers developed a ceremony in which a human skull was the object of worship. Usually practitioners gathered several skulls to chant and pray over. Followers painted the skulls red and white, colors representing female blood and male semen; they placed cinnabar inside the skull as a symbol of the nourishment provided by a mother to her fetus. Condemned by later clerics, this ceremony is a sample of the wide range of belief flourishing during the thirteenth century.

Another monkish practice drawing the ire of later thinkers was the institutionalized prostitution and rape of boys aged seven to fourteen.[10] Safe from the temptation of women in their mountain fastnesses, monks struck up love affairs with these boys, and the stories were later set down in satires. The real issue was not that the objects of clerical desire were so young or male but rather that the priests' behavior showed a lack of commitment to the faith and to the rules of monastic life. Unsurprisingly, the satirical pieces almost always ended badly for the boys—in suicide, duels, or battles.

In this context of despair, heterodoxy, and anticlericalism, charismatic religious figures appeared, opening new avenues to salvation. Almost every major reformer and his social movement reacted in one way or another to the palpable fear that believers could never obtain salvation because of the evil in the world. Some, such as Hōnen (1133–1212), Shinran (1173–1262), and Nichiren (1222–1282) emphasized human weakness and inability to attain salvation. Drawing on the Tendai doctrine of original enlightenment, they taught that humans could not rely upon themselves or their good deeds for rebirth in paradise. Instead, believers should place total trust in their innate Buddha nature and the Buddha's compassion as expressed in a simple, easy-to-repeat formula. Those who tried any other road to salvation were guilty of self-reliance and arrogance. All three of these men founded new sects—Pure Land (Hōnen), True Pure Land (Shinran), and the Lotus sect (Nichiren). The monk Ippen (1239–1289) learned from Pure Land doctrine, dancing ecstatically around Japan reciting "Hail to Amida." The patron saint of the Timely Sect, he advocated among other doctrines a greater role for women

The Buddhist Saint Ippen here preaches to a warrior in northern Kyushu. Kankikōji, Kyoto.

in Buddhism. His followers were said to have numbered more than 250,000 at the time of his death.

Others, such as Myōe (1173–1232), Jōkei (1155–1213), and Eison (1201–1290) were members of the "establishment schools" in Nara and Kyoto, but they had their own critique of society. They argued that the "Latter Day of the Buddhist Law" was precisely the time to reinforce religious discipline. Those who tried to abandon the old ways and use simplistic formulas were "irresponsible fatalists."[11] Each venerated the behavioral precepts of Buddhism and sought a return to the age of Shakyamuni. The monk Myōe, for instance, mutilated his right ear to test his resolve to sacrifice for the salvation of all sentient beings. At the same time, he recorded sexually charged dreams in which he had intercourse with a bodhisattva. Myōe died in 1232 from the failure of his digestive track, probably due to the Kangi famine. Jōkei led a major fund-raising campaign for Kasagidera, asking small holders, estate officials, and even poor peasants to donate just a little for a hall for the Buddha of the Future. His actions were part of a general movement to refurbish dilapidated temples throughout the realm. Eison, a monk of the Shingon order, expressed his determination to find salvation for all by tending to lepers at more than 1,500 temples throughout Japan. By feeding and treating them in baths containing medicinal plants, he attempted to convert the great unwashed to his version of Buddhism. He also strove to ordain more women by rebuilding nunneries that had fallen into disrepair.

Even the Zen Buddhism patronized by the Hōjō felt the impact of apocalyptic thought. Eisai (1141–1215) was the founder of Rinzai Zen and Dōgen (1200–1253) the patriarch of Sōtō. Both formed their sects at least partially in reaction to the feeling that the Buddhist law had declined. Each tried to make his practice of seated meditation easy and fit for all people and believed that simply one action (or nonaction) would bring about the stated goal of Zen—enlightenment. Dōgen, whose followers tried to achieve enlightenment through nonsense riddles (*kōan*) and dream stories, even praised the effectiveness of reciting Amida's name, just like Hōnen and Shinran.

Fueling this unprecedented religious ferment was greater contact among members of the Buddhist community throughout East Asia. Between 1168 and 1280, eighty Japanese priests studied in China. More than thirty Chinese masters arrived in the islands between 1250 and 1350. In effect, Buddhist religious complexes throughout China, Korea, and Japan created a network for the exchange of ideas, goods, technologies, and people. The initial impact was felt mostly among the elites of East Asia, but eventually these travelers helped to transform the material basis of life everywhere.[12]

The Hōjō, for instance, welcomed five famous Chinese Zen monks. Each one either founded or became the abbot of new temples in the Hōjō capital of Kamakura. Kakushin (1207–1298) was the most well-known Zen prelate to travel to China. Once there, he learned Chinese readily and wrote treatises, prose, and poetry in his adopted language. When these prelates returned to Japan, they used their newfound talents to enrich Japanese literature and painting. As will be described in chapter 6, the effects of these exchanges would eventually be felt in fields as disparate as diet, commerce, and architecture.

Artisans and traders retained the slightly elevated status of practitioners of the "fine arts." Many belonged to commercial organizations (*za*) that had originated in the late eleventh century and served patrons at court, among religious institutions, and even within the warrior class. Among their ranks were the usual metal casters, carpenters, blacksmiths, sword makers, and roofers as well as doctors, shamans, wrestlers, prostitutes, sutra copyists, and even experts at board games. Such "artists" usually made their products and marketed their services; commerce had not sufficiently developed to become a specialized operation. Some even farmed as a side occupation. To promote manufacture and trade, however, these wandering craftspeople/merchants received free passes at most toll barriers. After 1250, when the lords of Kamakura fully recognized the value of these people, they gave them free transit and other privileges to encourage them to settle in eastern Japan.

Of all the artisans, most is known about metal casters. After the incineration of Tōdaiji in 1180, the court poured all its resources into reconstructing the temple that symbolized the realm, and metal casters were in great demand. They organized themselves into at least two gangs, each led by a master craftsman. One group was composed of about fifteen artisans; a father, his son, and another relative held the top positions. A Chinese metal caster headed the other unit; when the Great Buddha was completed, he returned to Sung China. In fact, Chinese played a prominent role in much of the metallurgy done in thirteenth-century Japan.

Life for the fishing populace became more stable. Previously, they had wandered from cove to cove, taking their catch and then selling it at market or even from their boats. Beginning around 1180, the "people of the sea" started to settle for longer periods in houses grouped together and facing the ocean. These more permanent communities had a chief or elder who guaranteed that all members had the same fishing rights. When they made salt, on average twenty-five family heads shared the facilities. Nets were set and fishing zones designated. Most of these mariners were still tied to members of the elite, such as the heads of shrines, the imperial family, or various civil aristocrats. Within families that made their living from Japan's rivers, lakes, and oceans, labor was divided by gender, with the men sailing the boats and making the salt and the women in charge of sales. During a dispute over one fishing territory near the capital, the women of the losing side encountered the civil aristocrat responsible for the decision and berated him angrily along the road to his mansion.[13]

Those who survived by the old forager livelihoods were the bane of officialdom because they refused to settle down and farm. Woodsmen and hunters roamed the mountains and wilds. Those who collected berries, fruits, nuts, grasses, and wild vegetables also made a living beyond the reach of the tax collector. Some trapped fowl. These foragers occasionally offered their products to members of the elite, especially in the court and shrines. Others traded with cultivators, although they were rootless foragers and not considered merchants.

The material well–being of the great majority of the population—the cultivators—changed more deliberately during this century. Their clothes were still woven from pounded hemp or ramie fibers. Sanitation was abysmal. At Yuigahama, the port for Kamakura, archaeologists have found a mass grave including refuse and animal remains. Diet may have been somewhat better, as there were more side dishes such as salted fish and noodles, but the basic foods were still brown rice, barley, millet, various vegetables, bean paste, and a lot of rice wine. Within their pit dwellings, farmers in western Japan cooked at a boiler while those in colder eastern Japan developed a sunken fireplace (*irori*) to warm their houses in the colder climate of the thirteenth century.

Ōta Estate, once situated near modern Hiroshima, depicts rural life during 1180–1280 as well as any other place. Established in mountainous terrain, this tract of land descends gradually from north to south and cradles the Ashida River, which empties into the Inland Sea. Most of Ōta lay north of the river and encompassed one large valley readily suitable for rice agriculture. The river divided southern Ōta into innumerable valleys and swamps where farmers also tried their hands at rice farming. Ponds watered the paddies in the valleys while cultivators relied merely on rainfall for crops in the low-lying areas. As might be imagined, the swampy paddies suffered frequently from flood and drought, leaving agriculturalists victim to failed harvests and famine.

Taira no Kiyomori established Ōta for his son in 1166. At the time there were merely twenty-six houses, ninety acres of paddy fields, eighteen of dry fields, two hundred thirty-five mulberry trees, and six acres of chestnut groves. In other words, it was mostly wilderness. When the Taira were destroyed in 1185, the court donated Ōta Estate to the Buddhist monks living on Mt. Kōya. By 1190, Ōta had grown enormously, to almost two thousand acres, but even though some increase was undoubtedly the result of development, most acreage was already productive land merely withdrawn from the control of provincial officials. To supplement the large grain harvest, the cultivators at Ōta hunted in the mountains and gathered chestnuts. They collected lacquer from sumac trees, raised mulberry groves to produce silk, and grew ramie plants yielding fibers for clothes.

No one knows how many villages or people Ōta had, but in 1236 three villages totaled one hundred twenty-three dwellings, suggesting that the average village had twenty to fifty residences. Scattered throughout the many valleys, each house was surrounded by gardens and fields, over which the farmers held property rights. For taxation purposes, officials divided Ōta into name-fields ranging from less than one to fifteen acres. For example, three villages were composed of one hundred six name-fields. Occupants of these units were liable for a rice tax, a labor impost, and revenues assessed in diverse other items produced at Ōta.

Ōta was a rich estate—so rich that a thirty-kilometer road was constructed to transport its products directly to a port on the Inland Sea. Because of its wealth, the estate was the scene of incessant conflict. In 1190, two officials raised a military force, confiscated more than three hundred acres, and refused to forward the proceeds to Mount Kōya. The two officials, for their own benefit, also worked the residents day and night. Finally, in 1196, Yoritomo stepped in and fired the guilty parties and appointed a new warrior to be on-site landlord. The new supervisor agreed to a ten-point pledge to placate the monks of Mount Kōya, but in 1223 trouble erupted again and continued more or less for the next fifty years. As a rule, the warrior landlord could count on various rice and labor revenues, ramie from every household, wheat and other dry field products, a third of the mulberry leaves harvested, and vegetables from peasant gardens. Despite this seeming plentitude, throughout the thirteenth century he continually manipulated the rules to increase his share at the expense of the Buddhist monks.

Residents at Ōta must have watched these quarrels among members of the ruling class with a good deal of cynicism and bitterness. After all, no matter which side won, the cultivators paid the price. Combined with the daily task of survival in the face of war, famine, and disease, these various rents and taxes made life even harder. Housed behind moats in a large official compound, the samurai seemed virtually invulnerable to peasant resistance. Farmers who refused to accede to the warrior's demands quickly lost their property and their freedom. Some were banished. These unfortunate cultivators were the source of Japan's fastest-growing class—servants and slaves.

The farmers at Ōta or any other estate, however, were not powerless. They presented grievances to the court and Kamakura, complaining of demands for too much labor and rice. They protested warrior charges placed on those who wanted to buy back their freedom. Mostly, though, they fled, a tactic so popular that Kamakura courts were forced to enshrine it into law. Fleeing a rapacious warrior or proprietor was so effective that Kamakura became concerned enough to create conditions in which farmers could breathe a sigh of relief and tend to their enterprises without landlord interference. Few samurai-landlords paid much attention, however. When the abuse was just too much to absorb, as at Ategawa Estate mentioned above, the peasants pledged to act together: "Before [this] Buddhist avatar, we take an oath of unity, and burning the paper on which the oath is written, we drink holy water and feel the hair stand up on our bodies."[14] Then they fled or fought.

The beliefs of the peasants of Ōta Estate revolved around their homes. These dwellings served as both physical and spiritual refuges from the myriad threats of the outside world. For this reason, farmers often surrounded their homes with a gated fence and a bamboo thicket. Legally speaking, residents at Ōta possessed the right to refuse entry to anyone—even the on-site warrior landlord. During the daytime, farmers worked outside, but once the sun set, the quiet, dark night became a frightening place full of spirits and demons filtering in from nearby mountains. For protection, many homes had special rooms just for hiding. There cultivators kept what few possessions they had, and when the door was shut, the refuge functioned as the couple's bedroom. Every domicile also had its god, usually venerated in that same small room. These rooms were almost always under the charge of the woman, who stayed behind in this small cubicle with the children when the menfolk at Ōta pledged to strike, flee, or fight.

Near the bottom of the social pyramid resided the servile class, found not merely at Ōta but all over Japan and at all levels of society. They were deemed no better than livestock. Their duties were highly diverse; they might be personal servants, field hands in bondage, or assistants to samurai lords. Usually, they stayed in their station for life, and their descendants might remain servants for several generations. A commoner might lose his freedom through debt, war, or sale as a result of famine. For example, one commoner lost his freedom when he could not pay his labor dues as he was observing funeral rites for his grandparents. Warriors sometimes kidnapped an unsuspecting farmer, tying him up in a large gunnysack, and forcing him to serve as a porter or groom for horses.

The number of social outcasts and beggars expanded during this age of cold, wet weather and massive famines. In fact, as the incidence of Hansen's disease increased, many more "unclean" people appeared. As in the late Heian period, social outcasts were usually homeless and performed jobs considered to be associated with pollution, including preparing corpses for funerals and handling the carcasses of cattle and horses. For example, at Narazaka, overseen by Kōfukuji, there were seven separate dwellings for these nonpersons. Their leader was "a sick man," probably a leper.[15] Narazaka was a transportation hub, thus important in the butchery of animals.

Family and Gender

Superficially, marriage and family life among civil aristocrats remained much as they had during 1050–1180. Status still trumped gender in sexual relations. A low-ranking man had no hope for an affair with an exalted woman, and emperors and regents forced themselves on more humble ladies-in-waiting, as when the ex-emperor Go-Fukakusa coerced Lady Nijō in 1271.[16]

Yet a gradual transformation was underway. The nature of marriage and kin-ship continued to move toward a more patrilineal bias. Instead of the man mov-ing in with his wife's family, she frequently took up residence in his house. The mansion was then deeded over to the woman and most of the husband's relatives left. In essence, the external form of unions had not changed, but the husband was gaining advantages. At court, this change in marriage meant that women still held high rank, but their authority often derived from their husbands. The trend toward male unigeniture was another sign of the ascendancy of aristocratic men.

All samurai were members of both a small nuclear family and a larger house-hold composed of parents, their siblings, and their children. Chapter 4 noted that this larger unit had virtually no cohesion, especially because for most of the thir-teenth century inheritance was partible. Even daughters could inherit the rights and duties of estate landlords. As with the civil aristocracy, however, the warrior class gradually began to exhaust their resources and moved toward unigeniture, or at least all-male inheritance, by 1300.

The various religious movements of this age offered an outlet for the talents of women in all classes. Of interest, this social trend flew in the face of Buddhist doctrine. Authoritative texts such as the *Lotus Sutra* contended that women were inferior creatures leading men to temptation and attachment and incapable of salvation unless they were first reborn as men. This doctrine had never fit well with the lofty social and economic status of most women in Japan, even before this apocalyptic age. In the thirteenth century, one Tendai prelate wrote a tract entitled *A Companion in Solitude* telling of many women taking the tonsure and obtaining salvation.

Indeed, women such as the nun Eshinni (1182–1268?) made important re-ligious contributions. Born to a local notable in northern Japan, she married Shinran in 1207. While her husband was busy spreading his beliefs in the Kanto, Eshinni and her family provided him with virtually all his economic support. Ten letters from the nun portray the life and times of Shinran for his followers, helping to forge Shinran's legacy after his death. Eshinni was devoted to the practice of the *nenbutsu*, or recitation of Amida's name. She helped articulate the family-centered doctrines of Shinran's movement and contributed to the belief that women, too, could be saved. Eshinni even proposed that women's sexuality created an enduring bond leading both men and women to the Pure Land.[17]

Commoner families during this time were similar to those of previous eras. Bilateral kinship was the normal pattern. Sexual relations began with nocturnal visitation and then the man might go to live with his wife's relatives or some-times the new couple took up an entirely new residence. Rural families were usually nuclear and highly unstable. Because of the frequent famines, however, there were also many single-parent households, especially those headed by women. Even small families consisting of the parents and children came and went rapidly, and there was neither a single heir nor a family patrimony. Divorce and remarriage were the norm in a society where women kept their own surnames, had great power over their children, and held their own property. Adoption and remarriage were usual customs.

Normally, these easily fragmented nuclear families were loosely bound into a few large lineages within each settlement. In each village, there were only four or five such extended households with surnames originating in much earlier times. These lineages performed religious ceremonies at local shrines and acted as mutual aid societies during times of hardship. They held fields and rights to produce that could be loaned out to individuals or small nuclear families. Each lineage included several elders who helped make decisions for the group.

Commoner women led hard but interesting lives. They almost always had opportunities for sexual liaisons, and women who traveled or stayed overnight at inns found it especially easy to meet men. Once a woman had a husband, she took up the same duties as he, working in the fields and at trades. Because most women preferred to give birth during the winter months after the crop was in, they were often large with child when they worked in the fields, increasing the likelihood of miscarriages, premature deliveries, and stillbirths. Most villages had midwives and parturition huts to maintain the privacy of vulnerable women. Bearing a child took place under poor conditions, with a man present to read sutras, a shaman to purify the birthplace, and another person to twang a bowstring to chase off evil spirits. Children were usually not suckled for long, increasing the risk of infant mortality.

Some commoner women continued to opt for the sex trade, singing, dancing, and engaging in intercourse with their patrons. Courtiers like ex-emperor Go-Toba remained avid patrons. Warriors also hired women for songs and sex, as the trade spread throughout Honshu. Around 1250, however, Kamakura began to place restrictions on these women. The association with pollution became stronger, and even though these female entertainers were still considered artisans, their status began to fall. Concomitantly, more women simply performed sex for money, as they were unable to write poetry or dance. Still, even by 1300, the flourishing sex trade held virtually no stigma.

Young children during this century were considered "unattached" (*muen*), often having lost their parents or suffered abandonment. Those who survived were the more fortunate ones, as a saying of the time held that until the age of seven "infants and small children belonged to the realm of the gods," undoubtedly a reference to the high rate of infant mortality.[18] Those who survived worked at

Women worked alongside their menfolk, planting rice seedlings and doing other agricultural hard labor. The Historiographical Institute of Tokyo University.

tasks such as fetching and watching livestock. There was a brisk market in buying and selling children, and they were probably also rented and shared for their labor. This market in young children may have saved some lives, as it gave them food and shelter during famine years. If their masters were harsh, however, they may have been forced to be prostitutes or lackeys for warriors. Most children had no rooms of their own, and those who did were forced to live in unhealthful lean-tos. Unattached children and families broken by famine or divorce barely eked out an existence.

Both Kyoto and Kamakura had large orphanages; abandoned children flocked to them during the famines. The services at these orphanages were minimal, however, and they may have been the last alternative for those nearing death. Increasing references to orphans may indicate that more infants were surviving to youth, but they also probably reflected the growing number of broken households. According to Kamakura law, when families disintegrated and descended into the servile class, the sons went with the fathers and the daughters with their mothers. The number of single-parent households, especially those headed by women, increased.

The large and growing class of unfree lived their daily lives in conditions hardly conducive to large, stable families. The master or mistress could sell either mate away from the other at his or her whim. Some servants undoubtedly struck up sexual relations with their masters or mistresses, producing offspring as a result. Women headed a disproportionately large number of servant households, while husbands were conspicuous by their absence.

Japanese society between 1180 and 1280 encompassed both new and old elements. The trifunctional elite still held sway, although the civil aristocrats in Kyoto were beginning to lose out to the warriors of Kamakura. Both classes devised new strategies, such as unigeniture, to solve the problem of too many offspring for too few resources. The clergy defined and led apocalyptic social movements through the mechanism of the "Latter Day of the Buddhist Law." All sects of Buddhism rose to the challenge, but different monks and nuns offered varying solutions. There were also signs of a virulent anticlericalism, especially among the elites, who feared that salvation was impossible during their lifetimes. Commoners lived in unstable but highly varied familial arrangements; their women continued to hold high status and work right alongside men. Orphans were numerous, despite the high rate of infant mortality. A large and growing servile class probably preserved the lives of war captives, debtors, and famine victims, but at the price of a lower birth rate.

Was Life in the "Latter Days of Buddhist Law" Really So Bad?

Persons of different social classes believed that the period between 1180 and 1280 represented the end of the world, in which salvation was all but impossible. To be sure, the era witnessed its share of problems. Politically, the age-old rule of the civilian aristocracy was coming to an end. There was the protracted violence of the War of 1180–1185, which was unprecedented in the islands. The climate was colder and wetter, producing death through influenza outbreaks and disfigurement in the form of leprosy. Most significant, three long famines rocked society, resulting in death, broken families, and a large class of servile persons.

Yet life had always been hard for almost everyone. During prehistoric times, foragers suffered from chronic malnutrition, and once agriculture commenced, about 900 BCE, war and seasonal famine offered new dangers. Since the mid-eighth century, killer epidemics regularly carried off a quarter or more of the population in just two or three years—victims were mostly adults who would have worked, raised the children, and paid the taxes. Famine was frequent in the eighth and ninth centuries, while factional strife and rebellion had become intractable problems well before 1180.

Was everyday life during the thirteenth century really worse than it had been previously? Perhaps it was, but maybe this enduring image of suffering was merely the product of the most literate class, the civil aristocrats, whose outlook was predominantly pessimistic. Or maybe saying so was a useful tool for prelates trying to enhance their standing and increase their following. No one can be sure what combination of factors made for this apocalyptic fear in an age that saw its share of major disasters masking incremental improvements.

6 The Revival of Growth, 1280–1450

Reshaping the Polity under Warrior Hegemony

The Collapse of the Kamakura Dyarchy

The policies designed by Kamakura to thwart the Mongols had the paradoxical effect of strengthening the *bakufu* vis à vis Kyoto while placing new strains on Kamakura's finances and manpower. On the one hand, Kamakura demanded and received rights to collect dues and raise troops in western Japan, extending its reach and denying courtiers and religious complexes much-needed tribute items and labor dues. On the other hand, increased resources were necessary to pay for expanded responsibilities, as the fear of a Mongol invasion continued unabated until the early fourteenth century. The added financial burden incurred preparing for another attack weakened the shogunate, as did its inability to reward warriors adequately for slaughtering some of the invaders during mop-up operations. Many long-time Kamakura supporters became more willing to sever their bonds with the shogunate, now over a century old, and try something new.

In addition, beginning in 1285 the *bakufu* was rocked by internal dissension caused by growing Hōjō autocracy. Loyal subordinates were assassinated and the Hōjō appointed outsiders to run the *bakufu* and act as provincial officials. They also enacted a series of laws appearing to aid impoverished warriors but in effect giving their family more power over military courts, vassal property, and loans taken out by samurai.[1] In many provinces, the Hōjō took for themselves positions once held by other warriors.

The problems of long-time Kamakura vassals were particularly vexing. Many had become indebted to usurers and merchants, as they struggled to adapt to the increasingly monetized economy. Until 1300, most families still practiced partible inheritance, and, as a result of improved rates of survival, members of each generation received smaller and smaller pieces of property. Litigation was so prevalent among samurai that many took to carrying around their own guides to the legal system. As Kamakura retainers became impoverished, their resentment grew and the likelihood of a successful rebellion increased.

Outlawry became more common among groups known by the epithet "evil bands." These thugs, lapsed vassals, rich peasants, and famine victims alike, formed close-knit groups identifiable by unusual clothing and colorful scabbards for their swords. They attacked without warning, murdering, robbing, resisting taxation, stealing farmers' crops, and then building makeshift stockades to defend themselves. Stone throwing was a favorite tactic, and during the early fourteenth century a mass hysteria erupted involving dozens of people throwing rocks at authorities.[2] Between 1310 and 1330, there were at least fifty violent incidents all over Japan. Kamakura reinforced its police forces, but attacks multiplied as dissatisfaction with the Hōjō and their shogunate grew.

As in the case of the War of 1180–1185, factionalism at court in general and division within the royal family in particular provided the pretext for another round of extended violence. Although the imperial line had split in 1243, at first relations had been amicable. Beginning in 1272, however, the two houses quarreled over the throne. In 1317, Kamakura brokered a compromise whereby the two lines would alternate in power, but political strife in Kyoto worsened.

In 1318, an energetic young sovereign named Go-Daigo assumed power and tried to consolidate an independent power base by appointing his own men at court and tapping into the growing commercial sector. He soon contemplated using the numerous unhappy Kamakura retainers and "evil bands" to overthrow the warrior government. As early as 1324, an anti-*bakufu* conspiracy was brought to light. It came to nothing, but the Hōjō failed to heed the danger inherent in an imperially inspired revolt. When he tried again in 1331, Go-Daigo led military forces but was captured and banished. Even without their leader, the rebels continued fighting.

In 1333, Go-Daigo escaped from exile to lead the ongoing insurrection. Kamakura dispatched Ashikaga Takauji, a supposedly trustworthy vassal, to crush the revolt, but Takauji decided his interests were better served by siding with Go-Daigo. By the fifth month of 1333, Kamakura fell, and the Hōjō committed suicide en masse. The city was incinerated and never recovered its former size or political importance. Japan's first samurai government was no more.

The Founding of the Muromachi *Bakufu*

In the power vacuum created by the destruction of the Kamakura *bakufu*, two contenders vied for power. The first was Go-Daigo and his motley crew of supporters at court and within the warrior class. Inspired by a mixture of Sung Neo-Confucianism, tantric Buddhism, and a newly defined nativist Shinto cult,

Go-Daigo managed to assert his right to rule between 1333 and 1336. He tried to concentrate power in his own hands by appointing to office his own relatives and trustworthy scions of minor civil aristocratic families. He also cultivated warriors such as Takauji and Kusunoki Masashige and placed them under a new shogun, Go-Daigo's son Prince Morinaga. Go-Daigo was indeed trying to revive imperial rule, but not as it had been six centuries earlier.

During his years in power, Go-Daigo attempted to establish imperial supremacy in a newly conceived polity. His Claims Court, where warriors, religious institutions, and civil aristocrats went to receive confirmation of their landholdings, was the centerpiece of his rule.[3] The court required that all valid holdings have Go-Daigo's seal as legal foundation, meaning that those who had seized property during the revolt lost out. His religious policy dictated that all temple-shrine complexes become subservient to his word, and he struggled to resuscitate the centuries-old position of provincial governor and have them rule alongside warrior constables. Go-Daigo even tried to extend control over currency to siphon profits from a growing commercial sector.

In the end, Go-Daigo's revolution failed, primarily because he had neither the manpower nor financial resources to dominate the old trifunctional elite. Instead, his policies antagonized many factions. For example, when he created the Claims Court, myriad samurai journeyed to the capital to obtain the proper papers, and soon legal wrangling over lands filled Go-Daigo's courts. Staffed at first with only sixty-four people, the imperial courts borrowed judges from the moribund Kamakura judiciary. In the end, the Claims Court operated at cross-purposes, trying both to reassert age-old rights and to legitimize current occupancy. This alienated numerous military houses. Go-Daigo tried some forward-looking policies, but he never could ensure their enforcement.

In the meantime, the Ashikaga bided their time as the other serious contender for power. Takauji established his headquarters in Kyoto and rewarded his followers with land and political offices, in defiance of Go-Daigo. When Go-Daigo tried to assert his control over the Kanto, Takauji had his brother Tadayoshi take control there and eventually Tadayoshi murdered Prince Morinaga. By 1336, the Ashikaga were in open rebellion against Go-Daigo, and a full-scale conflict erupted.

Known as the Wars between the Northern and Southern Dynasties, these battles lasted from 1336 to 1394 and constituted the most prolonged and devastating violence that Japan had seen to date. The war took place in five phases. During the first stage, from 1336 until 1338, fighting occurred almost every day, and control of Kyoto shifted from one side to the other. To buttress their claim to power, in 1336 Takauji and Tadayoshi promulgated their own code of laws; in 1338 they created a second shogunate with Takauji as its titular leader. Based in the Muromachi section of Kyoto, the shogunate was known by that name. To legitimize their rule, the Ashikaga captured the imperial regalia and the senior or northern branch of the royal family, countering Go-Daigo's claim as head of the southern dynasty.

During the second stage, from 1339 to 1350, Go-Daigo and his major supporters among the samurai were killed or passed from the scene, and warfare took place on a regional basis; Go-Daigo's allies kept a base at Yoshino in Yamato just south of Kyoto. Hostilities during this second phase proved inconclusive. During 1350–1355, Takauji and his brother Tadayoshi, after a falling out over how richly to reward their vassals, made war against each other, mostly in eastern Honshu. During this third stage, the rough-hewn Takauji poisoned his administratively gifted brother, taking sole command of the *bakufu*. More intense fighting between the Ashikaga and supporters of the southern court erupted during the fourth phase, ending in 1363. During the fifth stage, from 1363 until the Muromachi shogunate reunited the two feuding royal lines in 1392, violence gradually ebbed, as the southern dynasty fought in guerilla style against the more powerful forces of the shogunate.

The Heyday of the Muromachi *Bakufu*

Although Go-Daigo lost his bid for power, the Muromachi *bakufu* managed to accomplish his major goal—hegemony over the other two partners in the trifunctional elite. To be sure, neither the temple-shrine complexes nor the civil aristocracy disappeared. Both still held considerable political and economic power, although most of it was concentrated in central and western Japan. The Muromachi shogunate was quintessentially different from the Kamakura regime: its establishment in Kyoto marked the ascendancy of the warrior class over its rivals.

The new shogunate reached its pinnacle under the third shogun, Yoshimitsu (r. 1368–1408). Assuming the title at the age of ten, Yoshimitsu received guidance from a capable vassal during his minority. Then Yoshimitsu went about creating a military government unrivalled in wealth and power. In 1378, he had the Palace of Flowers built for himself, a new complex twice as large as the imperial residence. He rode roughshod over the civil aristocracy, taking for himself the First Court Rank and aristocratic post of prime minister (*dajō daijin*). He reconciled the two dynasties in 1392 and built the sparkling Golden Pavilion between 1397 and 1407 as a symbol of his lavish patronage of the arts. He received the title "king of Japan" in 1402 from the Ming dynasty (1368–1644) and enjoyed donning Chinese clothing while riding his horse in parade. He may even have attempted to displace the emperor altogether, gaining for his father the title of retired monarch and attempting to make his son an imperial prince. After Yoshimitsu's death in 1408, the next three shoguns were especially dynamic and wielded considerable power until 1441.

During its heyday, lasting from 1363 to 1441, the government was essentially a balancing act between the shogun's central administration and thirty-seven or so local warlords known as *daimyo*. In this sense, it followed the fundamental form of previous Japanese governments: an alliance of a limited central administration with local notables. When the shogun was powerful, as he always was between 1363 and 1441, the balance tipped toward him. Three related daimyo households complied by supplying a prime minister (*kanrei*). Together, the shogun and these collateral houses oversaw the courts, a records office, and vassal affairs. They developed a corps of bureaucrats, which included magistrates and secretaries. The *bakufu* had its own army of about 3,000 equestrians and 25,000 foot soldiers, equal to the armies of about ten daimyo. The shogun maintained a landed base from which he drew rents in grain and cash and taxed merchants and usurers who traded or operated storehouses and rice wine breweries. The shogun could also require daimyo to contribute to construction projects and he sold offices to Zen monks and ambitious samurai.

Local warlords usually administered two to three provinces and their armies numbered about 300 cavalry and 2,500 infantry. Within his jurisdiction, the daimyo held power over criminal matters, land disputes, and local temple-shrine complexes. From 1352, daimyo were granted the right to one half the taxes due on all lands in the provinces they controlled, helping to enrich the *bakufu*'s vassals at the expense of the clergy and civil aristocracy. Few daimyo, however, fully controlled more than a handful of properties within their jurisdictions. Most daimyo families relied on the power and prestige of the shogunate to enhance their status and to enlist followers in their province. The Muromachi policy of leaving the daimyo and his men on the land to collect taxes and run provincial affairs essentially revisited Yoritomo's plan, a concept that was open to abuse and growing vassal disloyalty over time.

Even at its height, however, the Muromachi shogunate was never in complete control of the archipelago, exerting its strongest powers in central and western Japan. To oversee the Kanto, Kyushu, and northeastern Honshu—areas never firmly in its grasp—the *bakufu* appointed regional deputies. Daimyo who lived far from Kyoto ignored shogunal demands to take up residence in the old capital. To be sure, the Muromachi *bakufu* was something new, wielding powers never before held by a warrior government. It probably reaped a greater portion of the economic surplus than any previous regime, but this was mostly because of the widening demographic and economic transformation then sweeping central and western Japan.

Renewed Demographic and Economic Growth

Population

During 1280–1450, Japan's population began to grow again. The number of Japan's inhabitants increased by about sixty-seven percent, from around six million to more than ten million. Most of the growth took place in central and western Japan where urbanization expanded by leaps and bounds. At least fifty new towns and cities sprang up, totaling about 400,000 residents. Kyoto was the largest at 200,000, but seven others contained more than 15,000 people. Hakata (40,000), Tennōji (later Osaka, 30,000), Ōtsu (20,000), Anotsu (15,000), and Nara (9,000) bustled with activity. Altogether, persons residing in towns and cities represented at least four percent of the augmented population, making Japan one of the most urbanized areas in the world.

Among these cities, Muromachi-era Kyoto was still preeminent. It developed precisely on top of the eastern half of the ancient capital, with many more people in a smaller space. Yet Kyotoites still used the same sewers and roads as during

Kusado Sengen was an important port along the Inland Sea until wiped out by a flood in the late 1500s. *Source*: *Tenji annai* (Hiroshima: Hiroshima kenritsu rekishi hakubutsukan, 1989), p. 51.

the ninth century, suggesting continued problems with sanitation. Nara experienced a building boom under the leadership of its numerous Buddhist temples. Anotsu and Kusado Sengen were busy municipalities during the fourteenth and fifteenth centuries, but natural disasters wiped them out by 1600. Archaeologists have uncovered street grids for both centers, and thousands of wooden tablets recording everything from loan contracts to talismanic writing designed to ward off disease.

The revival of demographic expansion was the direct result of a general decrease in mortality and higher fertility and infant survival rates. The number and virulence of epidemic outbreaks fell off markedly, especially after 1380. Only smallpox, measles, and influenza were even recorded, so there were apparently no new microorganisms for the populace to contend with. Furthermore, immunity levels continued to rise. Occasionally, as in 1421, pestilence decimated the populace of Kyoto. When the shogun made a pilgrimage to a local temple in that year, the afflicted poured into the holy grounds, and the poor shogun fled for his life. People still conducted rituals to ward off illness, tying garlic cloves to their doorways, for example, or performing the favorite songs and dances of the smallpox god to calm the deity. Deaths of infants and small children, however, continued to drain the population.

The role of famine also diminished notably. There were no crises of the magnitude of the Kangi or Shōga disasters, and the frequency of widespread famine dropped to about once every ten years between 1280 and 1450, compared to once every six years between 1150 and 1280. There were still more local famines than ever before, and some of them had dire effects. Even then, the years from 1280 to 1333 and 1370 to 1420 were almost completely free of food shortages.

The advent of a more benign climate helped reduce the number and severity of famines. The thirteenth century had been a time of especially cold, damp weather, probably caused by volcanism. Beginning in 1280, however, the weather became warmer, and after an interlude of intermittent cold, wet conditions between 1350 and 1400, the climate once again apparently turned even balmier. The period between 1370 and 1420 appears to have been optimal. This salubrious climate encouraged more stable agricultural production.

Finally, merchants and political and religious institutions stepped forward in new ways to ameliorate the effects of those few famines that did occur. Prior to 1350 when a famine struck, the populace sold off their possessions for food and abandoned cities and villages for the mountains and seashores to find sustenance. When a severe famine struck during 1420–1421, however, the reaction of victims was quite different. They streamed into Kyoto in record numbers to find food relief, either from charitable organizations such as the *bakufu* or Buddhist temples or from merchants looking to make a profit during a time of grain shortage. In short, a major improvement had taken place in the ability and willingness of charitable institutions and mercantile houses to provide assistance to famine victims. Merchants could be unscrupulous, though, as during 1431, when the *bakufu* caught and tortured traders who had withheld grain to create an artificial subsistence crisis for their own benefit. The intervention of the shogunate immediately ended that shortage. Starvation victims now began to receive charitable aid and relief from merchants instead of having to fend solely for themselves.

Despite the relative improvement in food supply, however, most commoners were still never very far removed from starvation. In one region of the Kanto during 1276–1405, for example, many peasants ordinarily went hungry in the spring. In fact, the spring and early summer constituted a "season of death" when the threat of starvation was greatest. The population inhabiting the Japanese archipelago had not so much conquered hunger as received a reprieve. Chronic malnutrition would be the lot of the overwhelming majority until at least 1600.

Although mortality from disease and famine fell, war was a different story. The epochal struggle that was the wars between the northern and southern dynasties lasted with great intensity for about thirty years—from 1331 through 1363. Armies became larger and specialized into distinct units employing more deadly weapons, including the pike and a more powerful bow. Despite greater dispersion of knowledge about the treatment of war wounds, techniques were primitive and included smearing human feces or dried infant tissue on open incisions.[4] Even then the number of combatants succumbing to wounds was probably small— usually only ten percent or so.[5]

But once again the battles, marches, and provisioning activities of the various armies dealt considerable hardship to the general populace. War acted as a handmaiden to those two other killers, disease and famine. For example, all the major smallpox epidemics and most measles and influenza outbreaks occurred during the height of the fighting. Six major and fourteen localized famines accompanied the movement of armies and battles through 1370.

In particular, the armies' provisioning techniques inflicted considerable hardship on the populace at large. Between 1335 and 1386 there were at least seventy-one incidents of arson and harvests stolen by armies in the field. In one particularly egregious case, in Mino in 1340, samurai "attacked residences, stole the rice and other grain laid aside as seed, so that the peasants fled and there was no cultivation going on."[6] These incidents could have been largely avoided if some central authority had dispensed the necessary grain to their armies in the field. Time and again, however, warriors stole food, even after the imposition of the half-tax in 1352. Like its predecessor the Kamakura shogunate, the new Muromachi *bakufu* commanded neither the power nor resources to centralize and manage the feeding and maintenance of its military forces, and ordinary people paid the price.

In sum, overall mortality dropped during 1280–1450 despite the depredations of war. In particular, the age of Yoshimitsu—roughly from 1370 to 1420—witnessed optimal conditions for demographic and economic growth, as neither epidemics, famines, nor war inhibited expansion. In addition, the weather was likely warmer, and when more moderate temperatures combined with plentiful rainfall, it made for better conditions for food production. Chronic malnutrition was still the lot of many, but for a short period some commoners could rise above that harsh fate.

Agriculture and Industry

As the death rate declined, more babies were born and survived into adulthood because of numerous agricultural innovations yielding a greater quantity of better and more diverse foodstuffs. Wider dispersion of iron tools, greater employment of livestock, and the application of more and better fertilizers such as ash and manure had accelerated during the late twelfth and thirteenth centuries. These three advancements had the effect of inducing cultivators to practice more efficient and intensive soil and plant management, evident in several ways. The number of "island dry fields," described in chapter 5, increased, giving hard-working peasants a productive rice paddy as well as a dry field on what was originally marginal land. The relatively simple technology of double cropping dry fields, noted in chapters 4 and 5, spread as well, blessing hungry peasants with a spring and autumnal crop of wheat, soybeans, barley, or millet.

More important, for the first time cultivators consistently double cropped their rice paddies, even though it required a lot of extra work. Along the Ki Valley in central Japan, for instance, peasants planted so many paddies in a second crop of wheat or soybeans by the 1300s that the proprietor began to levy a regular "added tax." By 1350, thirty percent of the valley yielded two crops, and where drainage was optimal, as much as fifty or sixty percent of the lands were so farmed. When a visitor from the Chosŏn dynasty (1392–1910) in Korea toured Japan in 1420, he wrote that it was not unusual for farmers in the rich Kinai to harvest even three crops in a single year. The harvest of multiple crops in a year had immense benefits, because it meant a richer diet, the ability to fend off starvation during the "spring hungers," and the sale of surplus grain in the new markets springing up near farming villages.

As noted in chapter 5, however, this potentially critical development was restricted to certain types of land in western and central Japan because farmers had to wait for the paddy to dry completely before beginning a second planting. Where land was low lying or swampy, as it was in much of eastern Honshu, double crop-ping was impossible. So the agrarian development of eastern Honshu—potentially a rich region—lagged behind that of western Japan.

At about the same time that peasants were learning how to reap two crops from their rice paddies, a new and hardier species of rice appeared in the archi-pelago. Known as Champa rice today, this rice species (*Oryza sativa indica*) was in-troduced from Southeast Asia via Sung China. Unlike the *japonica* strains already available in Japan, it resisted blight and insects well and withstood damage from flood and drought. By the time the term first appears in 1397, Champa rice had probably been known in Japan for at least a century. Traders may have introduced the grain to northern Kyushu farms from Korea or into the Kinai through Japa-nese religious centers with ties to Sung China.

Sporting a characteristic red awn, Champa rice played a crucial role in help-ing peasants convert Japan's river plains and deltas into productive rice paddies. Unlike the many small, flat stretches of land tucked away in mountain valleys, where rice cultivation had started, these lands did not drain easily and were of-ten flood-prone. Despite these conditions, the soil was rich, if only it could be unlocked. Champa rice proved to be one key because of its resistance to flood, drought, blight, and insects. The only drawback was that it apparently did not taste as good as native strains, but starving people paid little mind to such a minor inconvenience.

Managing crops and the soil better was only one facet of the ongoing trans-formation of agriculture. Better irrigation engineering was another. For instance, at Tajiri Estate in northern Kyushu, farmers built sophisticated irrigation channels with sluices to increase their harvests manyfold beginning in the 1300s; at Hineno Estate in the Kinai, the construction of four new ponds expanded acreage fivefold by 1417. The excavation and construction of new and better irrigation works nec-essary to water crops more regularly and efficiently also occurred at innumerable parcels in estates and provincial lands located between these two farms in north-ern Kyushu and the Kinai.

Along with the digging and construction work necessary for better irrigation, Japanese cultivators also utilized a new device: the waterwheel. It is depicted in screens, scrolls, and narrative tales beginning in the 1300s. An observant Chosŏn dynasty emissary reported on the strange contraptions in a visit during 1428–1429, writing that the waterwheels often turned automatically as the river flowed. In other cases, farmers pedaled or cranked this ingenious machine to pump the precious liquid. The development of the waterwheel was an important innovation helping to reduce the incidence of drought and crop failure. In essence, farmers made watering their paddies easier and more effective than ever before.

The agrarian transformation affected village patterns, too. Prior to 1200,

Widespread use of the waterwheel starting at this time helped farmers irrigate lands more thoroughly and efficiently. Ishiyamadera.

rural folk had lived in dispersed settlements organized into groups known by their name-fields. During the century from 1250 to 1350, however, most settlements in the Kinai and immediate vicinity became clustered, with peasant homes side by side and often encircled by a moat. At the same time, the old name-field designations lost their meaning. Rural residential patterns became compact because it was more efficient to group dwellings in one place and the more intensively worked fields in another. Also, as villagers acquired more livestock, it made sense to tend to the animals in areas where they could not invade houses. The long round of violence from the late Kamakura era through the 1360s may have encouraged cultivators to band together to resist pillaging and marauding, too.

The development of compact villages also signaled a change in the way that farmers related to each other. As the countryside became more crowded and irrigation works more complex, cultivators soon saw the need to control access to water and enforce rules about repairing dams, channels, and sluices. Disputes over rights to forest land also encouraged peasants to work together. Farmers began making collective judgments about what crops to plant and how to police themselves. The village also worked together when it was necessary to petition a proprietor or protest a legal decision or samurai incursion. In other words, the peasant village was becoming a corporate entity as farmers started to manage their own affairs. Shrine associations conducted village festivals and various rituals, with distinctions based on age, status, and gender. The few villagers who were minimally literate wrote down rules about all these affairs; such regulations appeared first in the Kinai but had spread throughout western and central Japan by 1450. Peasants adopted identities based on community and began to take control of their lives in new ways.

Encouraged by all these developments, farming productivity grew between 1280 and 1450. In 1450, the average farmer could expect a forty-five percent more plentiful crop than the same cultivator would have reaped in 700. Between 1280 and 1450, yields improved five times faster than they had between 700 and 1280. This growth in productivity occurred as the acreage under cultivation expanded by as much as thirty percent. Blessed with a greater quantity of various foodstuffs, more people in all trades had a better chance of surviving. The proportion of "floating population" decreased as organized villages assured more certainty about issues such as personal security and food supply. The number of people resorting to the old forager livelihoods out of desperation decreased.

Demographic and agrarian growth also affected industry and the labor market. From a tight labor market defined by the application of labor-saving devices before 1280, the Japanese economy moved to a surplus of workers in new and expanding industries by 1450. A Muromachi construction boom led to more jobs for lumbermen even as it meant expanding deforestation and its attendant effects. Builders journeyed farther afield than ever to seek good timbers, shipping them from Shikoku and deep within the Japan Alps. For example, when builders raised a new pagoda at Tōfukuji in Kyoto in 1442, two hundred rafts and six thousand packhorses bore lumber down the Kiso River valley from central Japan. The building boom also found impetus from new inventions, such as better tools for marking off angles and lengths and more precise and efficient saws and planes.

Other industries took advantage of the growth in the work force. Salt production became more labor intensive, as workers now carried ocean water up the beach, dried it in lots, and boiled the brine in kettles, instead of merely relying on the sun to dry trapped seawater. Fishermen developed specialized nets and set them up in one place, suggesting greater occupational specialization and the settlement of these workers at a fixed location. The production of ceramics also grew dramatically, as some villages came to concentrate on the firing of a certain type of pottery. Many settlements had three or four kilns where laborers learned to apply glazes. According to a freight report for the port Hyōgo, about a hundred pieces passed through its busy harbors per month, indicating the significant place of ceramics in commerce.

Critical innovations in ship building and navigation also took place. The hollowed-out logs used as boats prior to 1300, described briefly in chapters 1 and 2, had a capacity limited to the width of the timber and were best suited for domestic traffic. They could make the crossing directly to south China out of sight of land only with the greatest daring. By the early 1400s, however, shipwrights learned to construct a real hull from planks braced by crossbeams within the hold. The new vessels had a capacity of three to seven times that of the traditional boat and boasted at least two masts for bamboo sails and deckhouses above board. These ships also used the compass and took advantage of seasonal winds blowing to and from China. Merchant families plying the Inland Sea constructed these more capacious and seaworthy ships and then chartered them to religious complexes, daimyo families, and the shogunate for official missions to China. Many boats of the old variety still sailed within domestic waters, but with the development of this new ship design, residents of the archipelago could travel and trade abroad as never before. In sum, the period from 1280 to 1450 was the most innovative and productive for Japanese industry in almost a thousand years.

Domestic and Overseas Trade

A larger population and higher farming output meant that regional specialization occurred in Japan as never before. When people of various areas do what they can do best, the result is often a greater volume of trade. In fact, the era between 1280 and 1450 constituted a commercial boom in Japan, in which merchants and markets made the growing supply of foods and other commodities available to a hungry populace.

Old markets came back to life and new ones sprang up as never before. In the eighth century, provincial capitals had had their own markets, some quite active. They declined, however, when the population shrank in the mid-Heian period. After 1280, markets associated with the old provincial capitals at Wakasa and Hitachi, for example, revived; they sold silk, cloth, swords, and other items, often for cash. In addition, there were at least 113 new markets scattered throughout the islands, mostly concentrated in the Kinai or adjacent provinces, but also prominent along the Inland Sea and northern Kyushu. In the popular consciousness, these markets had more than a purely economic meaning. Each was believed to have its own god and was considered a bridge between this world and the next.

In order for the commercial sector to grow, more efficient transportation was imperative. The improvement in ship construction has already been noted. On the other hand, the technology for land transportation changed little, still dependent on packhorses and foot traffic traversing dirt or sand roads. The Muromachi *bakufu*, however, took an exceptional step to aid merchants and artisans by reducing or eliminating barrier fees wherever possible. These tolls had become burdensome, as they charged as much as ten percent of the value of commodities, and unfortunate merchants encountered as many as twenty of them in one trip. During Yoshimitsu's reign, however, the shogunate relied on property and land taxes paid in cash and abolished many fee barriers. This action lowered the cost of doing business precisely during the period when both the population and economy grew most rapidly.

Kyoto, the ancient capital and now home to the *bakufu*, was the hub of commercial activity. Buyers there could find stalls offering all sorts of grains, vegetables, and processed foods, as well as silk and hemp thread, various dyes, and perilla oil to light lamps. The demand of a large consumer class in Kyoto led to regional specialization in certain products sold just to Kyotoites. Nara sent rice wine; central Japan traded in swords and knives; the northern Japan Sea littoral marketed hemp cloth.

Kyoto was home to a sizable mercantile class, represented by forty organizations (*za*). They included Kitano malt brewers, Ōyamazaki oil producers, and Gion silk weavers. There were at least three hundred fifty moneylenders, formerly brewers and warehouse owners, charging as much as sixty percent interest for a term. They loaned to samurai, religious complexes, the old aristocratic class, and local farmers, and they bribed the shogunate to guarantee repayment.

During the boom, monetization developed even more rapidly than it had during the 1200s. Urban proprietors began to prefer receiving their rents in cash, as it was fungible and cost only 2.5 percent as much as shipments of rice. Throughout the 1300s, temple records and other sources show more and more transactions being conducted in cash. The same Chosŏn dynasty ambassador who noted the efficacy of the waterwheel wrote that travelers in Japan carried money belts containing large sums of cash to pay for lodging, transportation, and barrier fees. They also purchased food and even a hot bath with coins.

The commercial boom eventually affected almost all levels of society. In western Japan, even small cultivators started to sell their excess grain, hemp, and other commodities produced especially for the market. At Tara estate near the Kinai, for instance, a class of merchant-farmers numbering fifty-nine members traded at market by the mid-fourteenth century. Not coincidentally, these same cultivators listed many more family possessions, often acquired at market, in 1450 than they had a century earlier.

Although many anonymous commoners benefited from growing commercialization, others did not. Because the supply of cash could not meet the demand for liquidity for a growing number of transactions, the period 1280–1450 was a time of price deflation. For those unfortunate enough to contract a loan and have their crop or business venture fail, flight or resistance became attractive alternatives to imprisonment or to having the investor seize homes and property.

Debt riots erupted regularly. In the first major case, in 1428, crops failed and teamsters stormed the capital, incensed by the loss of freight and fees. Angry mobs of farmers soon followed, streaming into Kyoto looking for handouts. In the process, they destroyed the warehouses of wealthy merchants, repossessed collateral, and ripped up debt contracts, which they undoubtedly could not repay. The shogunate sent samurai to quell the violence, but it is interesting to note that many sided with the rioters.

The uprising of 1441 was even worse. Indebted peasants numbering in the thousands closed off the seven entrances to the city and occupied nearby temples. For two months they attacked pawnshops and moneylenders, using sophisticated battle tactics. Eventually a factionalized shogunate capitulated to demands for debt relief for all. There were similar large-scale riots in 1454 and 1457, marking the advent of widespread market activity in Japan just as surely as the appearance of more shops and stalls throughout the islands.

Western Japan, the center of domestic commerce, felt most keenly the impact of growing overseas trade. China left the biggest and most lasting impression because of its size and wealth. Trade and travel between China and Japan received a major boost in 1368, when the powerful Ming dynasty (1368–1644) emerged.[7] Like the Tang court, the Ming demanded that Japan accept tributary ties and send missions. According to the agreement hammered out between the Ming and the *bakufu*, only authorized ships from China and Japan could participate in commerce. The Ming would regulate trade through tallies, with each ship carrying half a slip fitting into a booklet; voyages would be limited to once a decade. Until the end of the fourteenth century, however, the wars in Japan and the rapacity of pirates based in the land-poor islands between northern Kyushu and Korea retarded the development of relations. In particular, hungry pirates looking for food drove up costs by requiring greater security for merchantmen.

When Yoshimitsu assumed power, however, he was eager for better relations with China and suppressed piracy as best he could. Beginning in 1395, several trading parties sojourned between China and Japan. Normally consisting of three ships—each manned by a crew of two or three hundred—these missions sent horses, fans, sulfur, gold, ink stones, sappan wood, copper ore, lacquerware, folding screens, and suits of armor to China. In return, the Ming court doled out hundreds of silver ingots, thousands of copper coins, and myriad bolts of silk cloth, along with jade, pearls, porcelain vases, and incense boxes. Zen monks played an especially crucial role in facilitating the exchange. Trade missions soon proved so popular in both China and Japan that boats sailed nearly every year until 1410. After Yoshimitsu's death, an eighteen-year hiatus occurred, but from 1426 until 1451, several more flotillas set sail.

These missions turned out to be especially lucrative for those living in western and central Japan. They also helped monetize Japan's cash-poor markets, thanks to all the silver, copper, and other precious objects flowing into the archipelago from the Ming. For instance, in 1433, Japanese traders took home 74,310 strings of cash, with each string holding a thousand coins. In 1453, the profit was 69,502 strings. The drain on Ming finances was so serious that the dynasty was forced to debase its currency. By itself the Ming trade was not enough to monetize the Japanese economy fully, but it provided a strong stimulus to domestic exchange.

Although their economies were much smaller, trade with the Chosŏn dynasty and the kingdom of the Ryukyus affected western Japan, too.[8] From the outset the *bakufu*'s relations with the Chosŏn dynasty were greatly troubled by the brigandage of pirates; they commanded more than three hundred ships, stealing grain, burning houses, and enslaving residents living in coastal provinces. They slowed economic activity in the Korean capital to a trickle, almost resulting in the termination of intercourse between 1350 and 1400. Attempts at resettling the outlaws, such as in 1368 when about two thousand were given residence in southern Korea, were fairly effective remedies for their behavior, however.

As piracy waned after 1400, the new Chosŏn dynasty adopted policies favorable to trade with Japan. With the daimyo of Tsushima acting as a middleman, the two states managed twenty-two missions per year during the first half of the fifteenth century. Cargoes per ship were small, but because commercial ventures were so common, the impact was sizable. Japanese merchants sent cinnabar, medicines, sulfur, metals, and military and artistic items to Korea. Koreans shipped ginseng, honey, tiger skins, Buddhist sutras and icons, and eventually cotton cloth to the archipelago.

The Ryukyu kingdom was a new player in East Asian affairs and trade, having been unified in 1429. Its economy was largely dependent on commerce, especially with the Ming. Merchants in the southern kingdom also did business with Southeast Asia, especially Thailand, Java, Malacca, and Vietnam. Ryukyu ships carrying

Southeast Asian dyes, woods, and spices called on Hyōgo and Hakata. Ryukyu merchants also acted as intermediaries in the Ming-Muromachi trade, reselling Chinese goods in Japan. Ryukyu-Japan trade was so significant that it induced the *bakufu* to form an office specifically to deal with these transactions.

By 1450, Japan was a much different place from what it had been in 1250. The population had grown sizably, especially in the cities. New and old agrarian techniques combined to reduce hunger and create a healthier populace. Industry became even more innovative and prolific. A commercial boom with both domestic and overseas components spread the new and more plentiful products to consumers of nearly all classes. To be sure, the effects of this transformation were much less robust for people dwelling in southern Kyushu and eastern or northern Honshu. Yet this geographically differentiated growth gradually came to have important ramifications for the social structure, family, and gender relations of many areas.

Social Relations: Class, Family, and Gender

Class

The social pyramid during 1280–1450 showed the effects of the political, demographic, and economic changes described above. For the first time in more than five hundred years, elites and local rulers could draw on a growing surplus of rents and revenues in the form of grain, labor, cash, and commodities. Warriors were best positioned to take advantage of the new conditions, becoming the richest and most dominant component of the ruling elite. The civil aristocracy suffered political and economic eclipse as their incomes dwindled. The religious movements of the 1200s expanded and became institutionalized but also more subservient to warrior power. The huge class of commoners increased dramatically and became more highly differentiated into occupational and income groups. Finally, there was still a substantial servile class near the bottom, clinging to a status just above Japan's outcasts.

As social upstarts, samurai were "extravagant, rambunctious, and lawless."[9] Having no sense of good breeding, they gambled and spent all their time partying, drinking, and engaging loose women. Legislation promulgated in 1336 tried to curb such behavior, but to little avail. Sasaki Dōyo was one such "extravagant" samurai. Born in 1306, Sasaki served first the Hōjō and then Go-Daigo. In 1335, he switched sides again and adhered to Takauji. For his service, he was named a daimyo, and ironically, helped to write the very law codes that he came to flout so freely.

In 1340, for example, when Sasaki was throwing one of his many parties, he and his followers admired some maple trees on an excursion, so much so that they ripped the branches off the trees. The garden happened to belong to a temple headed by the brother of a retired emperor, and his servants beat the branch gatherers. When Sasaki heard about the thrashing, he led three hundred mounted soldiers back to the temple and set it on fire. The priests demanded Sasaki's head, but the Ashikaga merely ordered him into exile. On the day when he left for distant parts, Sasaki placed three hundred members of his family and retainer band in an entourage showing off the latest in martial finery, including quivers covered in rabbit skin. They brought along quantities of sumptuous food and had courtesans waiting at every inn along the exile route. It became a pleasure excursion, not the punishment for a grave crime.

Men like Sasaki could afford to be so brazen because they benefited from both the economic growth of the age and the redistribution of resources away from the civil aristocracy. Sasaki's residence in Kyoto was elegant, filled with hanging scrolls, flower vases, incense burners, and teakettles. The floor was covered in rush matting sporting his crest. He slept in silken garments on a pillow of aloe wood. The guardhouse was filled with food—chickens, rabbits, pheasants, and quantities of rice wine. Visitors were offered a free drink. Sasaki was also a connoisseur of the arts, possessing Chinese articles (*karamono*) fashioned by famous artists and calligraphers. An avid participant in tea parties, he competed to taste and name as many brands as possible. He patronized the theater of his day and was responsible for introducing Noh drama to Yoshimitsu.

Although extravagance, lawlessness, and arrogance were the terms most frequently associated with these upper-class samurai, there were also models of decorum among them. Imagawa Ryōshun, who had played a pivotal role in pacifying Kyushu for the Ashikaga, left behind admonitions for his son after Ryōshun's death.[10] They are idealized, but advocate a sound grasp of the arts of peace, including Chinese philosophy, Japanese history and law, and the teachings of Zen masters. He warned his son not to waste his time hawking, putting minor offenders to death, living in luxury by fleecing the people, or disregarding moral laws. Ryōshun admonished his offspring to treat retainers equally, listen to sound advice carefully, and avoid drinking bouts. While he recognized that the warrior's way consisted of expertise in archery, horsemanship, and strategy, he also emphasized the capacity to manage men and affairs soundly.

Few samurai held such exalted positions as daimyo. Most lived on the land and behaved as local notables had for ages. Growth in the number of these petty warriors holding small pieces of land was substantial between 1280 and 1450. The Kawashima, for example, were just one such family; they lived southwest of Kyoto and reached the status of Muromachi vassal in 1336.[11] They received from the Ashikaga titles bolstering their local power and in turn served in the shogun's army. As local authorities, the Kawashima suppressed peasant uprisings, litigated land disputes, helped administer irrigation rights, acted as moneylenders, and added to their holdings through purchase.

Samurai were known above all for their fighting prowess. Nomoto Tomoyuki, for instance, fought for Takauji in over a dozen battles ranging from the Kanto to the Kinai during 1335–1337. Boasting repeatedly of his valor, he killed numerous enemies and managed to topple a tower single-handedly. He also watched, however, as first one and then another of his comrades fell. Finally, confused and lost in a particularly bloody battle near Kyoto, he fled back to the Kanto, where he encountered stiff resistance from allies of Go-Daigo. His brother was killed in a battle there in 1337, the same year that Tomoyuki died of unknown causes. His support for the Ashikaga cause "accomplished nothing of strategic consequence" and his family probably received almost no compensation for his exploits.[12]

Meanwhile, the civil aristocracy suffered considerable decline. The old court political structure still existed, but warriors held all the important posts. Civil aristocrats became poorer, as the Wars between the Northern and Southern Dynasties, together with the new half-tax, siphoned off a greater portion of rents once belonging to them. Many aristocrats, however, were still rich enough to participate in the ceremonial and artistic activities of the court. Upstart samurai sought approval for their social pretensions and artistic efforts from courtiers. Samurai made large gifts to the court, hungered for meaningless court ranks, and even intermarried with the old aristocracy.

Ichijō Kaneyoshi (1402–1481) led a life both representative of and exceptional for a civil aristocrat of his age.[13] Born during the height of Yoshimitsu's power, Kaneyoshi received a classical education in ritual and the arts. He lived in a large mansion surrounded by high walls filled with the accustomed halls connected by walkways, located just southwest of Yoshimitsu's Palace of Flowers. He played in the gardens and streams that his father used for parties. As a young man, Kaneyoshi probably knew only indirectly of the bustling city around him, hearing about but never touring the warrior district, the teahouses and baths in the mercantile sector, or even the homes of other aristocrats.

Kaneyoshi's family was born to rule, an exalted lineage extending through both his father and mother. He advanced rapidly through the ranks until at the age of thirteen he already held a high appointment. Kaneyoshi's father suddenly died when the boy was fourteen; despite this setback, Kaneyoshi managed to cultivate the new shogun. At twenty he ascended to the First Rank and was named Regent, a position he held off and on until his retirement in 1450.

The clergy during the 1300s concentrated on expanding and institutionalizing the various religious movements of the thirteenth century, as fears accompanying the "Latter Day of the Buddhist Law" faded while the age-old emphasis on practical worldly benefits reasserted itself. For example, Rinzai Zen, guided by Chinese émigré monks and the renowned Musō Soseki (1275–1351), found avid patrons at court and among the Muromachi shoguns. Looking for a religious force to counterbalance older recalcitrant sects and protect the realm, the *bakufu* organized, sponsored, and appointed the leaders of the so-called Five Mountains, or systems of Zen temples in Kyoto and Kamakura. These temples quickly became major landholders, traders, and moneylenders, and a three-tiered organization reached into the countryside. By 1450, there were more than three hundred Rinzai Zen monasteries and perhaps fifty thousand clerics.[14] Zen monks were the leading intellectuals and travelers of their day, engaging in cultural pursuits such as the tea ceremony, garden design, poetry and painting, and the study of Chinese thought. They introduced Japan's residents to many new aspects of Chinese material culture.

Musō Soseki's academic and economic connections to China and his willingness to accept political support and control in the Five Mountains system are illustrative of many clerics of this era. Born of a warrior family, Musō read widely in Buddhism, Confucianism, Daoism, and secular texts. He became a monk at eighteen and studied with Chinese émigré Zen masters for much of his life. At twenty-five, he achieved enlightenment, the goal of all Zen prelates. He then spent some time as an itinerant ascetic. Eventually, he rather hesitantly adopted the patronage of the Hōjō to help in his quest to build religious hermitages. His need for political and economic support led Musō to cultivate Go-Daigo and then the Ashikaga. He became the teacher for Takauji and was instrumental in the construction of Tenryūji in southwest Kyoto, garnering materials through the China trade. When he died at seventy-seven in 1351, he had been a monk for sixty-nine years and boasted more than thirteen thousand disciples.[15]

Other religious movements prospered, too. True Pure Land Buddhism developed from a relatively small following restricted to the Kanto after Shinran's death in 1262 to a powerful institution with adherents mostly in western Japan and along the Japan Sea littoral.[16] Shinran's sect benefited from the creation of numerous religious meeting places, where the faithful convened once a month before an altar over which hung a large inscription of Amida's name. There they chanted the *nenbutsu*, listened to sermons, and sang hymns. The most important temples did not appear until the early 1300s, when Shinran's gravesite became an object of pilgrimage and soon the home of a major temple called Honganji. Dōgen's Sōtō Zen school and even Ippen's itinerant movement of *nenbutsu* chanters embraced large followings and eventually established temples, too.

The wave of Buddhist institutionalization also resulted in the formation of independent schools based on new interpretations of the ancient talismanic writings of the old native cult now called Shinto. Spurred by Go-Daigo's revolt and Ki-tabatake Chikafusa's *Chronicle of Gods and Sovereigns* defending the legitimacy of that emperor, several new sects evolved centering on Ise Shrine or Mt. Yoshida in Kyoto. These new schools overcame Buddhist doctrinal domination and benefited from the demise of apocalyptic, pessimistic views. They eventually incorporated large followings of pilgrims destined for sacred sites.

The expansion and growing differentiation of the commoner class into new occupations and varying income levels was another significant development. Material life improved for most of these people during the fourteenth and fifteenth centuries, albeit slowly and unevenly. Among the farming populace—still the largest single group—some became wealthy leaders of corporate villages and sold their surplus products at market. Others were much poorer, falling victim to crop failure or indebtedness. Most were somewhere in the middle.

The most widely shared advances in material comfort concerned diet and cleanliness. Agricultural advances led to three dietary improvements. The spread of double-cropping and Champa rice made grain more plentiful. The custom of drinking green tea became popular among commoners. Recognized today for its ability to fight cancer and heart disease, the green herb had a more direct effect during this epoch—commoners began boiling their water to kill harmful micro-organisms. Finally, soybean curd became a prominent part of the diet and supplied an additional source of protein. It is notable that Buddhist temples with ties to China, where these items had been popular for centuries, introduced all three foods to Japan at about the same time (1100–1300).

Although toilets were still primitive and streets were not regularly cleaned, urban sanitation may have improved somewhat. For the first time people began to collect and sell excrement (night soil) but probably not on a widespread basis. At the same time, personal cleanliness became a daily habit for many. There were bathhouses in Kyoto by the 1360s. The Chosŏn dynasty ambassador of 1428–1429 observed that "people liked bathing and cleaning their bodies," with each city and village having a communal bath.[17] When the water was hot, an attendant blew a horn. Even welfare agencies, inns, bridges, and hospitals had their own baths.

Other changes had a more limited effect. For example, most people still wore cold and scratchy hemp or ramie clothing, but by the early 1400s, the cotton plant introduced from Korea spread into western Japan as a cash crop. Soon even wealthy commoners wore warm, soft cotton cloth. Housing for wealthier peasants made great improvements, too. Instead of the traditional pit dwelling, rich peasants built farmhouses plastered with mud, with a thick ridgepole to support a thatched roof. Pillars were planted at regular intervals, and the floor was covered in planks laid at ground level. The main residence might measure twenty by forty meters, depending on the wealth of the owner, and included a kitchen, bathroom,

Improved farmhouses like the one pictured above are clear signs that Japanese agriculture was becoming more productive for many cultivators. The Ehime Prefectural Museum of History and Culture. *Source:* Ishii Susumu, ed., *Fukugen gijutsu to kurashi no Nihon shi* (Shin jinbutsu ōrai sha, 1998), p. 39.

living space, and storage area. There were also small sheds and lean-tos where servants lived. These magnificent farmhouses, some of which still stand today, were the exception. The pit dwelling was still the home for most peasants, especially in eastern Honshu.

Because of the commercial boom, sizable new classes of artisans and merchants were created. In artisan organizations, for example, relations were equitable and horizontal. All members selected the officers and shared in profits from joint ventures. They had their own rules of behavior, analogous to those of the corporate village. Moneylenders lived in neighborhoods having considerable responsibility for their own affairs, such as defending their city against rioters, organizing for garbage disposal, naming people for guard duty, and mediating arguments among neighbors. Wealthy moneylenders adopted pursuits such as poetry, art collecting, and the tea ceremony, and sponsored and participated in the many festivals organized for Kyoto and other major cities. In all these activities, artisan and mercantile families established ties with their social betters, especially civil aristocrats and warriors, mixing with differing social classes as never before. Meanwhile, the urban poor went on rent strikes and joined one of the new sects of Buddhism.[18]

Beneath this prospering class of commoners of all descriptions, substantial groups of servile people and outcasts suffered their fates. Servants appear frequently in stories, comic sketches, popular songs, and Buddhist sermons of this era. A Chosŏn dynasty visitor observed that "in Japan where there are many people and little to eat, they sell lots of slaves, even children in secret."[19] Outcasts included leatherworkers and some artisans such as dyers and plasterers. The job of urban clean-up also fell to outcasts and others of lowly status associated with particular shrines or temples because no one else could be found to labor in the filthy cities.

Artists were a special subgroup of outcasts or marginal people. Often dwelling on the riverbanks in Kyoto or other cities, they included dancers, musicians, and magicians. They entertained the gods through performances of Noh plays and linked verse poetry. To show their solidarity with the unclean, they donned bamboo or rush hats symbolic of outcasts or mendicant monks. In effect, as Japan became more agrarian and commercial and more people rose out of poverty, social intolerance of marginal peoples, including sex workers, hermits, and shamans, increased.

As patrons of the arts, however, the elite could not do without the outcasts. In 1349, for instance, troupes of dancers were scheduled to perform on a large stage. The shogun and civil aristocrats were in attendance. Wearing costumes, these outcast/artists danced, played music, and did acrobatic feats. When a young boy wearing a monkey suit did tricks, the audience became so raucous that sixty stands collapsed. More than a hundred spectators died. The shogun received the blame for the disaster, as his enthusiasm was believed to invite divine punishment.[20]

Family and Gender

Family and gender relations among almost all classes saw the growing power of men and a consequent decline for women. Warriors of exalted status lived in households dominated by a male head. His wife (and concubines) came to live in his house. The wife frequently attained her status as a result of a political alliance with another samurai family. Prospective wives were expected to present their mates with a dowry. By 1450, most samurai practiced unigeniture. Sometimes there was also a primary daughter who could inherit property in perpetuity. Eventually, however, all siblings except the male heir lost out. Daughters were married out to other families or took the tonsure. Secondary sons tried to build their own territorial bases and frequently quarreled with the heir over property. As was true earlier, most families included servants and vassals bound by fictive kinship ties. Each main family had cadet lines on which they counted for support but which were often sources of political and economic competition.

Among the civil aristocracy, Kaneyoshi's family life was exceptional. He married the daughter of a prominent aristocrat, and she bore him five children in a decade, the eldest son becoming the sole heir. At twenty-five, Kaneyoshi was the head of a household in which both his parents were dead, his siblings had all become clerics, and his immediate family employed numerous servants, retainers, wet nurses, and other menials. He inherited the family mansion, took other wives, and eventually had fifteen children, most of whom became monks or nuns. He learned to support this relatively lavish lifestyle by managing what was left of the once imposing total of fifty estates deeded to the Ichijō family. Most aristocrats were neither as wealthy nor as powerful as Kaneyoshi.

Before 1280, commoner kinship had been bilateral, the status of women had been high, families were unstable, and divorce and remarriage were usual. The decrease in the death rate and improvements in the economy during 1280–1450 encouraged the formation of more stable farming families settled in the same village for several generations. Instead of extended lineages based on ancient surnames, nuclear families took last names based on the place where they lived, such as Mizoguchi ("mouth of the ditch") or Fujino ("wisteria moor"). The greater wealth of individual commoner families meant not only geographical stability, but also a patrimony to pass along to an heir.

These new units were called stem families, or *ie*, and were fairly common in central and western Japan by 1450. Stem families placed great value on the lineage and passed along property and the family's occupation to a male heir. They also cared for their elders and kept ancestral tablets to commemorate the dead. The head of the *ie* was responsible for taxes and often served as a member of the village shrine association. In these stem families, there was a new emphasis on the conjugal pair, with the male now more dominant. He was almost always the head of the *ie* and named one of his sons as heir, ordinarily the eldest son. The adoption of a male from another family was also common. Depending on their wealth, these households might include unrelated people such as servants.

Even the treatment of death changed. Corporate villages came to have their own cemeteries, and cremation was more commonly practiced. Because villagers knew each other well, funerals became a community-wide event, in which people gave gifts, read sutras, dug graves, made ritual implements, and washed the remains for placement in a coffin. Even the time of day for these funerals shifted from night to day. These changes had as much to do with penetration of Buddhism into the countryside as the formation of the stem family and the corporate village.

Marital practices also changed. The old custom of uxorilocal residence disappeared and women instead went to live with their men. Divorce slowly evolved toward becoming the privilege of the male, though not exclusively. Wives gradually came to be considered no better than the possession of the male head. More women kept their childhood or husband's name, which suggests infantilization. Females at all levels of society lost the right to inherit and control property. Fewer widows remarried, and it became more difficult for women to become members of village shrine associations. Male adultery went unpunished while female extramarital relations could earn both the woman and her lover the death penalty. Prospective brides often had to provide the husband's family with a dowry.

Women were valued almost solely for their ability to produce children, especially a male heir. In addition, giving birth took on new meaning as a form of pollution, further diminishing women's status. Conversely, mothers merited special veneration for making such a sacrifice to continue the family line. Of course, the worst fate for a female was to be barren or lose an infant in childbirth.

To be sure, women still worked in the trades and on the farm. In addition, although the slow formation of stem households may have meant less freedom for a woman, for those lucky enough to be designated legal wives, their security as the managers of the household may have increased in comparison to the older, loose marital arrangements. Unfortunately, many men also took concubines, whose position was anything but fixed in the family. As the number of concubines multiplied late in the period, so did the number of vulnerable women.

Literature and religious doctrine reveal the decline of women's status during this epoch. For example, Tomoe, the heroic woman warrior of 1180, became a cross-dressing shaman in fourteenth-century theater.[21] In Buddhism, women were more closely associated with death, decay, and pollution, and one picture scroll depicts women as "evil, lascivious, and furious when rejected."[22] Stories written in the fourteenth and fifteenth centuries explained the proper behavior for women and made them obedient to their fathers and mates. One monk wrote *A Mirror for Women* in 1300, listing the seven serious faults of women and prescribing ways to overcome them. Even a separate spoken and written language evolved exclusively for females.

The slow decline in women's status beginning in the late thirteenth century was too much for some. Sixty percent of all nunneries in Japan were established between 1270 and 1470. When women took the tonsure and resided exclusively with other women, many may have found that they could manage property, create a business, and run their own lives, options not available to a woman living in an *ie*. During this era, these women came to be known as "those who did not form a family." Religion also provided other comforts to females. For instance, Murōji, mentioned briefly in chapter 2, became known as "the Mount Kōya for women." Females went on pilgrimages there and placed votive offerings in the shape of breasts on the walls.[23]

No religious site better reveals the ambivalent treatment of women in society than the shrines at Mount Kumano. There women were revered as deities of fertility and the mothers of Buddhist saints such as Saichō and Ryōgen. Courtly females including Izumi Shikibu were even reported to have made pilgrimages to Kumano, one of the few religious destinations remaining open to women throughout the fourteenth and fifteenth centuries. At the same time, however, itinerant nuns at Kumano preached that females were sources of pollution and transgression. Graphic representations of "blood-pool hell" showed these unfortunates their ultimate fates.

Some single women reacted by finding other outlets for their talents. Wandering performers, including the ones based at Kumano, journeyed from village to village providing entertainment by juggling, dancing, doing acrobatics, or acting out or vocalizing popular stories and Buddhist sermons.[24] They told tales guiding their listeners past fierce animals, hungry ghosts, never-ending battles, and the other realms of hell on the way to Amida's Paradise. They thrilled their audience with accounts of famous warriors such as Yoritomo and his brother Yoshitsune. Using various props such as flowers, picture scrolls, and musical instruments, they helped to link persons of diverse stations in a more unified culture of storytelling. They also raised donations for local Buddhist temples. Many of the women were blind; it was believed that their very blindness gave them powers to see suffering and religious truths that the sighted could not. Female jongleurs are known to have sold drugs to induce abortions, too.

Children continued to suffer from high mortality rates, and when they died the corpse was simply placed in a sack and abandoned in the wild. The wider

Female storytellers like the one pictured here provided entertainment and excitement as they traveled from village to village. Kankikōji, Kyoto.

dissemination of medical texts, especially books specializing in obstetrics and pediatrics, may have helped to save some infants. If the infant survived, for the first few years mother and child were united in a love free from the guilt inherent in sexual love. When the child was old enough, however, he or she was expected to work. Few children of the commoner class received much education. The orphanage in Kyoto continued to operate, but there are fewer references to unattached children during this era, perhaps because they were better cared for in stable familial and village units.

Like children in all eras, they enjoyed using their imaginations and playing games, too. Popular toys were whistles, tops, boats, miniature carts, bamboo horses, small bows, and wooden dragonflies. Youngsters played stickball and marbles, and chased flocks of birds, too. During the winter, snowball fights broke out, and when the iris bloomed, boys donned iris helmets and wielded iris swords at a horizontal pole. The first one to knock down the pole was declared the victor. Little girls enjoyed floating bamboo boats down small streams, and during the autumn, they divided into groups and played in the mud or a local stream. Regardless of gender, children kept dogs, cats, and small birds, too. Even adults played games: *go*, dice, and chess for the upper classes and wrestling for commoners and those lower in the social hierarchy. Adults were also fond of whistles, because they believed that the toys could chase away evil spirits bringing disease or vile insects such as mosquitoes.

In sum, Japanese society in 1450 was a more finely specialized and tightly organic structure than even two centuries earlier. Besides the ruling elite now dominated by the samurai, commoners adopted diverse occupations in industry and commerce. The stem family and the corporate village coalesced to provide more stability in a wealthier economy. At the same time, the status of women started to plummet and social prejudice surrounded those living on the margin. Like all periods, the era 1280 to 1450 had its share of those who prospered and those who did not.

Why Did the Status of Women Begin to Fall?

The relatively lofty position of women was a hallmark of Japanese society until about 1300. Women of all classes had economic power, owned their own homes, held political rank and power, and could engage in sexual relations fairly freely. Beginning around 1300, however, many lost the independent bases of their power and influence.

Why did this happen? Was it related to the rise of the military and the length of wars, where men excelled? Yet there had been skillful women warriors from the

Tomb age through the fourteenth century, as suggested by suits of armor with room for breasts. Did population growth and the rise of a labor surplus encourage women to become specialists in birthing and child-raising, as occurred in Southeast Asia? Even so, a good number of females still supplied a high proportion of back-breaking work on the farm and at various trades. Did a new Buddhist emphasis on pollution condemn menstruating women to lose their once great powers? Women had escaped religious disapproval earlier, but why not now? Did the social trend toward unigeniture lead to the devaluing of daughters and the need to enforce fidelity to ensure paternity? Unigeniture, however, was by no means fixed and universal during this epoch. Or were the reasons a complex mixture of all these factors? As historians unfortunately must write too often, no one knows for sure.

7 Uneven Expansion in an Age of Endemic Warfare, 1450–1600

The Deterioration of Shogunate Control

In 1441, a disgruntled daimyo assassinated the despotic shogun Ashikaga Yoshinori and ended the period of assertive *bakufu* leadership. Although the assassin was eventually caught and executed, the shogun's army did not dispatch him, but a rival warlord coveting the assassin's territory killed the murderer. Yoshinori's death effectively brought to a close the period of shogunal autocracy that had begun under Yoshimitsu. Yoshinori's successor died of dysentery at the age of three.

The next shogun, Ashikaga Yoshimasa, was only seven when he was chosen in 1443 and was dominated by first his wet nurse and then his wife's family. Upon reaching adulthood, he relied heavily on the advice of his fiscal and household administrator and beginning in 1454 the *bakufu* was wracked by a series of succession disputes among important allied daimyo families. Yoshimasa tried to settle the various claims, but political strife within the government and among these warlords only worsened. In 1465, the contention among daimyo families reached into the shogun's household itself, where two claimants to the succession appeared. Daimyo families took sides and Yoshimasa tried to resolve the conflict, but dithered. Yoshimasa's indecisiveness eventually resulted in several warlords sending armies to Kyoto and sustained violence erupted in the capital.

This conflict, known as the Ōnin War (1467–1477), launched a period of more than one hundred years of violence in Japan. As in the case of earlier contests, the trigger was a succession dispute, but a more important problem lay beneath the surface. To be specific, most daimyo families had failed to consolidate control of their jurisdictions. They had only weak economic bases and each faced several power-hungry rival samurai known as "men of the province" (*kokujin*). Daimyo held little of the land in their bailiwicks exclusively, and they had trouble enticing competing "men of the province" to become their vassals. The backing of the shogunate had always been an important component in daimyo power, and once the shoguns were no longer aggressive adults, daimyo positions became ever more vulnerable. At its root, the long "war of all against all," starting in 1467, was a struggle to create and maintain more effective control over the economies and manpower of the hundreds of local regions comprising the archipelago.

During the decade-long Ōnin War, eastern and western camps battled for supremacy in Kyoto.[1] Each army numbered in the tens of thousands and employed foot soldiers fighting in a ferocious style. These urban guerillas moved stealthily and quickly, wielding pikes and often wearing little armor. They inflicted massive damage to the city, especially through arson. They put venerable temples and shrines to the torch, and by the end of the first year almost the entire northern half of the city lay in ruins. Troops sacked moneylenders' shops and Buddhist altars, commerce dried up, and residents fled the inferno to find food. Those who remained behind constructed walls around their neighborhoods to protect themselves. The two camps fought fiercely until 1473, by which time the commanders of both armies had died and Yoshimasa had settled on an heir. From 1473 through 1477, soldiers took up positions behind barricades and a stalemate ensued. Ultimately, both armies simply gave up and went home. By the end of the conflict, Kyoto was a burned-out shell of its former self.

Still, both Kyoto and the Muromachi *bakufu* survived. The population returned in 1476 and started to rebuild the old capital, but two widespread fires, in 1494 and 1500, destroyed new homes and shops. Repeated incursions of hungry peasants also hindered revival of the city. By the mid-sixteenth century, Kyoto was shaped like an hourglass, with two large blocks in the north and south connected by a narrow strip in the middle.

The gravely weakened shogunate, for its part, tried to exercise its old authority throughout the archipelago but largely failed. Provincial warriors united and chased daimyo out of their jurisdictions. During the most famous insurrection in Yamashiro province during the late 1400s, "men of the province" ejected the daimyo by refusing to participate in battles concerning a succession dispute. Once in control, local warriors held mass meetings and appealed to peasants by seeking the repeal of toll taxes and the transfer of all estate dues to the farmers. Yamashiro province remained under local control for a decade, and such rebellions spread throughout the capital region.

The Muromachi *bakufu* could barely manage effective control of Kyoto. The numbers of reliable administrators shrank, as the *bakufu* struggled to make its payroll. The government tried valiantly to regulate currency and raise funds by erecting toll barriers, but even those efforts ceased by the early 1500s. The once formidable Muromachi shogunate was a government in name only.

Warring States: The Process of Destruction

Even while hostilities focused on Kyoto, sporadic violence erupted throughout the provinces. When the Ōnin War ended in 1477, the rival daimyo armies
returned to their jurisdictions to reassert control, but they could not put an end
to the fighting. Instead, Japan entered the most devastating and prolonged period of warfare to date, known as the Warring States Era. From 1477 until 1590,
battles took place at a dizzying pace, but this long epoch can be usefully divided
into four phases. Between 1477 and 1490, the Muromachi shogunate writhed in
its death throes as local warfare commenced in many provinces. From 1490 until 1530, the first stage of intense hostilities yielded self-contained principalities,
known as domains, headed by new families of daimyo. These incipient domains
were concentrated in central and eastern Honshu, along the Japan Sea littoral, on
the western tip of Honshu, and in northern Kyushu. During 1530–1560, a second
wave of domain formation occurred in northeastern Honshu and Shikoku, even
as established daimyo began to fight among themselves to expand their spheres
of control. From 1560 until 1590, the rising warlord Oda Nobunaga (1534–1582)
and his chief lieutenant Toyotomi Hideyoshi (1537–1598) subdued all comers and
brought peace to the islands in the form of a more unified polity.

These wars encompassed a process of both destruction and construction.
Massive armies fighting according to group tactics brought ruin wherever they
marched or fought. By the sixteenth century, daimyo could field hosts numbering
in the tens of thousands. For example, three well-known daimyo—the Takeda,
GoHōjō, and Mōri—regularly organized forces of fifty thousand or more by the
1550s. These large armies fought in a new and more effective way, as coordinated
units of specialized troops in the open field. Most units were composed of humble
foot soldiers, because they were more cost-effective and responsive to central control than riders. The itinerant poet Sōchō (1448–1532) frequently encountered
battles in his journeys throughout Japan, always commenting in his diary on the
"tens of thousands" engaged in hostilities.[2] These military developments matched
trends toward larger and more lethal military forces around the world.

In 1543, the Portuguese, having arrived in Japan seeking trade and Christian
converts, introduced the blunderbuss to the warring daimyo. While it took time
for Japanese artisans to master its manufacture and for commanders to organize
the battle formations necessary to use the new weapon effectively, ultimately the
musket proved deadly. By 1556, there were at least 300,000 of them in the islands.[3]
Famously, in 1575 at the Battle of Nagashino, the shielded musketeers of Oda Nobunaga slaughtered the renowned cavalry of the Takeda. Cannon were not introduced until later; armies trained them on siege works beginning in the 1580s.

Warlords fought nearly all of the time. Prior to the stabilization of the various

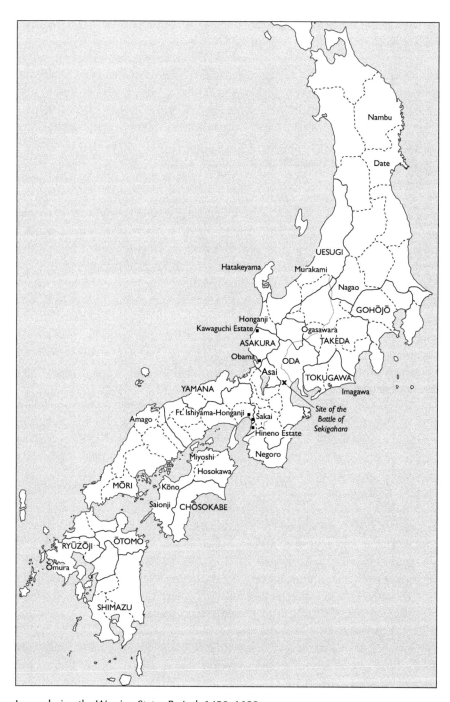

Japan during the Warring States Period, 1450–1600

domains in the 1520s, small but frequent local battles pitted samurai units against each other in an internecine free-for-all. Once a daimyo consolidated his domain, he went on military campaigns almost every year. Uesugi Kenshin (1530–1578) led his armies outside his domain located along the northern Japan Sea littoral in nineteen of twenty-three years between 1555 and 1577. His bitter rival Takeda Shingen (1521–1573) resided at home in Kai province just west of the Kanto only five times between 1541 and 1569. To be sure, wise daimyo concluded alliances with their peers and negotiated settlements with weaker "men of the country" to avoid battle and the resulting death and destruction whenever possible. In the end, however, almost all warlords gained substantial portions of their domains by force.

The frequency and length of these campaigns were usually dictated by the availability of food. For instance, the northern location of Kenshin's domain meant that his farmers could harvest only a single crop. When the harvest was good and he had plentiful food, Kenshin went on long campaigns south to the Kanto. When crops failed—as they often did during these war-torn years—Kenshin fought much closer to home and stole the food he needed. Shingen, too, took his armies with him in the spring, when the grain from the previous year had been exhausted, calling that season "the time when we have no provisions."[4] An advantage of leading sizable armies outside the domain was that it lessened the potential for starvation at home by reducing the resident population. In this sense, the wars were an expression of peoples' most elemental instinct to fill their bellies.

There is no doubt that these battles killed more combatants than ever before. Previously, few soldiers had died in the single combat of the twelfth century or even the more organized fighting of the fourteenth. During the Warring States Era, however, combatant casualties mounted steadily. For example, the Mōri, a powerful daimyo family living in western Honshu, lost 921 men in a battle in 1540, but in 1600 the death toll was over 3,200. When the foes were implacable enemies, as the neighboring Takeda and Uesugi were, deaths could reach three or four thousand for each side in a single battle. Casualties were still not nearly as high as the most lethal modern wars, such as the U.S. Civil War or World War I, but soldiering was becoming an increasingly hazardous occupation. This rising death toll was an important component in the process of destruction accompanying the wars.

The effects on noncombatants were even harsher. Ever since the revolt of Masakado in the mid-tenth century, innocent bystanders had suffered from arson and pillage at the hands of marauding troops. With the expansion of armies and the employment of new tactics and weapons, "collateral damage" grew exponentially. In the battles he witnessed, Sōchō wrote that the multitude of fleeing men and women was a pitiful sight.[5]

Pillage, arson, and rape took place from one end of the archipelago to the other. In western Honshu, the Mōri left behind a legacy of glory arising from an annual cycle of devastation. Their armies plundered fields during the spring planting, mowed down wheat crops and interfered with farmers during the busy summer, stole the harvest in the fall, and broke into granaries, burned peasant homes, and left their victims to freeze or starve to death in the winter. At Hineno Estate in the Kinai, soldiers repeatedly burned residences, raped women, kidnapped and pressed unsuspecting cultivators into service, and pilfered peasants' personal belongings, tools, and livestock. Just west of the Kanto, Takeda Shingen was among the most creative in profiting from the war—capturing the enemy's women, children, and disabled and offering them for sale back to their relatives. Shingen's brand of war-profiteering shattered families and undoubtedly resulted in the death of many captives, even as it fed his war machine.

Daimyo ranging from southern Kyushu to northeastern Japan participated in the same process of pillage and plunder. To the extent that these ruinous activities occurred on a widespread basis, the wars were a disaster for Japan. This does not mean that there was no demographic or economic growth during this era, but it suggests that violence, pillage, arson, kidnapping, and forced conscription are not conducive to the welfare of the region where they are conducted.

Warring States: The Process of Construction

While the wars during 1477–1590 were highly destructive, there was a process of construction going on at the same time. This constructive aspect featured the pacification and consolidation of domain control under the various new daimyo (few were descended from their Muromachi predecessors). The first step was to put an end to the mayhem. As early as the 1550s, daimyo adopted policies to counter pillage, arson, peasant flight from the land, and the needless devastation of common lands within their nascent principalities. The GoHōjō, for example, issued more than one hundred twenty orders against plundering and nearly thirty dealing with cultivators' departure from their fields. In what might seem a reversal of policy bordering on sheer hypocrisy, the Mōri in 1557 ordered that samurai units caught pillaging within Mōri territory were to be executed on the spot. All the major leaders, including Nobunaga and Hideyoshi, practiced scorched earth tactics to pacify an area and then turned right around and banned those very practices once the region was theirs.

Daimyo formulated these new arts of peace not out of generosity, but economic necessity. They required the populace's rents, revenues, and conscripted labor as much as the people needed any contributions toward peace or prosperity that the samurai might make. During the long Warring States period, commoners forced the warriors' hand by actively opposing pillage and plunder and developing their own strategies to counter the deleterious effects of marauding armies. Often they fled their lands or went on strike. They hid their belongings in the mountains or in temples, sacred spaces where warriors dared not tread. They constructed mountain hideaways, stowed grain and other necessities there, and took up residence in the hideouts until the samurai left. They played opposing forces against each other, switching sides as often as grasses wavered in the winds. When all else failed, they barricaded their settlements, took up weapons or even tools, and tried to repel the predatory host. The pacification and creation of stable domains was not simply the work of the warrior elite, but it was the result of give-and-take between rulers and the ruled.

Conceived through the efforts of the entire populace—not only the samurai elite—these new domains became rock solid. Many lasted for more than three hundred years. For the first time since the district magistrate had dominated local politics during the eighth century, these new daimyo were able to create coherent, contiguous domains that they knew and oversaw closely. The continuous warfare had the effect of eliminating the gap between legal authority and effective control of these regions, as each warlord could exercise power only in the places he had pacified.[6] By 1590, the long-standing system of layered absentee rights to the land, epitomized by the estate and provincial land tenure system, had been abolished.

In place of the old arrangements, daimyo gradually took direct control of the land or managed to confirm "men of the province" in their own or new lands. Daimyo made these grants in return for military service and administrative assistance. Much more successful in recruiting and organizing bands of warriors than the Muromachi daimyo, the new, more powerful warlords drew lines of political authority that were "short and taut."[7]

Within their domains, the daimyo soon could act as mini-monarchs. Many conducted land surveys, offering residents a choice between serving in the military or paying higher taxes levied in rare, fungible coins. At least ten daimyo also had law codes written for their domains, claiming to rule their "country" according to official authority. These laws placed warriors in a status hierarchy and regulated various aspects of vassal behavior such as marriage and inheritance. Most daimyo prohibited self-redress, whereby samurai avenged any act besmirching their honor. The law also stressed absolute loyalty to the daimyo. Several daimyo, including GoHōjō Sōun and Takeda Shingen, left lists of moral precepts to guide their heirs.

Daimyo tried to bring many other domain affairs under their direct supervision. They always asserted control over temples and shrines within their jurisdiction. They regulated travel by issuing passes to those crossing domain borders, and they acted as the enforcers of law and order by policing diverse crimes. They attempted to unify weights and measures and the width of roads in their domains.

Daimyo also set wages for some artisans. Commerce was of particular interest, since samurai could obtain war materiel (especially muskets) only from outside their principalities. In the matter of trade, these warlords were mercantilist, taxing exports and encouraging merchants from afar to import valuable products. They also levied transport and business taxes. Daimyo were especially eager to encourage the expansion and regulation of irrigation works and commanded farmers to take up immediately the planting of abandoned fields. They were also careful to guard the resources of the mountains and seashores.

In short, the process of construction during the Warring States Era was a product of the lengthy and often bitter tug-of-war among the samurai and between them and the rest of the populace. For this reason, warlords seem like Janus-faced figures, responsible for massive destruction while trying simultaneously to consolidate and develop their own domains. The dual character of these warlords was one reason that these one hundred forty years witnessed streaks of lackluster demographic and economic performance along with binges of accelerated expansion. Eventually, however, between 1560 and 1600, the process of construction won out. The denouement of this struggle, known as the Warring States Settlement, will be described at the end of this chapter.

An Epoch of Fitful Demographic and Economic Growth

Population

The size of Japan's population around 1600 grew to 15–17 million, adding 50–70 percent more inhabitants. As a result, the archipelago became even more urbanized than before. More than 150 new towns and cities appeared between 1450 and 1600, including 67 political centers, 51 temple or shrine towns, 47 post stations, 26 ports, and 11 marketplaces. Given an overall population of 15–17 million, perhaps 750,000–850,000 dwelt in towns or cities containing at least 5,000 residents. In other words, by 1590 there were twice as many city dwellers as in 1450. Japan had become one of the world's most highly urbanized regions.

The effects of city life on population and the economy were diverse. The construction of so many new urban centers created more jobs; possibly this stimulated fertility, but it may also have had the opposite effect by separating spouses when one mate went to look for work. Even relatively clean cities like Japan's were still inveterate foci of disease, with deaths spiking during the summer months in big centers like Kyoto. Cities received a constant influx of hungry, poor, or curious migrants from the countryside, which countered the higher urban mortality.

Sakai, located in modern Osaka, was one of the most important ports during the sixteenth century.[8] As late as the Ōnin War, the city was simply an entrepot for shipping rents to Kyoto. By 1484, however, Sakai established a council of local autonomous commoners and clergy ruling over its residents. It divided the city into administrative units to organize festivals, keep public order, and collect taxes. Eventually, the council was composed exclusively of merchants made rich by Sakai's standing as a major foreign port. Despite the efforts of the council, Sakai almost always faced fierce warrior armies eager to control it. In return for the merchants' business, warlords promised protection. This community of interest preserved Sakai from attack even though it had no defensive earthen works. In 1569, the council capitulated to the powerful warlord Nobunaga when council members were implicated in a plot with his enemies.

Obama, situated due north of Kyoto on the Japan Sea, was another growing city.[9] A village in the 1200s, Obama specialized in transshipping rice by the 1300s, and its wealth and trade potential led the Ashikaga to seize control of it. During 1450–1550, the port became part of the overseas commercial network linking Japan to China, Korea, and Southeast Asia. Like Sakai, Obama escaped the ravages of warfare and prospered greatly between 1520 and 1570. The port developed both long-distance and local trade in rice and lumber with other daimyo. Its merchants gained special status, tax exemptions, and the privilege of collecting local rents and revenues. The city reached its zenith in 1592, when it became a major center for a Japanese invasion of Korea.

Overall population growth occurred unevenly because of large, periodic fluctuations in mortality arising from disease, famine, and the war itself. Demographic expansion between 1450 and 1550 was a puny .2 percent per year; unsurprisingly, disease, famine, and war were frequent, lethal killers during that century. Between 1550 and 1600, however, the growth rate accelerated 2.5 times, as fewer plagues and crop failures occurred and the war wound down.

Epidemic outbreaks, for example, were most frequent and virulent amid the devastation and social dislocation wrought by the warring armies. Between 1450 and 1540 when the conflict was at its height, smallpox raged in nine years, measles in seven, and influenza in two. Massive hosts promoted the spread of pathogens by roaming over the countryside and blocking travel arteries. Then, too, units of soldiers often came from the same village and campaigned together, all having the identical susceptibility to microorganisms that none had ever encountered before. For instance, in the Takeda domain in 1550, fifty percent of one such village unit died from smallpox, undoubtedly their first exposure to the virus. To be sure, immunities to such killers continued to climb, but repeated contacts between the afflicted and susceptible helped to spread lethal microorganisms more widely. As stable domains were established after 1540, however, the same three maladies combined to ravage the populace in only seven years, none of them severe.

Beginning in 1512, the populace faced a new threat: syphilis. Possibly originating in the New World, syphilis spread around the globe with astounding speed, aided by the revolution in nautical technology in Western Europe. The sexually transmitted disease initially produced harsh effects on its European victims, killing them by destroying their palate, uvula, jaws, and tonsils. The inhabitants of Japan dubbed the new affliction "the Chinese pox," presumably because of its association with the China trade. After 1512, however, outbreaks happened only twice, in 1515 and in 1522.

Skeletal remains from cemeteries in the Tokugawa era reveal that the sexually transmitted disease had hardly disappeared. An astonishing 54.5 percent of the adult commoner population had syphilis by that time. The malady had become endemic and was rarely fatal by then, but as was true in Europe, syphilis had probably been quite lethal when it was first introduced to Japan during the early 1500s.

The constant warfare characterizing this time also encouraged the dispersion of the disease. Soldiers on campaign undoubtedly picked up and spread syphilis through the sexual favors obtained from infected prostitutes desirous of food as payment. The afflicted of both sexes then unwittingly carried the disease back home, becoming sterile or transmitting it to their babies. The sexual nature of the malady may have discouraged people from talking or writing about what may have been a raging epidemic, just as in Western Europe.

Like pestilence, famine returned to haunt the islands. Between 1450 and 1600, there was a major subsistence crisis almost twice as often as during the preceding one hundred seventy years. In other words, starvation and chronic malnutrition typified the Warring States Era. The return of cooler and damper weather may have been an important contributing cause, but climatologists are divided on this issue, with some envisioning a more temperate climate, encouraging agricultural expansion.

The chronology of hunger supports the pattern of fitful growth outlined above. Between 1450 and 1540, starvation reappeared as a common scourge for most people. In eastern Honshu, deaths spiked during the 1450s and 1460s and then again between 1490 and 1520. For these people, deaths clustered during the first half of the year, after the grain from the autumnal harvest had run out. The age-old pattern of "spring hungers" afflicted large segments of the rural population, as they faced starvation or chronic malnutrition even in the late 1500s.

The Kanshō Famine of 1459–1461 symbolizes the return to hard times. Hungry people began to enter Kyoto as early as 1457, seeking food and debt relief. The year 1458 was apparently a lean time, because early in 1459 Buddhist clerics began to ask Shogun Yoshimasa for cash to make gruel for the starving. Drought hampered cultivation in 1459, and by 1460 people in provinces stretching from

Shikoku and western Honshu to northeastern Japan were in distress. During 1461, there were stories of corpses jamming irrigation ditches and mass burials in Kyoto. At Kawaguchi Estate, located along the Japan Sea coastline, about fifteen to twenty percent of the peasants dropped their farming implements and fled for less afflicted regions to forage or obtain a handout. One tally of the dead in Kyoto was 82,000. Relief did not come until 1462.

As was true for pestilence, war exacerbated the effects of famine. For example, in 1458 there was a major rebellion in the Kanto, with people complaining that "the roads are blocked and bands of merchants cannot get through."[10] The Kinai and Japan Sea littoral were also scenes of ferocious combat, as armies trampled fields, destroyed and consumed crops, and killed peasants. Troops also attempted to keep rioters out of the old capital, cutting the city off from its lifelines to the country.

The Kanshō Famine indeed signaled that Japan's inhabitants were more vulnerable to crop failure and starvation, but not so much so as during the hungry 1200s. The effects on Kyoto with its large literate populace were dire, but in other parts of the countryside, death seems to have been less widespread. For instance, at the aforementioned Kawaguchi Estate, only about two percent of residents succumbed to hunger. Both the shogunate and religious institutions continued to feed and shelter victims. Wealthy merchants put the hungry to work refurbishing temples and bridges and in return gave them food and wages. Famine had returned, but the agrarian and commercial transformation that had begun during the previous epoch kept mortality from spiraling out of control.

Food supplies were generally adequate until the end of the century, but between 1498 and 1540 famine had its harshest effects on the populace. Crop failure and starvation occurred almost every other year in an unparalleled stretch of bad harvests. In 1504, for example, provinces located from western to northeastern Honshu reported severe distress, made worse in the Kanto by military upheaval. Snow fell five times during the summer and early autumn in a province just west of the Kanto, ruining the harvest in the process. The whole tragedy was "beyond words," according to contemporary observers.[11] Other particularly bad times included 1511–1513, when battles around Kyoto worsened the death toll there, and 1518–1519, when extraordinarily cold weather produced crop failure and starvation in various provinces throughout the realm.

As noted above, during 1490–1540 daimyo were engaged in pacifying their domains. Local samurai families contended for power in numerous internecine battles raging throughout the islands. Armies blocked roads and provisioned freely from the land. The wars critical to the establishment of these new domains gave a generous assist to the famines afflicting many inhabitants at this time.

During 1540–1600, people still starved to death, but most subsistence crises

were local in character. The weather seems to have been milder and the formation of stable domains opened transportation routes for merchants selling food
and encouraged the establishment of more relief agencies feeding the hungry. In
particular, the last quarter of the sixteenth century was nearly free of widespread
famine. It is no accident that the population increased at a much faster rate during
those decades than it had in the century before.

The wars made yet another contribution to the pattern of fitful growth. When
armies went on campaign, men left their wives behind. To be sure, soldiers might
engage prostitutes and procreate with them. Yet the lengthy campaigns had the
same effect as long-distance job commuting does today, because men had less
chance to impregnate their wives. In other words, warfare reduced fertility in subtle ways.

Agriculture and Industry

Developments in agriculture and industry bolstered the expansion that had
begun around 1280, when conditions permitted. In the countryside, farmers went
on clearing small parcels of land, building more and better irrigation works, and
raising a variety of crops. For example, isolated in southern Kyushu, Kiyoshiki
Village witnessed its share of rice fields more than treble from sixty-one to one
hundred ninety-two units by 1500. In Shikoku, residents produced the first guide
to more scientific agriculture, the *Agrarian Instructions*. The manual explained
important points about irrigation procedures, the application of fertilizer, and
the preparation and planting of early-ripening rice. In Imabori Village near the
Kinai, the number of rice paddies expanded from two in 1351 to twenty-five by
1570. In the Takeda domain, farmers and engineers tamed the badly behaved
Ryūō River in a massive project of irrigation construction. And in the GoHōjō
domain in the Kanto, farmers opened fifty-seven new lands for cultivation. From
the valleys of southern Kyushu to the Kanto plain, advances in agronomy, irrigation works, and social organization begun at an earlier date endured and diffused
to new areas.

Aggregate figures from around 1600 tell an even more impressive story. The
acreage under cultivation increased by as much as twenty-eight percent between
1450 and 1600. While farmers were clearing all those new fields, they were also improving rice productivity, by as much as twenty-five percent. The rate of productivity growth measured about .15 percent per year, much faster than between 700
and 1280 (.05 percent per year), but slower than the rate for the years 1280–1450
(.24 percent per year). The gains in agriculture were substantial and helped to support the notably larger population. Access to more and better food was another
major reason for the sizable increase in the number and size of cities.

Innovation in industry also led to continued economic growth.[12] For instance, the manufacture of cotton cloth increased substantially during these one hundred forty years. Chapter 6 noted that this plant was introduced from Korea to northern Kyushu some time prior to 1429. It spread so rapidly that by the Ōnin War rival armies were wearing cotton uniforms. Cotton was no longer imported from Korea, as farmers tended it in the Kinai by 1480 and as far east as the Kanto by 1580. Even the Jesuit João Rodrigues remarked on how quickly cotton clothing spread after 1542.[13] Although cultivation required large amounts of fertilizer and involved great risk, by 1600 peasants in many regions were shipping raw cotton to the Kinai to be woven into cloth.

There was also a boom in large-scale construction. By the mid-1500s, the great daimyo resided in immense stone castles several stories high, hinting at progress in stone-cutting and -fitting. A burgeoning population was also necessary to move and implant the boulders for these castles. For example, Oda Nobunaga's Azuchi castle, completed in 1576 in Ōmi Province, boasted a stone wall twenty-two meters high at its base and an arched dome thirty-two by thirty-seven meters. The castle keep was forty-six meters high. Ichijōdani, located in a domain in the central Japan Sea littoral, was an impressive feat of engineering skill, guarded by an outer wall and trench at least seventy meters long. Great stones formed the western wall, and rounded stones laid the foundation. Inside, the castle had gardens, temples, and samurai homes.

Greater use of saws and planes accompanied the building boom. These tools produced larger, flatter boards and helped separate the planks from the bark more readily. Builders eventually developed a uniform system of measurement based on the distance between posts, improving a building's balance, safety, and beauty. Carpentry skills could more readily be learned and passed on to others.

Mining and metallurgy encompassed the newest and most important advances. Japan was the world's leading producer of silver between 1570 and 1670, all based on technology learned from China. First came the techniques for sinking, reinforcing, draining, and ventilating horizontal mining shafts. These ideas had probably been initially employed in tunneling beneath siege works. Once miners had acquired the ore, the Chinese also taught Japanese artisans to use lead and then ash in a large furnace to produce high-grade gold and silver. This purification process was fully developed by the 1540s. The Jesuits were especially impressed by the large amounts of silver and gold then being produced in Japan.

Japanese ironworkers also improved their skills. They built a larger furnace with more advanced bellows, often cranked. This mud-plastered furnace could achieve much higher temperatures than ever before, raising productivity by making repeated castings unnecessary. By the early 1600s, the Englishman Richard

Before it was completely destroyed upon his death. Nobunaga's magnificent Azuchi Castle revealed his wealth and power. Copyright Naitō Akira. *Source:* Ishii Susumu, ed., *Fukugen gijutsu to kurashi no Nihon shi* (Shinjinbutsu ōrai sha, 1998), p. 115.

Cocks wrote that iron products made in Japan were as good as those of his native land. The additional high-grade iron supplied metal pieces for farm and carpentry tools as well as weapons.

Improvements in ferrous technology spawned a small munitions industry. Introduced into an isolated, pirate-infested island south of Kyushu, the musket took a long time for Japanese artisans to duplicate successfully. The Portuguese, however, were only too willing to sell the weapons in large quantities to warlords. Kyushu, Sakai, Ōmi province, and the Takeda domain emerged as major centers

Among the industries showing marked improvement during the 1500s, iron smelting in a furnace as shown above helped make possible the production of better tools and weapons. The Kita Hiroshima-chō PTA. *Source:* Ishii Susumu, ed., *Fukugen gijutsu to kurashi no Nihon shi* (Shin jinbutsu ōrai sha, 1998), p. 128.

for making matchlocks. In addition to muskets, the improved iron industry also encouraged daimyo to cast field pieces and armor plating for their ships.

Of course, firearms needed gunpowder, made of saltpeter, charcoal, and sulfur. Japan had no saltpeter; the merchants of Sakai led the way in acquiring the chemical from China. They mixed the ingredients in the very same utensils they employed for the tea ceremony, an art then popular with both mercantile and warrior elites. Ironically, new types of stoneware such as raku ware were produced for tea, but use of stoneware in making gunpowder gave it a new—and potentially much more dangerous—purpose.

Domestic and Overseas Trade

The commercial boom continued and spread even more readily than improvements in farming and industry, with daimyo acting as the chief organizers and beneficiaries. Kyoto and the Kinai remained the most developed regions, but each new domain became its own trade hub, pulling the boom that had commenced in western Japan deeper into the hinterlands. For example, monetization reached into the Kanto region, especially the Takeda and GoHōjō domains. These daimyo assessed taxes in coins because they could exchange the rare cash for war materiel and other goods they needed from the more highly commercialized Kinai. Markets sprang up in even greater numbers—three hundred were established in the Musashino plain in the Kanto alone. After the Muromachi *bakufu*'s ill-fated attempt to throw up more toll barriers after the Ōnin War, daimyo and merchants created twenty-six unrestricted markets from northeastern Honshu to Hakata in northern Kyushu in the sixteenth century. As noted above, Sakai became a free city, managed by merchants for their commercial advantage. To connect the markets, shipwrights laid the hulls for more seaworthy ships and labor gangs built more and better roads and bridges and refurbished old ones. Wholesalers gathered at post stations to deliver precious commodities originating from outside the domain.

Commerce played an important role in domain formation all over Japan, as daimyo tried to turn trade growth to their advantage. The Mōri, for example, improved their roads and ports and remitted taxes for artisans and merchants involved in construction and the arms industry. They borrowed from merchants, so much so that one daimyo said that the loans were more important to the war effort than weapons. By 1590, special local products such as iron, lacquer, paper, and vegetable oils became everyday household items throughout their domain, mostly through purchase at market. In Ise and Kii, two provinces bordering on the Kinai, the daimyo of eastern Japan found a valuable market where they could ship the raw cotton their farmers raised in exchange for rice, cash, and war materiel. One rich trader in indigo dye used his considerable prestige to curry favor for the Uesugi with the Kyoto elite, and buttressed the daimyo's rule by overseeing urban construction and stockpiling gold and silver bullion in the domain treasury. The

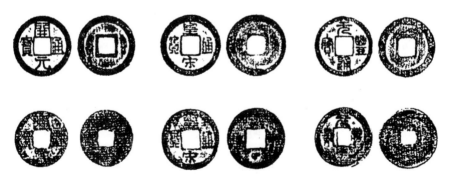

People scrambled after coins, whether struck in China or Japan, in the cash-poor economy of the fifteenth and sixteenth centuries. A string or wire was meant to go through the holes in the centers of the coins. *Source*: Ono Masatoshi, ed., *Zukai Nihon no chūsei iseki* (Tokyo daigaku shuppankai, 2001), p. 179.

Takeda also relied on mercantile families, rewarding them for their loyalty and business with land, boats, rank, and tax remissions.

The expansion of overseas trade reinforced trends in the domestic market. Once again, commerce with China had the greatest impact. In 1451, Shogun Yoshimasa dispatched a trade mission consisting of nine ships and over a thousand members, led by Zen monks. He sent along a memorial begging for liberal prices for Japanese commodities, but his request was rebuffed. The shogun tried to outfit another mission in 1460, but by the time it was underway in 1469 he needed money from daimyo to finance it. Other daimyo and Zen traders bound for China sailed six times between 1476 and 1547.

Eventually, however, Japanese demands for higher prices for their goods strained relations with the Ming to the breaking point. Although the Muromachi shogun was willing to accept the trade terms of the Ming emperor, the various merchants, Zen prelates, and daimyo wanted no part of such an arrangement. Quarrels took place over the balance of payments, which were favorable to cash-hungry Japanese traders. These entrepreneurs became so angry that they inflicted deadly injuries on disagreeable Chinese merchants and officials in incident after incident. In 1511, for example, retainers of two daimyo heading a mission fought several battles in China. In the end, official trade with the Ming court ended in violence and disputed exchange rates.[14]

These official problems combined with a re-emergence of piratical raids attributed to residents of the islands around northern Kyushu. Between 1552 and 1559, pirates, often led by Chinese smugglers and bandits, captured ten walled Chinese cities and occupied part of the Yang-tze delta. The teetering Ming court was barely able to restore control, but the Japanese, Chinese, Koreans, and newly arrived Portuguese colluded with rich Chinese gentry and practiced smuggling throughout the 1500s.[15]

With the suspension of friendly relations between China and Japan in 1547, merchants of the two sides needed a middleman. The Portuguese, newly arrived in Japan in 1543 and looking for profit, fulfilled that role for the rest of the sixteenth century. In 1557, they established a key base at Macao in southern China and began calling on Japanese ports regularly. At Macao, Portuguese ships bought goods for Japan, almost exclusively raw silk and silk fabrics, and sailed to the islands, preferring Sakai or the new Kyushu port of Nagasaki, then controlled by Christian missionaries. They exchanged the silk goods for Japanese gold and especially silver, at that time being mined in record amounts. From Japan, the Portuguese returned to Macao and bought more Chinese silk goods to ship back to their base in India (Goa) and on to Europe. This trade kept the Japanese in elegant Chinese silk, filled China with Japanese precious metals, and netted the Portuguese profits of seventy to eighty percent.[16]

Japanese entrepreneurs also traded with the Chosŏn dynasty in Korea.[17] Between 1450 and 1500, sixty-seven trade missions took place *per year* between merchants of the two regions. An uprising led by permanent Japanese residents in three Korean ports, however, in 1510 curtailed these lucrative ventures. During the sixteenth century, the daimyo of Tsushima conducted what commerce existed, importing cotton, porcelain goods, Buddhist sutras and icons, and rice and other grains. In exchange, Japanese merchants offered minerals such as copper, tin, and sulfur along with medicines and spices transshipped from the Ryukyus and Southeast Asia. Japan's invasion of Korea beginning in 1592 terminated relations between the two regions.

Commerce with the Ryukyu Islands and Southeast Asia brought new and wondrous products to Japan. The Kingdom of the Ryukyus acted as it had before, trading with China and Southeast Asia and then transshipping exotic goods such as Southeast Asian dyes, woods, and spices to Kyushu ports. The Japanese sent copies of Buddhist sutras acquired in Korea to the Ryukyu elite. Japanese traders also conducted business with various regions in Southeast Asia, including northern Viet Nam, Cambodia, Siam, and the Philippines.

Throughout East and Southeast Asia groups of Japanese merchants and warriors formed a diaspora. Unlike the widespread Chinese mercantile communities in Asia, however, the Japanese diaspora had no future, because almost all the migrants were men and intermarried with local women, losing their ethnic identity in the process. Of course, this sizable emigration of erstwhile residents of Japan to far-flung places is another indication of the strength of demographic increase at home.

The Warring States Era was a period of uneven growth. In other words, the good years, when harvests were plentiful and the economy expanded, outnumbered and outweighed those when disease, famine, and military depredations raised mortality and cut fertility significantly. Historians can only wonder how great the overall increase in population and the economy might have been had the archipelago not been wracked by warfare and the accompanying higher incidence of pestilence and famine.

Society: Class, Family, and Gender

Class

The class structure of Warring States Japan resembled that of the former epoch, but was evolving in new directions. An age of endemic conflict gave wide latitude for the samurai to become unrivalled masters of the elite and the islands.

The old civil aristocracy, however, barely made ends meet. Clerical institutions grew apace, but lost their bid to retain significant power in a polity dominated by samurai. The commoner class grew in both size and specialization, and the wars produced more slaves and outcasts than ever before.

The warrior class consisted of several hundred daimyo at the top, high-ranking local "men of the province" in the middle, and a multitude of everyday soldiers at the bottom. The daimyo Takeda Shingen was born in 1521 to Nobutora, who spent most of his life quelling insurrections by rival "men of the province." To firm up an alliance with one of these local families, Nobutora took one of their daughters as his wife, who later gave birth to Shingen. The year of Shingen's birth witnessed a crucial battle in the Takeda's quest to pacify their home province, and when Nobutora won, he named his new son "the Divine Child of Victory."[18] Shingen repaid his father by conspiring to banish him in 1541, when Shingen was only twenty, and then ceremoniously assumed leadership of the Takeda household.

Shingen's relations with his vassals were complex. There were individual loyalists, hereditary followers serving the Takeda for generations, and those who remained with the Takeda for only a year or two, preferring to change lords then.

Takeda Shingen was one of the most famous Warring States daimyo. His motto was "swift as the wind, silent as a forest, destructive as fire, unmovable as a mountain." Seikeiin of Mt. Kōya.

Ties between the first two groups and the Takeda were direct and personal, and all of the men held lands granted by the daimyo. Shingen had better control of his followers than the samurai of previous eras, but even the strongest and most charismatic Warring States daimyo could not guarantee complete loyalty.

Locally powerful samurai families known as "men of the province" represented a second level of warriors. They were common in most provinces and usually fought would-be daimyo for control of the domain in the early stages of the war. In Takeda territory, for example, the Hemi household held lands in the northwestern section of the province. They claimed descent from the Minamoto, as did the Takeda, and were brought to heel in the 1450s. Even when subdued, these locally powerful families retained direct control of their ancestral lands and their consent was important in administering their bailiwicks. "Men of the province" also commanded their own home units in battle, retaining a military autonomy few others had. Like the Kawashima discussed earlier, these local power holders put down peasant rebellions, oversaw irrigation works, acquired lands, and lent money.

Only a sketchy picture survives of the ordinary soldiers fighting in the massive armies of the age. Some held a tiny plot of land, hardly sufficient to support them. Many were mercenaries, changing lords as often as they pleased to obtain more money, food, or other emoluments. They wore almost no armor and went barefoot, wearing their long hair bound at the neck. Most possessed swords and pikes, although they might also use other weapons. They sometimes fought in guerilla style, engaging in the pillage, arson, and rape described above.

In contrast to most samurai, civil aristocrats suffered greatly during the one hundred forty years of upheaval.[19] Court offices went unfilled and many nobles were unable to serve because of their penury. One sovereign waited ten years to ascend the throne, and there was not enough money for the timely funeral of another. Even though the imperial palace survived, nearly everyone lost property in the fires that devastated Kyoto between 1467 and 1500. Each noble house lost huge parcels of rent-producing lands; one family went from fifty-five to just five properties by 1500. The income of the imperial house fell from 7,500 strings of cash in 1450 to just 620 between 1521 and 1569. To support themselves, aristocrats turned to donations, tolls, fees for offices and literary lessons, and still they were forced to place almost all their sons and daughters in temples. Ichijō Kaneyoshi obtained clerical posts for seventeen of his children.

Under such duress, courtiers left Kyoto and returned to their rent-producing lands in the country. During the Warring States Era, 338 aristocrats went to live in the country and another 600–700 spent considerable time there. Court councils lacked a quorum. This behavior drew the wrath of the emperor, who reclaimed their ranks and offices. Aristocrats apparently paid no mind—it was every man for himself. Those of the middle rank or even the monarch's guards began reporting directly to the emperor.

Even without much income or most of its members, the court tried to keep up appearances. It conducted poetry sessions, flower viewing, kickball tournaments, and bathing ceremonies. Annually, the court held about fifty rituals, compared to the one hundred seventy-nine listed for 1422. One reason was that most aristocrats lost their elegant clothes in the fires during the mayhem in Kyoto, and their budgets for clothing dropped on average from thirty to two strings of cash per year. By the 1550s, all but a few courtiers lived in small, dispersed families that they struggled to support. Conditions did not begin to improve until after the 1570s, as Nobunaga took control of the capital and a modicum of peace was restored.

For the clergy, the Warring States Era was a time of intense competition for believers and confrontation with the military authorities. In general, the older sects in Nara and Kyoto lost out; Rinzai Zen became weaker with the collapse of the Muromachi *bakufu*. On the other hand, believers in Sōtō Zen, the Pure Land, and the Lotus Sutra increased greatly. Jesuits brought Roman Catholicism to Japan and they succeeded in making many converts. The emerging thought system, Shinto, chose its sacred texts and drew pilgrims to shrines at Ise and Mount Yoshida in Kyoto.

The fate of Enryakuji, headquarters to the Tendai faith, symbolized the hard times faced by older sects. Already in the 1400s, Enryakuji had begun to lose its lands to warriors and to lose revenues to Kyoto moneylenders. The Muromachi *bakufu* generally ignored the frequent demonstrations so frightening to the court in the twelfth century. Finally, in 1571 after the warlord Nobunaga had taken control of Kyoto, he had his troops surround Mount Hiei where the temple complex was situated and, shockingly, ordered them to burn the mountain, ending Enryakuji's pretensions to independent political and economic power. One of the most venerable institutions in Japanese history had been reduced to cinders.

By contrast, Sōtō Zen expanded rapidly into the countryside between 1450 and 1590, primarily because of warrior patronage.[20] Along the Japan Sea littoral, local "men of the province" founded new temples, even as prelates promised them salvation and worldly benefits. The population in Sōtō Zen monasteries and temples grew exponentially in the 1500s, partly because Buddhist monks ignored their behavioral precepts and served potential warrior patrons rice wine in elaborate rituals.

True Pure Land Buddhism benefited from the enlightened rule of its eighth head, Rennyo (1415–1499), who had five wives and twenty-seven children.[21] He proselytized far and wide, writing hymns and pastoral letters to guide his followers. He was especially successful around his home temple Honganji near Kyoto, in eastern Honshu, and along the Japan Sea littoral. The families that became his followers formed congregations as grassroots units, and soon they were known for their cohesion. For example, during a famine, farm families would reserve grain for like-minded artisans and merchants. These congregations numbered between twenty and a thousand and met monthly for religious discussion and worship. They also received rules checking wild behavior, such as slandering other sects or attacking political leaders. By the early 1500s, True Pure Land Buddhism had emerged as a powerful religious organization.

Eventually, this sect came to be known as the "Single-minded" (*Ikkō*) school because of its adherents' devotion to Amida Buddha. The cohesion of believers made them difficult for daimyo to control, and in 1488 between 100,000 and 200,000 of the faithful drove a warlord from his domain in Kaga located along the central Japan Sea.[22] The Kaga devotees established an "estate of the Buddha," resisting local warrior rents and labor dues. Like-minded local samurai willing to accept the new regime soon joined, sharing power with the *Ikkō* sectarians. Warrior armies failed to suppress the wayward province until 1580, slaughtering thirty to forty thousand religious soldiers in fierce battles.

Meanwhile, the focus moved to the *Ikkō* sect's headquarters in the Kinai. When Honganji was burned in Kyoto in 1532, the tenth patriarch had it rebuilt as a fortification in Osaka and recruited an army of twenty thousand. Soon the Single-minded sect became a rallying point for all those opposing warrior rule. During the 1570s, the warlord Oda Nobunaga launched an all-out war against Honganji, using armored ships brimming with cannon to blockade the fortress. In the face of such overwhelming military power, the sect sued for peace on Nobunaga's terms in 1580. Warrior power had triumphed over the religious network of the Single-minded sect.

The Lotus Sect was no less militant, espousing an ideology of "succeeding in this world."[23] Kyoto merchants and moneylenders joined in droves, because they felt that the Lotus Leagues, as they were known, helped to protect their profits. These radicals were also popular because they rejected the rents and labor dues imposed by warriors and clamored for the abrogation of urban taxes. Thousands of adherents chanting "Hail to the Lotus Sutra" demonstrated in the streets in long, circular processions, frightening commoners and aristocrats alike. Eventually they came to occupy twenty-one temples protected by moats and earthen walls.

Finally, between 1532 and 1536, the Lotus Leagues in Kyoto revolted against a powerful warrior in the region. Taking over the administration of the city, they kidnapped aristocrats, decided lawsuits, apprehended arsonists, and blocked rent payments. A type of "popular justice" meted out by the Lotus sectarians reigned in the city.[24] In 1536, however, the tide turned against them, as Enryakuji, supported by samurai and the older Buddhist sects, counterattacked. Enryakuji and its allies burned many Lotus temples over a period of thirty-six hours. Survivors fled to the imperial grounds but were nevertheless killed there. Like the Single-minded believers, devotees of this urban religious movement succumbed to the forces of order.

Jesuit missionaries introduced Christianity in the 1540s. Just as the Single-minded sect had done, Christianity stressed the kinship of all believers, giving them a similar cohesiveness that warriors detested. Jesuits also operated social welfare institutions, such as hospices for those afflicted with Hansen's disease. As long as they were granted latitude to proselytize by daimyo and the toothless Muromachi shogun, missionaries were able to make converts. Wellborn samurai were baptized partly out of conviction and partly for benefits in the lucrative trade with the Iberians. Ordinary peasants facing starvation and war also converted. By 1579, when a leading daimyo in northern Kyushu accepted Christianity, eight thousand people—a third of his domain's population—followed the same faith. By 1582, Jesuits claimed 150,000 converts and two hundred churches in Japan. Warrior leaders ignored this growth until the 1580s, when they decided Christianity posed a threat similar to the Single-minded and Lotus sects and began to suppress the movement.

Shinto continued to differentiate itself from Buddhism. During the Warring States Era, thinkers articulated new doctrines and sought funds for the reconstruction of several shrines. They claimed that their Shinto was Japan's original faith, grounded in certain esoteric rituals and texts. By the late 1500s, the leading lineages controlling the lands around Ise and Mount Yoshida granted licenses to shrine officials throughout Japan. The intellectual importance of the Shinto movement lay in its claims that Japan was a land of the gods ruled for ages eternal by an unbroken line of divine sovereigns. In 1590, however, it was better known for the numerous pilgrims sojourning in shrines at Ise, Mount Yoshida, and Mount Iwaki (in northeastern Honshu).

Farmers comprised the largest segment of the commoner population. By 1590, corporate villages, in which age ranking was common, covered much of central and western Japan. Adult males performed the heavy duties of construction and fighting. Wealthy peasants dealt with warriors and other proprietors to decide the amount of a village's revenues and divide the burden among the various households, each one of which was a single tax unit. In these corporate villages, peasants attached great importance to the continuation of the family line, because fewer households meant a heavier burden for those remaining. Of course, these villages continued to decide life-and-death issues such as self-defense, irrigation rights, and access to the commons.

During the late fifteenth and early sixteenth centuries, when famine and disease were common, farmers from these villages took united action to save their lives and their lands. Like their forebears from the thirteenth century, these groups swore written oaths appealing to a Buddhist deity and then drank from a communal bucket to solemnize their actions. Then they abandoned their fields and fled to the city looking for aid. During the Ōnin War, they joined daimyo armies as poor foot soldiers, pillaging battle sites to fill their bellies. The uprisings of these peasants added another dimension to the violence of the era.

In eastern Honshu, settlements were more loosely arranged, and they were often home to "men of the province" who held sway over the farming populace. Pliable local notables proved helpful in the daimyo's quest to control the peasantry. Warlords used local samurai families and the wealthiest cultivators residing in the villages to resolve disputes over borders and water rights. In the process, the village acknowledged daimyo rule. In one important respect, however, settlements in eastern Japan resembled those in the western part of the archipelago: warriors and peasants alike were concerned to keep households and lineages intact to facilitate taxation.

The dramatic increase in occupational specialization, trade, and cities encouraged the formation a sizable class of merchants and artisans.[25] Just as peasants formed corporate villages, urbanites developed their own social organization, composed of households facing each other from two sides of a street. These block units joined associations, giving cities like Kyoto a cellular structure. The members of each unit formed assemblies led by the wealthy and were responsible for fire and crime prevention and mutual defense. They also issued building permits, administered urban lands, and forbade the barracking of soldiers and the levying of extra taxes. As the Ōnin War, arson, and smaller but more frequent riots afflicted Kyoto after 1467, these units became more cohesive and joined with rich, secularized, and increasingly autonomous moneylenders in defense of the capital. Even some aristocrats joined the urban associations.

Imai Sōkyū (1520–1593) was a Sakai merchant during this epoch.[26] After developing a relationship with the warlord Nobunaga, Imai was allowed to exploit the rich silver and iron reserves in a province just west of Sakai. In turn, Imai produced firearms and gunpowder for Nobunaga. The strongest link between the warrior and the merchant, however, was their mutual interest in the tea ceremony. They attended gatherings together and learned from tea masters. Nobunaga also ensured Imai's acquisition of valuable tea utensils, enhancing the merchant's wealth.

For both farmers and urbanites, gains in material culture from the previous age continued and spread, making survival more likely. As food production increased, diet improved, so that by the end of the wars in 1590 malnutrition and starvation were not as likely. A general rise in caloric intake, indicated by a shift to three meals a day, helped lessen the chances of the "spring hungers." More commoners adopted warm, soft cotton rather than cold, scratchy hemp for their clothing. The construction of dwellings moved toward greater size, with more storage space, and more houses had roof tiles, plastered walls, and wooden planks for floors. Boilers heated homes in western Japan as did fireplaces in eastern Honshu. João Rodrigues, the Jesuit mentioned above, described "the privy as very clean and without any bad smell at all."[27]

As Japan's cities became cleaner, the incidence of epidemics lessened. A Spanish visitor remarked in 1609 that "one cannot see streets and homes this clean anywhere else in the world."[28] The custom of bathing spread through the erection of urban and village bathhouses. The monk Sōchō, for example, was almost always offered a bath as he wandered the countryside. In Kyoto, there were twenty bathhouses by 1600, charging eight coins per session.[29]

In addition to greater physical comforts, most residents of Japan benefited from intellectual advancements. Literacy and numeracy grew, so much so that one Jesuit priest noted that "all the children in Japan study at temples."[30] The abacus was introduced from China, making it easier for merchants to calculate their profits. Jesuits brought cartography, the mechanical clock, and the movable type press, technologies affecting the ruling elite most profoundly.

These various improvements had less effect on the servile and outcast classes. As a result of the wars and famines, more people fell victim to servitude all over Japan. Daimyo skirted the issues of kidnapping and slavery in their law codes, suggesting such behavior was rampant. The Portuguese were participants in slaving, although Jesuit priests condemned it. The lives of those in the servile class were undoubtedly hard, but many had their own parcels to farm and small huts or lean-tos in which to carry out their daily lives. Numerous lawsuits indicate that many fled their masters.

Outcasts performed tasks designated by daimyo law, such as making bowstrings and bamboo brushes for the tea ceremony. Some were fairly rich, like a mercantile outcast specializing in leather goods in the Mōri domain. They also cleaned towns and ports, undoubtedly scooping out toilets and sweeping streets. Interestingly enough, outcasts had their own bathhouses segregated from the rest of the population. Other marginal groups included shamans, wandering ascetics, traveling storytellers, and those afflicted with Hansen's disease.

Family and Gender Relations

In general, families in all classes continued their patriarchal tilt and women suffered a decline in status. Among the samurai, a woman was most powerful when her daimyo son listened to her. Shingen's mother, for example, exerted a strong influence on her son throughout his life, even joining his vassals to help plan strategy. Otherwise, siblings were useful primarily for political purposes. Shingen used his four brothers in various military capacities and his four sisters as wives for rival warlords. He himself was married at twenty-two to the daughter of an ally in his father's battles with the nearby GoHōjō family, but she died a year later during childbirth. His second marriage was also a political arrangement, permitting the Takeda better access to Kyoto. Shingen also kept three concubines, all taken from locally prominent samurai families. Though she derived her power from her warlord husband, the main wife still had important duties within the household. She managed family ceremonies and etiquette, supervised the storage of weapons, and dealt with visiting vassals and traveling merchants.

Shingen's eldest son was named heir, but, like Shingen, he tried to oust his father. He failed and committed suicide at the age of thirty. In addition, Shingen had six other sons and six daughters, two of whom died in childhood. Most of his male children were killed in battle, including his fourth son and heir Katsuyori. The daughters were all used as political pawns in marriage alliances. In addition to his wives, concubines, and children, Shingen's household contained the usual contingent of wet nurses, servants, and menials.

Most civil aristocrats could no longer afford more than one wife, and extra females usually became Buddhist nuns or they married warriors.[31] Even though the households were smaller, women were still defined by their marriage. Despite (or perhaps because of) the penury of the Kyoto court, however, aristocratic women made a comeback. Ironically, the political and economic disarray provided an opportunity for women to emerge on the political stage they had once shared with powerful men. As court officialdom became an empty shell of its former self, about fifty women obtained rank and office and served the sovereign directly. The chief financial officer was female, and she held the keys to the imperial house's reception of petitions and donations. She even drafted imperial letters.

Among commoners, the stem household continued to spread as the basic family unit. It was more common in central and western Japan by the 1580s, and households there named a male head and kept ancestral tablets. This kinship organization was still fluid even in the late 1500s, however, as distinctions between the main and branch families, so important in the Tokugawa period, were not so clear-cut and brothers were more nearly equal. In other ways, too, household units remained diverse, with many having female heads and still practicing partible inheritance. Noninheriting siblings had to fend for themselves, usually clearing their own lands and forming new families.

Male headship and patrilineal succession were salient characteristics of the stem household. As noted in chapter 6, women suffered in this arrangement, losing for the most part the right to inherit and control property. Many provided a dowry to the male's family and were valued merely for their ability to produce a healthy son. The wars were especially bad for women, as the incidence of rape increased and the commodification of sex and the importation of syphilis made their lives more dangerous.

Although the stem household and male power were in ascendancy, a peasant woman's lot may not have been so harsh, especially when compared with their betters' lives in the samurai and noble classes. Women worked the fields right alongside their husbands, and even made land transactions and managed fields, albeit through a male guarantor. They had considerable latitude to engage in sex when young and divorce their husbands after marriage. A few abandoned their children, trying to escape an unwanted duty. Some were members of the shrine association deciding crucial issues in the village. In the end, commoner males and females mostly faced the same overriding hardship—survival in a world of war, famine, and disease.

Children likewise had difficult and uncertain lives. Infant mortality remained so high that babies were not considered fully human until age seven. More women turned to medicinal drugs or other means for abortions and infanticide. Armies regularly captured and enslaved the young because they were vulnerable. Starving farmers still sold their children for food, breaking up their families and leaving the sale item to an uncertain fate. Jesuit priests were particularly disturbed by the sale of children into prostitution. Children who lived beyond age ten worked demanding and dangerous jobs in the fields and at trades.

Like women, however, children may have been better off than is usually supposed. Continued improvements in material life along with the dispersion of corporate villages and stem households may have had a salutary effect on mortality. By preserving lineages intact through war, famine, and disease, cultivators undoubtedly helped more children and youths to survive to adulthood. This enhanced the chances of survival for orphans and children in single-parent households. Some youths even acquired the rudiments of education, learning to read and write and do simple arithmetic. Youthful sexual practices, including masturbation, sodomy, and premarital relations, remained free and untainted by shame, much to the chagrin of Christian missionaries.

In sum, Japanese society in 1590 was more complex than ever before. The elite had long ago split into military, religious, and civil aristocratic functions, but now warriors had become dominant. Several different income and social groups composed the farming populace, and city dwellers were likewise diverse. The servile class expanded and outcasts produced goods crucial to war. The status and economic powers of women fell, but the same basic problem of survival hounded both sexes. Most important, people all over the archipelago founded cohesive social organizations, including urban block units, corporate villages, stem households, and even the congregations of the Single-minded and Christian sects. As the wars ended, even greater change lay ahead.

The Warring States Settlement, 1560–1600

The final phase of the Warring States Era, lasting from 1560 to 1590, resulted in a political settlement that at last brought peace and stability to the archipelago. Conventionally, three men—Oda Nobunaga, Toyotomi Hideyoshi, and Tokugawa Ieyasu—are credited with effecting these changes, a Great Man Theory of Japanese history. While each man was remarkable and made significant contributions, the Warring States Settlement was actually the product of a slowly and painfully worked out arrangement not just with the great daimyo but also with the rest of society. In return, warriors were rewarded with the most thorough control of the countryside since the eighth-century court had enforced a census. Although these three men put their reforms into place because they had much to gain from them, ultimately the Warring States Settlement benefited all classes in Japanese society.

By 1560, several powerful daimyo had a chance to forge ahead in the wars. Nobunaga, who has become renowned for his cruelty, happened to be the one vaulted into the cat's bird seat. A minor warlord in 1560, he defeated a force more than ten times the size of his own as it marched through his small territory—he immediately became a major player in the wars. Geography favored Nobunaga because his base was located in mountainous central Japan within marching distance of Kyoto, but not so near that he became embroiled in the daily warfare engulfing the capital. In 1568, he entered Kyoto at the head of an army of sixty thousand. At once, he declared himself the protector of the emperor and the last Ashikaga shogun, but Nobunaga made all the decisions.

Until his assassination in 1582, Nobunaga was almost constantly at war. In 1571, he had his soldiers burn Mount Hiei, destroying more than three thousand buildings and eliminating the monks of Enryakuji as a political force. In that same year, he began fighting the adherents of the militant Single-minded sect throughout Japan. In 1573, he crushed two daimyo with domains near Kyoto and chased the final Ashikaga shogun out of the capital when he uncovered a shogunal plot against him.

During 1574–1579, Nobunaga concentrated his efforts on destroying the adherents of the Single-minded sect, slaughtering them first in Ise and then along the Japan Sea littoral. Beginning in 1577, he blockaded the sect's base at Fort Ishiyama (Honganji) located in modern-day Osaka with seven ironclad ships bristling with cannon and musketeers. Later that year, he decided to move against the Mōri in western Honshu because they were running supplies to the beleaguered occupants of Fort Ishiyama. To deal with the Mōri, Nobunaga dispatched his best general, Hideyoshi. In 1580, Fort Ishiyama finally capitulated to Nobunaga's army of 100,000, and later that year he plundered the temples of the Lotus Sect to render them powerless.

At this same time, Hideyoshi found the Mōri a fierce foe and called for rein-forcements. As soon as Nobunaga had destroyed the Takeda in 1582, he rushed his armies to aid Hideyoshi but was trapped in a temple in Kyoto and murdered by a treacherous general. Hideyoshi broke off his campaign against the Mōri, killed the traitor, and soon assumed the mantle as Nobunaga's successor.

By the year of his death, Nobunaga controlled about a third of Japan—the economic heartland of the islands. Like many Warring States daimyo, Nobunaga developed his resources and inaugurated policies to take firmer control of his do-main. He built the impregnable Azuchi Castle on Lake Biwa to house his kin and personal aides. Nobunaga retained for himself the best lands in his territory, en-fiefing around him his most trusted soldiers as vassals while destroying the castles of wayward "men of the province." He had small surveys carried out to determine the productivity of some lands. He unified weights and measures in his domain and maintained trade policies encouraging free competition for those who mar-keted goods there.

Nobunaga had sought to ensure his legacy for a grandson, but by 1584 Hideyoshi had subdued all comers. Between 1585 and 1590, he conducted a series of campaigns on the eastern and western flanks of his domain, ensuring his leader-ship of a federation of daimyo. It took 200,000 men to defeat the lords of Shikoku and 280,000 to crush resistance in northern Kyushu. Faced with such massive forces, the daimyo of southern Kyushu sued for peace. Finally, in 1590 Hideyoshi destroyed the recalcitrant GoHōjō of the Kanto with an army of 100,000.

Like other warlords, Hideyoshi constructed large castles, one in Kyoto and the other in Osaka on the site of Fort Ishiyama. Although by 1590 no daimyo would have been foolish enough to wage war against Hideyoshi, he was no dictator. In-stead, he sat atop a federation that included about three hundred warlords residing throughout the islands. Hideyoshi himself controlled a relatively small amount of land producing around two million units of rice. His long-time vassals, arranged from just west of the Kanto to northern Shikoku, numbered about two hundred daimyo and together held sway over eight times the resources of their lord. Most of their domains were small, however, ordinarily yielding less than 100,000 units of rice. Daimyo who had at one time resisted Hideyoshi in battle were also part of the federation, often ruling large domains. For instance, the Tokugawa were granted the lands of the defeated GoHōjō in the Kanto and actually controlled more acreage than Hideyoshi. No matter what their relationship to the hegemon, however, all daimyo swore oaths of allegiance to him and sent him their wives and heirs as hostages. To bolster his authority, Hideyoshi, a man of humble origins, had religious centers reconstructed and took names, rank, and official titles from the Kyoto court.

As the fighting ended, Hideyoshi launched a series of far-reaching reforms guaranteed to prevent the outbreak of another round of hostilities. Beginning in 1589, he had his men and those of the daimyo survey most of the productive land throughout the realm. Although not always accurate and subject to evasion, these cadastres gave Hideyoshi and other daimyo a relatively firm grasp over the agricultural resources of Japan. Surveyors noted the location, grade, area, productivity, and cultivator of each parcel. They used unified measurements for both acreage and yield. Even mountains, moors, and seashores were assessed. The village became the unit of taxation, a policy building on the development of corporate settlements in many parts of the archipelago.

The most important aspect of these surveys is that they labeled all cultivators as commoners. In one moment, those servile people who farmed parcels attained their freedom. Like other commoner farmers, they gained cultivation rights and incurred responsibility for paying taxes. By freeing the considerable class of rural servants and slaves, the surveys helped to raise their standard of living and encouraged them to produce more children, adding momentum to other forces stimulating sizable population growth.

Village assessments became units of soldierly enfiefment, but most samurai no longer lived on the lands from which they drew their incomes. Instead, many lords moved them to the growing castle towns where they could keep an eye on them. At the same time as the cadastres defined peasants as a class of cultivators living on the land, they designated samurai as those who bore weapons and collected agricultural rents. Daimyo ranked their vassals according to their income from the land. High-ranking warriors might receive several hundred units of rice to support themselves, while lowly fighters who had been part-peasant and part-samurai prior to 1590 collected just a few units. To emphasize the new division between commoner cultivators living in the country and ruling samurai dwelling mostly in the castles with their lords, Hideyoshi implemented a sword hunt, confiscating more than ten thousand weapons.

Another fundamental reform accompanied the widespread land survey, the separation of peasant from warrior, and the sword hunt. Along with the daimyo, Hideyoshi established among his lands certain fields designated especially for provisioning troops on campaign. Hideyoshi and other daimyo doled out grain and other supplies directly to soldiers on the march, putting an end to the centuries-old practice of wanton pillage and plunder. In 1590, for example, when Hideyoshi defeated the GoHōjō, his final samurai enemy, he immediately prohibited his massive army from taking up lodging in peasant villages, stealing women, or pillaging fields. Peasants were at last left alone to farm their parcels on their own, away from the daily interference of marauding warriors. Though conflicts between peasants and samurai did not disappear, even in the more placid 1600s, peasants free to farm as they thought best soon proved to be inventive, industrious, and productive.

The Warring States Settlement of the 1590s was an important turning point for Japanese society. Through the survey, the elite had a better grasp over the land and muscle of Japan than at any time since the 700s. Peasants and warriors became distinctive classes in most parts of Japan, creating a society based on status. Farmers were free to cultivate their lands in peace while samurai became a hereditary urban ruling class.

Unfortunately, there was too much of the megalomaniac in Hideyoshi to allow him to stop fighting. After asserting control over major ports such as Osaka and Nagasaki, he decided to conquer the known world. Of course, that meant Ming China, but Hideyoshi's army required safe passage from the Chosŏn dynasty in Korea to reach China. Based in northern Kyushu, his horde launched an invasion force of 200,000 against the Korean state. Despite the heroics of Korean guerilla fighters and Chosŏn Admiral Yi Sun-sin, Hideyoshi's armies slaughtered thousands of residents of the peninsula, cutting off their ears as souvenirs. His hosts drove toward the Yalu River, where they encountered an even bigger army under the Ming Emperor. Stalemate ensued. Hideyoshi took a Chinese princess as a consort, declared victory, and his men went home. He tried once more in 1597 but died before the misadventure went very far.

Hideyoshi did not live long enough to profit from the long-term effects of the newfound stability and peace within the islands. When he died in 1598, Hideyoshi left behind a council of regents that he hoped would ensure leadership for his heir. By 1600, the council had disintegrated into warring factions and a major battle took place at Sekigahara in central Japan not far from the site where Emperor Tenmu had rallied his forces almost one thousand years earlier. Tokugawa Ieyasu (1542–1616) won a smashing victory and became the real beneficiary of Nobunaga's and Hideyoshi's efforts. The Tokugawa *bakufu* (1603–1868), the last of Japan's warrior governments, rested firmly on the foundation laid by the Warring States Settlement.

Epilogue

The Seventeenth Century in Historical Perspective

This book has traced two major themes. Economically, it has shown how the peoples of Japan gradually moved from a forager-collector subsistence pattern to an agrarian base integrated with sophisticated industries and a booming commercial sector. Socially, it has described how three thousand years of population growth resulted in an increasingly complex and specialized class system characterized by more tightly knit corporate organizations. Important subthemes have included the growing power and increasing intricacy of the islands' political structure, the development of sophisticated religious institutions, and the closer connectedness of Japan to East Asia and the world.

The seventeenth century was in many ways the climax of all these trends. Politically, the new Tokugawa *bakufu* was still a confederation, with the shogun serving as the leader of the coalition. Controlling more than a quarter of the productive land of all Japan, as well as its big cities and mines, however, the Tokugawa qualified as by far the most powerful ruler of any federation in Japanese history. Though there were about 255 to 275 independent great daimyo, most of them were bound tightly to the Tokugawa shogun as vassals. Such institutions as the system of alternate attendance, wherein domain lords spent every other year at the shogun's capital in Edo (modern Tokyo) reinforced conformity. Finally, during the seventeenth century, several powerful shogun, beginning with the founder Ieyasu himself, wiped out open resistance, caused the populace to be registered at local Buddhist temples, and erected a transportation system designed to keep the daimyo in line. The reign of the fifth shogun, Tsunayoshi (1688–1704) witnessed the pinnacle of Tokugawa power.

The dynamism of the first century of Tokugawa rule was made possible first of all by substantial demographic growth. The population nearly doubled to thirty-one million by 1720. Moreover, vital statistics showed their first noticeable improvement in more than a thousand years. Infant mortality dropped to about thirty-five to forty percent, leading to a rise in life expectancy at birth to thirty-five to forty. Fertility rose to new heights, as single people and the newly freed servile class moved out of extended families to their own lands, got married, and had

families. By 1720, Japan was a land of countless independent small farmers, cultivating their own fields and having their own households.

Extraordinary causes of mortality plummeted, as both epidemics and famines
took a much smaller toll on the populace. Far fewer people were afflicted by the
"spring hungers," as a new and more benign pattern of mortality took hold. And,
of course, the end to endemic warfare cut the death rate. Much of the demographic explosion appeared as a dramatic increase in the number and size of cities and
towns, totaling ten percent of the population by 1720. The shogun's capital at Edo,
as well as Kyoto, Osaka, and over two hundred castle towns home to the daimyo,
were fed by a constant migration from the countryside, making them havens for
single males. Edo alone housed one million residents by 1700.

Extensive gains in agriculture and industry fueled population growth. The
archipelago finally became a fully agrarian society and old forager livelihoods effectively disappeared. The amount of arable land increased by as much as forty-
two percent, while the yields for rice paddies expanded by fifteen to thirty percent.
Massive extension of irrigation works, the wider dispersion of transplanting techniques, and the cultivation of more diverse crops all played a major role. Double-
cropping also diffused more widely. Peasants commonly used night soil as fertilizer for the first time and learned to raise more cash crops. A scientific agrarian
literature made these advancements known on a wider scale. In industry, mining,
fishing, construction, textile weaving, dye making, ceramic manufacture, and rice
wine and soy sauce brewing witnessed great expansion. Free labor set by contract
replaced corvée gangs.

The commercial sector also grew, encouraged by the low rate of taxation
on trade. The Tokugawa *bakufu* minted an adequate supply of gold, silver, and
copper coins and along with the domains, issued more than 1,600 types of paper money. The new transportation system encouraged more long-distance trade
and greater regional specialization. The number of merchants multiplied many
times over and they kept better records detailing purchases and sales, orders and
deliveries, cash reserves and receipts, wages and salaries, and operating expenses.
Osaka became the chief mercantile center with a market in commodities futures,
and Edo, home to 500,000 samurai, the major area for consumption. Overseas
trade grew most noticeably through 1650, and there were hundreds of missions
to China, Korea, the Ryukyus, and Southeast Asia. As during the 1500s, the main
trade continued to be in Japanese silver for Chinese silk, but after the Iberians
were expelled in 1639, the Dutch took over as middlemen, confined to an artificial island in Nagasaki.

Socially, seventeenth-century Japan was divided into the most complex status
hierarchy residents had ever seen. Samurai were the undisputed hereditary rulers
of Japan and a strong barrier separated them from all other groups. They num-

bered about two million, and ranged from the shogun and daimyo who owned huge estates with large incomes, to less fortunate samurai living in modest residences with only a kitchen, tearoom, and small living space lit by unscreened paper windows. Most grappled with what it meant to be a warrior in an age of peace. They tried to live according to the "way of the samurai" (*bushidō*), an austere philosophy stressing the martial arts, absolute loyalty to one's lord, the duty to rule over hapless commoners, and the willingness to face death at any moment.

Civil aristocrats benefited greatly from peace, as the Tokugawa shogunate restored their incomes. The *bakufu* watched them closely, however, and urged them to follow harmless artistic pursuits. Religious institutions lost their independence and became an arm of the new samurai order. Christianity was banned in 1639 after its adherents were implicated in a rebellion in northern Kyushu. All residents were then commanded to register at a Buddhist temple, guaranteeing a following for more than 500,000 institutions. As a thought system, however, Buddhism lost its intellectual vitality to Neo-Confucianism. Yet the populace remained staunchly Buddhist in its outlook, using Buddhist vocabulary for the cult of the ancestors and making pilgrimages to holy sites such as Shikoku and Kumano. Wandering ascetic priests remained popular. Shinto also garnered pilgrims, but its major purpose was as an ideology to bolster the state.

Most people benefited from continued improvements in diet, housing, clothing, literacy, and sanitation. Farmers cultivated on average about three acres. Villages contained complex arrangements of main and branch families sharing tools, seed, and labor, and village shrine associations decided the central issues of agrarian life. The massive increase in cities meant that there were more merchants, artisans, and laborers than ever before. Most noticeable was a new urban proletariat made up of servants, shop hands, and day laborers, constituting twenty to thirty percent of all urbanites. Beggars, outcasts, religious mendicants, and wandering female storytellers lived on the fringes of this theoretically rigid class system.

The status of women living in families of warriors and wealthy merchants continued to wane. Daimyo women, for example, had even less authority than they held during the 1500s. Their husbands kept concubines, while philosophical tracts warned women to maintain proper behavior at all times. Gender roles were strictly defined, and samurai women had limited freedom of movement, control of property, and marital rights. They could be divorced for such offenses as talking too much and faced death if caught in an adulterous affair. Wives of rich merchants also had powerful husbands, but they were better off than samurai women. Some enjoyed considerable freedom to manage and own property rights in land and household goods and even ran their own businesses. Many learned to read and write.

Among peasants, conditions for females were even better and restrictions fewer. The "marriage revolution" launched by Hideyoshi's reforms in the late sixteenth century created many more stem households with more children. Husbands and wives united as able-bodied teams, sharing work in the family enterprise as well as in household chores. Each sex participated in housekeeping, childrearing, and fieldwork, yet women's wages for farm work were only about half that allotted to men. In cities, however, where men comprised a substantial majority, working females benefited from better conditions than their male counterparts.

Sex, marriage, and divorce among peasants were also more favorable to women. Premarital sex was extensive and sanctioned as a way to "shop around" for a suitable mate. To this end, girls were taught to be obedient, gentle, clean, and hardworking and joined sewing associations to learn domestic virtues from local farmwives. Marriage meant the union of two households of roughly equal status and income. It was a major milestone for a woman, marked at times by elaborate ceremonies. The new wife was primarily responsible for maintaining peace within the household and was duty-bound to produce a male heir, bearing a child on average about every three years. Infants benefited from a much longer period of breast-feeding—as long as three years—undoubtedly helping to reduce mortality. Divorce rates were high at fifteen percent, but far from being a male prerogative, dissolution of a marriage took place only after intense discussion among family members. Divorced women were free to remarry and the man might even pay his ex-wife money.

The shogunate was overtly misogynistic in its views of women, condemning them for abortion and infanticide and characterizing females as objects of pollution. In its view, women were created primarily for reproduction and a philosophical tract entitled *The Greater Learning for Women* exhorted wives to submit to their husbands. Yet the shogun and daimyo maintained a double standard by tolerating red-light districts, known as the "gay quarters." They were meant for townsmen, but samurai frequented them, too. In these zones, male homosexuality was rampant and celebrated in print and art. Female prostitutes performed in a cult of pleasure symbolic of a woman's other role as sexual temptress. They, too, were graphically portrayed in art and print and even ranked in catalogues. By regulating sexual images and practices, the Tokugawa *bakufu* apparently hoped to promote a happy consciousness in a society dominated by a strict Confucian moralism.

Finally, during the 1600s substantial commercial expansion brought Japan into closer contact with nearby peoples. To the north, residents of Honshu encountered and largely subdued the Ainu of Hokkaido. To the south, the Shimazu, a daimyo of southern Kyushu, invaded the formerly independent Kingdom of the

Ryukyus in 1609 and tried to impose its culture on the natives. Even as Japan had grown more politically powerful, populous, wealthy, and socially specialized, it was becoming more closely knit into both the East Asian and global communities. This rich social and economic legacy provided ample basis for later historical developments.

Notes

SZKT = Shintai zōho kokushi taikei (A Library of Japanese History, Newly Revised)

Chapter 1: The Building Blocks of Japan

1. Mark Hudson, "Japan's Beginnings," unpublished paper, May 2006.
2. Ibid.
3. J. Edward Kidder, "The Sannai-Maruyama Site: New Views on the Jōmon Period," *Southeast Review of Asian Studies* 20 (1998): 29–52.
4. Tsude Hiroshi, "Early State Formation in Japan," in Joan Piggott, ed., *Capital and Countryside in Japan, 300–1180* (Ithaca, N.Y.: Cornell University Press, 2006), pp. 13–53.
5. Yoshie Akiko, "Gender in Early Classical Japan," *Monumenta Nipponica* 60 (winter 2005): 437–477.
6. "Account of the Wa," *History of the Wei Dynasty,* cited in Ryusaku Tsunoda, trans., and L. Carrington Goodrich, ed., *Japan in the Chinese Dynastic Histories: Later Han through Ming Dynasties* (New York: P. D. and Ione Perkins, 1951), pp. 8–21.
7. Gina Barnes and Mark Hudson, "Yoshinogari," *Monumenta Nipponica* 41 (summer 1991): 211–235.
8. "Account of the Wa," in *History of the Wei Dynasty,* cited in *Japan in the Chinese Dynastic Histories,* pp. 9–10.
9. Ibid., p. 16.
10. Ibid., p. 13.
11. "Account of the Wa," in *History of the Liu Sung Dynasty,* cited in *Japan in the Chinese Dynastic Histories,* pp. 22–26.

Chapter 2: An End to Growth

1. "Account of the Wa," in *History of the Sui Dynasty,* cited in *Japan in the Chinese Dynastic Histories,* p. 32.
2. William Aston, trans., *Nihongi Chronicles of Japan from the Earliest Times to A.D. 697* (Rutland, Vt., and Tokyo: Charles Tuttle, 1972), 2: 262.

3. The estimate for Nara's population comes from W. Wayne Farris, *Sacred Texts and Buried Treasures: Issues in the Historical Archaeology of Ancient Japan* (Honolulu: University of Hawai'i Press, 1998), p. 164. The other figures are best-guess estimates based on the city plans.

4. Jerry Bentley and Herbert Ziegler, *Traditions and Encounters* (New York: McGraw-Hill, 2000), p. 261.

5. *Chronicles of Japan*, 2: 104.

6. *SZKT, Shoku Nihongi,* cited in W. Wayne Farris, *Population, Disease, and Land in Early Japan, 645–900* (Cambridge, Mass.: Harvard University Press, 1985), p. 59.

7. Order of the Council of State in *SZKT, Ruijū sandai kyaku,* cited in Hotate Michihisa, "Traffic between Capital and Countryside in *Ritsuryō* Japan," in Joan Piggott, ed., *Capital and Countryside in Japan, 300–1180*, p. 170.

8. W. Wayne Farris, *Sacred Texts and Buried Treasures*, p. 192.

9. "Account of Japan," in *New History of the T'ang Dynasty,* cited in *Japan in the Chinese Dynastic Histories*, p. 41.

10. Bruce Batten, *Gateway to Japan* (Honolulu: University of Hawai'i Press, 2006), pp. 55–78.

11. Stanley Weinstein, "Aristocratic Buddhism," in William McCullough and Donald Shively, eds., *The Cambridge History of Japan: Heian Japan* (Cambridge: Cambridge University Press, 1998), p. 452.

12. Yoshida Kazuhiko, "Revisioning Religion in Ancient Japan," *Japanese Journal of Religious Studies* 30 (2003): 11–12.

13. Order of the Council of State 7/11/797 in *SZKT, Ruijū sandai kyaku,* (Tokyo: Yoshikawa kōbunkan, 1974), p. 591.

14. Nakamura Kyoko, trans., *Miraculous Tales from the Japanese Buddhist Tradition* (London: Routledge Curzon, 1997), pp. 257–258.

15. Kenneth Hall, "Economic History of Early Southeast Asia," in Nicholas Tarling, ed. *The Cambridge History of Southeast Asia* (Cambridge: Cambridge University Press, 1992), 1: 190–191, notes that in Southeast Asia where wet-rice agriculture and bilateral kinship were predominant, the high status of women coincided with a lack of workers.

Chapter 3: State and Society in an Age of Depopulation

1. Both quotations in this paragraph come from the Owari Protest of 988, cited in W. Wayne Farris, *Heavenly Warriors: The Evolution of Japan's Military, 500–1300* (Cambridge, Mass.: Harvard University Press, 1992), p. 179.

2. William McCullough, "The Heian Court, 794–1070," in McCullough and Shively, eds., *The Cambridge History of Japan: Heian Japan*, p. 45.

3. William McCullough and Helen McCullough, trans., *A Tale of Flowering Fortunes* (Stanford, Calif.: Stanford University Press, 1980), 2: 496.

4. John Hall, *Government and Local Power in Japan, 500–1700* (Princeton, N.J.: Princeton University Press, 1966), p. 99.

5. The estimate for Heian's population comes from William McCullough, "The Capital and Its Society," in McCullough and Shively, eds., *The Cambridge History of Japan: Heian Japan*, p. 122. For the other cities, see chapter 2.

6. *A Tale of Flowering Fortunes*, 2: 112.

7. Ibid., 2: 520.

8. Order of the Council of State, cited in W. Wayne Farris, *Population, Disease, and Land*, p. 90.

9. The first two quotes in this paragraph are Orders of the Council of State. The third is correspondence sent from Fujiwara Sanetō. All three are cited in W. Wayne Farris, *Daily Life and Demographics in Ancient Japan* (Ann Arbor: University of Michigan Press, 2009), p. 40.

10. *Tales of Times Now Past*, cited in ibid., p. 50.

11. *SZKT, Shoku Nihon kōki*, cited in W. Wayne Farris, "Famine, Climate, and Farming in Japan, 670–900," in Mikael Adolphson, Edward Kamens, and Stacie Matsumoto, eds., *Heian Japan: Centers and Peripheries* (Honolulu: University of Hawai'i Press, 2007), p. 295.

12. Order of the Council of State in *SZKT, Ruijū sandai kyaku*, cited in Farris, *Population, Disease, and Land*, p. 100.

13. *SZKT, Nihon kiryaku*, cited in Farris, *Heavenly Warriors*, p. 94.

14. *The Tale of Masakado*, cited in ibid., p. 136.

15. W. Wayne Farris, *Japan's Medieval Population: Famine, Fertility, and Warfare in a Transformative Age* (Honolulu: University of Hawai'i Press, 2006), pp. 68–71. The quotations in the following two paragraphs also come from the same source.

16. Yoshito Hakeda, *Kūkai* (New York: Columbia University Press, 1972), p. 54.

17. *SZKT, Nihon kiryaku*, cited in Farris, *Daily Life and Demographics in Ancient Japan*, p. 81.

18. McCullough, "The Capital and Its Society," pp. 142–159.

19. Fujiwara no Michinaga's diary *Midō kanpakuki*, cited in Farris, *Heavenly Warriors*, p. 174.

20. Jacqueline Stone, *Original Enlightenment and the Transformation of Medieval Buddhism* (Honolulu: University of Hawai'i Press, 1999), p. 111.

21. Paul Groner, *Ryōgen and Mt. Hiei* (Honolulu: University of Hawai'i Press, 2002).

22. *Lady Murasaki's Journal*, cited in John Wallace, *Objects of Discourse* (Ann Arbor: University of Michigan Press, 2005), pp. 150–151.

23. A story from *The Tales of Ise,* cited in Joshua Mostow, "Female Readers and Early Heian Romances: *The Hakubyō Tales of Ise Illustrated Scroll Fragments,"* *Monumenta Nipponica* 62 (summer 2007): 163–164.

24. Royall Tyler, "Rivalry, Triumph, Folly, and Revenge," *Journal of Japanese Studies* 29 (summer 2003): 273; Charo D'Etcheverry, "Out of the Mouth of Nurses: *The Tale of Sagoromo* and Midranks Romance," *Monumenta Nipponica* 59 (summer 2004): 153–154.

25. Sei Shōnagon, *The Pillow Book,* trans. Ivan Morris (New York: Columbia University Press, 1991), p. 254.

Chapter 4: Rising Social and Political Tensions in an Epoch of Minimal Growth

1. Order of the Council of State in *SZKT, Ruijū sandai kyaku,* cited in Farris, *Heavenly Warriors,* p. 105.

2. *SZKT, Shoku Nihon kōki,* cited in ibid., p. 92.

3. Cameron Hurst, "Insei," in McCullough and Shively, eds., *The Cambridge History of Japan: Heian Japan,* p. 585.

4. Mimi Yiengpruksawan, *Hiraizumi: Buddhist Art and Regional Politics in Twelfth Century Japan* (Cambridge, Mass.: Harvard University Press, 1998).

5. Farris, *Daily Life and Demographics in Ancient Japan,* p. 42.

6. Mimi Yiengpruksawan, "The Visual Ideology of Buddhist Sculpture in the Late Heian Period as Configured by Epidemic and Disease," in *Iconography and Style in Buddhist Art Historical Studies* (Kōbe: Kōbe University Press, 1995), pp. 69–79.

7. *Chūyūki,* the diary of Fujiwara no Munetada, cited in Farris, *Daily Life and Demographics in Early Japan,* p. 57.

8. Ibid., p. 71.

9. *SZKT, Honchō seiki,* cited in ibid., p. 77.

10. Charlotte von Verschuer, "Japan's Foreign Relations 600 to 1200: A Translation from *Zenrin kokuhōki,"* *Monumenta Nipponica* 54 (spring 1999): 35.

11. *SZKT, Hyakurenshō* Jishō 3/6 (Tokyo: Yoshikawa kōbunkan, 1929), p. 98.

12. Thomas Conlan, "Thicker than Blood: The Social and Political Significance of Wet Nurses in Japan, 950-1330," *Harvard Journal of Asiatic Studies* 65 (June 2005): 175–178.

13. Mikael Adolphson, *The Teeth and the Claws of the Buddha: Monastic Warriors and Sōhei in Japanese History* (Honolulu: University of Hawai'i Press, 2007).

14. Amino Yoshihiko, *Chūsei minshū no seigyō to gijutsu* (Tokyo: Tokyo daigaku shuppan kai, 2001), p. 213.

15. *Shinsaru gakuki*, cited in Hotate Michihisa, "Traffic between Capital and Countryside in *Ritsuryo* Japan," p. 183.

16. Amino Yoshihiko, *Chūsei minshū no seigyō to gijutsu*, p. 31.

17. *Ryōjin hishō*, cited in Eiko Ikegami, *Bonds of Civility: Aesthetic Networks and the Political Origins of Japanese Culture* (Cambridge: Cambridge University Press, 2005), p. 88.

18. Janet Goodwin, *Selling Songs and Smiles* (Honolulu: University of Hawai'i Press, 2007). The quotation comes from Ōe Yukitoki's *Seeing asobi*, a late tenth-century source, but surely applies to this later era, too.

Chapter 5: Economy and Society in an Age of Want

1. *Hachiman gudō kun*, cited in Farris, *Heavenly Warriors*, p. 331.

2. *An Account of My Hut*, trans. Donald Keene, in Keene, ed., *Anthology of Japanese Literature from the Earliest Era to the Mid-Nineteenth Century* (New York: Grove Press, 1955), p. 201.

3. *Rakugaki*, or lampoon, cited in Farris, *Japan's Medieval Population*, p. 53.

4. *Mirror of the East (Azuma kagami)*, cited in ibid., p. 62.

5. Janet Goodwin, *Alms and Vagabonds* (Honolulu: University of Hawai'i Press, 1994), pp. 67–106.

6. Karl Steenstrup, *Hōjō Shigetoki (1198–1261) and His Role in the History of Political and Ethical Ideas in Japan* (London: Curzon, 1979).

7. Haruko Wakabayashi, "From Conqueror of Evil to Devil King," *Monumenta Nipponica* 54 (winter 1999): 481–507.

8. Mark Teeuwen, "The Creation of a *honji suijaku* Deity: Amaterasu as the Judge of the Dead," in Teeuwen and Fabio Rambelli, eds., *Buddhas and Kami in Japan* (London: Curzon, 2003), pp. 115–144.

9. James Sanford, "The Abominable Tachikawa Skull Ritual," *Monumenta Nipponica* 46 (spring 1991): 1–20.

10. Margaret Childs, "*Chigo monogatari*: Love Stories or Buddhist Sermons," *Monumenta Nipponica* 35 (summer 1980): 127–151.

11. Jacqueline Stone, "Seeking Enlightenment in the Last Age: *Mappō* Thought in Kamakura Buddhism," *Eastern Buddhist* 18 (spring 1985): 49.

12. Charlotte Von Vershuer, "Japan's Foreign Relations 1200 to 1392: A Translation from *Zenrin kokuhōki*," *Monumenta Nipponica* (winter 2002): 421.

13. Pierre Souryi, *The World Turned Upside Down* (New York: Columbia University Press, 2001), pp. 93–95.

14. Gomi Fumihiko, *Taikei Nihon no rekishi 5 Kamakura to Kyō* (Tokyo: Shōgakkan, 1988), p. 279.

15. Nagahara Keiji, "The Medieval Origins of the Eta-Hinin," *Journal of Japanese Studies* 5 (summer 1979): 393–394.

16. Hitomi Tonomura, "Coercive Sex in the Medieval Court," *Monumenta Nipponica* 61 (autumn 2006): 283–338.

17. James Dobbins, *The Letters of the Nun Eshinni* (Honolulu: University of Hawai'i Press, 2004).

18. Farris, *Japan's Medieval Population,* p. 89.

Chapter 6: The Revival of Growth

1. Ishii Susumu, "The Decline of the Kamakura *bakufu,*" in Kozo Yamamura, ed. *The Cambridge History of Japan: Medieval Japan* (Cambridge: Cambridge University Press, 1990), pp. 155–158.

2. Souryi, *The World Turned Upside Down,* p. 108.

3. Andrew Goble, *Kenmu* (Cambridge, Mass.: Harvard University Press, 1996), p. 171.

4. Andrew Goble, "War and Injury: The Emergence of Wound Medicine in Medieval Japan," *Monumenta Nipponica* 60 (autumn 2005): 298–338.

5. Thomas Conlan, *State of War* (Ann Arbor: University of Michigan Press, 2003), pp. 48–92.

6. Correspondence from the Ōtomo family, cited in Farris, *Japan's Medieval Population,* p. 124.

7. Wang Yi-tung, *Official Relations between China and Japan* (Cambridge, Mass.: Harvard University Press, 1953).

8. Kawazoe Shōji, "Japan and East Asia," in Yamamura, ed., *The Cambridge History of Japan: Medieval Japan,* pp. 423–466.

9. H. Paul Varley, "Cultural Life of the Warrior Elite," in Jeffrey Mass, ed., *The Origins of Japan's Medieval World* (Stanford, Calif.: Stanford University Press, 1997), p. 194.

10. Karl Steenstrup, "The Imagawa Letter: A Muromachi Warrior's Code of Conduct," *Monumenta Nipponica* 28 (autumn 1973): 295–316.

11. Suzanne Gay, "The Kawashima: Warrior-Peasants of Medieval Japan," *Harvard Journal of Asiatic Studies* (1986): 81–119.

12. Conlan, *State of War,* pp. 12–46.

13. Steven Carter, *Regent Redux* (Ann Arbor: University of Michigan Press, 1996).

14. Martin Collcutt, *Five Mountains* (Cambridge, Mass.: Harvard University Press, 1981), pp. 115–117.

15. Martin Collcutt, "Musō Soseki," in Mass, ed., *The Origins of Japan's Medieval World,* pp. 261–294.

16. James Dobbins, *Jōdo Shinshū* (Bloomington: Indiana University Press, 1989).

17. *Veritable Records of the Yi Dynasty,* cited in Farris, *Japan's Medieval Population,* p. 162.

18. Suzanne Gay, *The Moneylenders of Kyoto* (Honolulu: University of Hawai'i Press, 2001).

19. *Veritable Records of the Yi Dynasty,* cited in Farris, *Japan's Medieval Population,* p. 159.

20. Ikegami, *Bonds of Civility,* p. 107.

21. Steven Brown, "From Woman Warrior to Peripatetic Entertainer: The Multiple Histories of Tomoe," *Harvard Journal of Asiatic Studies* 58 (1998): 183–199.

22. Virginia Waters, "Sex, Lies, and the Illustrated Scroll," *Monumenta Nipponica* 52 (spring 1997): 64.

23. Farris, *Japan's Medieval Population,* p. 156. On Murōji, see Sherry Fowler, *Murōji* (Honolulu: University of Hawai'i Press, 2005), pp. 66–74.

24. Barbara Ruch, "Medieval Jongleurs and the Making of a National Literature," in John Hall and Toyoda Takeshi, eds., *Japan in the Muromachi Age* (Berkeley: University of California Press, 1977), pp. 279–309, pioneered study of these storytellers.

Chapter 7: Uneven Expansion in an Age of Endemic Warfare

1. Paul Varley, "Warfare in Japan, 1467–1600," in Jeremy Black, ed. *Warfare in the Early Modern World* (London: University College of London Press, 1999), pp. 59–60.

2. Sōchō, *Journal of Sōchō,* trans. Mack Horton (Stanford, Calif.: Stanford University Press, 2002), pp. 98–99.

3. Delmer Brown, "The Impact of Firearms on Japanese Warfare, 1543–98," *Far Eastern Quarterly* 7 (May 1948): 238.

4. Farris, *Japan's Medieval Population,* p. 197.

5. Sōchō, *Journal of Sōchō,* pp. 98–99.

6. John Hall, "Foundations of Modern Daimyo," in Hall and Jansen, eds., *Studies in the Institutional History of Modern Japan* (Princeton, N.J.: Princeton University Press, 1968), p. 70.

7. Ibid., p. 71.

8. V. Dixon Morris, "The City of Sakai and Urban Autonomy," in Elison and Smith, eds., *Warlords, Artisans, and Commoners* (Honolulu: University of Hawai'i Press, 1981).

9. Isao Soranaka, "Obama: The Rise and Decline of a Seaport," *Monumenta Nipponica* 52 (spring 1997): 295–316.

10. *Hekizan nichiroku,* cited in Farris, *Japan's Medieval Population,* p. 179.

11. *Masamoto kō tabi hikitsuke,* the diary of Kujō Masamoto, cited in ibid., p. 183.

12. Nagahara Keiji and Kozo Yamamura, "Shaping the Process of Unification: Technological Progress in Sixteenth- and Seventeenth-Century Japan," *Journal of Japanese Studies* 14 (winter 1989): 77–109.

13. Michael Cooper, *They Came to Japan* (Berkeley: University of California Press, 1965), pp. 205–208.

14. Wang Yi-tung, *Official Relations between China and Japan, 1368–1549.*

15. So Kwan-wai, *Japanese Piracy in Ming China during the Sixteenth Century* (Lansing: Michigan State University Press, 1975).

16. Iwao Seiichi, "Japanese Foreign Trade in the Sixteenth and Seventeenth Centuries," *Acta Asiatica* 30 (1976): 1–18.

17. Kawazoe Shōji, "Japan and East Asia," pp. 443–445.

18. Sasamoto Shōji, *Takeda Shingen* (Tokyo: Chūkō shisho, 1997), p. 10.

19. Lee Butler, *Emperor and Aristocracy in Japan, 1467–1680* (Cambridge, Mass.: Harvard University Press, 2002).

20. William Bodiford, *Sōtō Zen in Medieval Japan* (Honolulu: University of Hawai'i Press, 1993), pp. 108–139. On the serving of rice wine, see p. 127.

21. Dobbins, *Jōdo Shinshū,* pp. 133–156.

22. Souryi, *The World Turned Upside Down,* pp. 192–195. Note also Carol Tsang, *War and Faith: Ikkō ikki in Late Muromachi Japan* (Cambridge, Mass.: Harvard University Press, 2007).

23. Souryi, *The World Turned Upside Down,* pp. 198–199.

24. Mary Elizabeth Berry, *The Culture of Civil War in Kyoto* (Berkeley: University of California Press, 1994), pp. 145–167.

25. Gay, *The Moneylenders of Kyoto,* pp. 172–200.

26. Andrew Watsky, "Commerce, Politics, and Tea," *Monumenta Nipponica* 50 (spring 1995): 47–65.

27. Cooper, *They Came to Japan,* p. 221.

28. Farris, *Japan's Medieval Population,* p. 258.

29. Lee Butler, "Washing Off the Dust," *Monumenta Nipponica* 60 (spring 2005): 1–41.

30. Farris, *Japan's Medieval Population,* p. 259.

31. Butler, *Emperor and Aristocracy in Japan.*

Suggestions for Further Reading in English

General Works

Students interested in reading more in English on the topics covered in this social and economic history of pre-1600 Japan should first consult the notes at the end of every chapter. In addition, they should refer to the *Bibliography of Asian Studies,* now accessible online through http://quod.lib.umich.edu/b/bas. A third general work is John Dower and Timothy George, eds., *Japanese History and Culture from Ancient to Modern Times,* 2nd ed. (Princeton, N.J.: Markus Wiener, 1995). For information on more detailed bibliographies, see "Appendix D: Supplemental Reading" in Conrad Totman, *A History of Japan,* 2nd ed. (Oxford: Blackwell, 2005). These various bibliographies are also invaluable guides to the storehouse of good translations of Japanese literature, often especially insightful sources for social history.

Surveys covering pre-1600 Japan from more traditional cultural and institutional perspectives have always been popular. George Sansom, *A History of Japan,* 3 vols. (Stanford, Calif.: Stanford University Press, 1958), is the classic study of elite culture. John Hall, *Government and Local Power in Japan, 500–1700* (Princeton, N.J.: Princeton University Press, 1966), still offers the most coherent explanation of political and institutional change. Conrad Totman, *Japan Before Perry* (Berkeley: University of California Press, 1981), offers a broadly synthetic approach. Volumes 1–3 of *The Cambridge History of Japan* (Cambridge: Cambridge University Press, 1992–1998) summarize the progress of the field as of the late 1970s. More recently, Paul Varley, *Japanese Culture* (Honolulu: University of Hawai'i Press, 2000), has published a comprehensive and stylish history of Japan's aesthetic traditions.

Other works specialize in diverse perspectives on pre-1600 Japan. Ian Reader and George Tanabe, eds., *Practically Religious* (Honolulu: University of Hawai'i Press, 1998), argue for the pragmatism of general religious values. Two comprehensive collections of essays on women's history are Hitomi Tonomura, Anne Walthall, and Wakita Haruko, *Women and Class in Japanese History* (Ann Arbor: University of Michigan Press, 1999), and Wakita Haruko, Anne Bouchy, and Ueno Chizuko, eds., *Gender and Japanese History,* 2 vols. (Osaka: Osaka University Press, 1999). Pierre Souryi, *The*

World Turned Upside Down (New York: Columbia University Press, 2001), is a refreshing survey of the medieval period (1100–1600) from a prominent European scholar. Glenn Trewartha, *Japan* (Madison: University of Wisconsin Press, 1965), is the most accessible guide to Japan's geography.

Politics

Both archaeologists and historians have concentrated on ancient state formation. Walter Edwards has written extensively on the Yamatai controversy, most recently in "Mirrors on Ancient Yamato," *Monumenta Nipponica* 54 (spring 1999): 75–110. J. Edward Kidder, *Himiko and Japan's Elusive Chiefdom of Yamatai* (Honolulu: University of Hawai'i Press, 2007), has analyzed the debate using mythological, historical, and archaeological evidence. The so-called "horse-rider theory" was first presented in English by Gari Ledyard, "Galloping Along with the Horseriders," *Journal of Japanese History* 1 (spring 1975): 217–254. Joan Piggott, *The Emergence of Japanese Kingship* (Stanford, Calif.: Stanford University Press, 1997), is of fundamental importance with its felicitous combination of historical and archaeological sources. Gina Barnes, *State Formation in Japan* (London: Routledge, 2006), is a recent valuable addition to the field.

Politics in the Nara and Heian periods is woefully underrepresented, the most evocative monograph being Robert Borgen, *Sugawara no Michizane* (Cambridge, Mass.: Harvard University Press, 1986). Also note John Hall and Jeffrey Mass, eds., *Medieval Japan: Essays in Institutional History* (Stanford, Calif.: Stanford University Press, 1974). G. Cameron Hurst, *Insei* (New York: Columbia University Press, 1976), is a path-breaking book on the system of ex-emperors. More recently, Joan Piggott, ed., *Capital and Countryside in Japan, 300–1180* (Ithaca, N.Y.: Cornell University Press, 2006), and Mikael Adolphson, Edward Kamens, and Stacie Matsumoto, eds., *Heian Japan: Centers and Peripheries* (Honolulu: University of Hawai'i Press, 2007), treat a wide variety of topics for the Heian period.

By contrast, the origins and development of the samurai class have been thoroughly explored in English. Excellent studies include Karl Friday, *Hired Swords* (Stanford, Calif.: Stanford University Press, 1992) and *Samurai, Warfare and the State in Early Medieval Japan* (London: Routledge, 2004); and Paul Varley, *Warriors of Japan* (Honolulu: University of Hawai'i Press, 1994). These monographs contain references to many important primary sources. Jeffrey Mass was the premier historian of Kamakura political institutions, and his *Yoritomo and the Founding of the Kamakura Bakufu* (Stanford, Calif.: Stanford University Press, 1999) contains references to his extensive research and writings. Also note the collection of essays in Mass, ed., *Court and Bakufu in Japan* (Stanford, Calif.: Stanford University Press, 1982). On the fourteenth century, see the collection of articles in Mass, *The Origins of Japan's Medieval World* (Stanford, Calif.: Stanford University Press, 1997). For the middle Muromachi period, see especially John Hall and Toyoda Takeshi, eds., *Japan in the Muromachi Age* (Berkeley: University of California Press, 1977).

John Hall, Nagahara Keiji, and Kozo Yamamura, eds., *Japan before Tokugawa* (Princeton, N.J.: Princeton University Press, 1981), is a collection of essays dealing with diverse aspects of the Warring States' Period, as is Bardwell Smith and George Elison, eds., *Warlords, Artisans, and Commoners* (Honolulu: University of Hawai'i Press, 1981). Neil McMullin, *Buddhism and the State in Sixteenth Century Japan* (Princeton, N.J.: Princeton University Press, 1984), examines the Single-minded sect. The unification process from above is well represented by Elizabeth Berry, *Hideyoshi* (Cambridge, Mass.: Harvard University Press, 1982), and Jeroen Lamers, *Japonius Tyrannus* (Leiden: Hotei Publishing, 2000). Finally, the debate about the effect of firearms is reflected in Robert Morillo, "Guns and Government: A Comparative Study of Europe and Japan," *Journal of World History* 6 (spring 1995): 75–106, and Olof Lidin, *Tanegashima* (Copenhagen: NIAS Press, 2002).

Economy and Material Life

Since the 1980s, Anglophone scholars have evinced a growing interest in Japanese archaeology, critical to a better comprehension of material life. Prior to that date, J. Edward Kidder, the father of this field in English, worked nearly alone, producing numerous foundational books and articles. The best surveys of Japanese archaeology to date include Richard Pearson, ed., *Prehistoric Japan* (Washington, D.C.: Smithsonian Institution Press, 1992); Gina Barnes, *China, Korea, and Japan* (London: Thames and Hudson, 1993); and Imamura Keiji, *Prehistoric Japan* (Honolulu: University of Hawai'i Press, 1996).

Regarding more specialized works, the reader should be aware that paleolithic archaeology was rocked by scandal in the late 1990s, when scholars discovered that evidence from many sites had been planted. Everything currently available in English is inaccurate, although Mark Hudson and Fumiko Ikawa-Smith are in the process of correcting the literature. Habu Junko, *Ancient Jōmon of Japan* (Cambridge: Cambridge University Press, 2004), made a major contribution by writing a theoretically sophisticated, comprehensive study. Mark Hudson, *Ruins of Identity* (Honolulu: University of Hawai'i Press, 1999), deals with the problem of ethnicity during the Yayoi age utilizing the most current methods and data.

Demographic and economic history is underdeveloped for the ancient era. W. Wayne Farris, "Disease in Japan, 500–1600," in Kenneth Kiple, ed., *The Cambridge History and Geography of Human Disease* (Cambridge: Cambridge University Press, 1993), pp. 376–385, presents an overview of the history of disease to 1600, focusing on the age of epidemics between 700 and 1150. Farris, "Trade, Money and Merchants in Nara Japan," *Monumenta Nipponica* 53 (autumn 1998): 303–334, is the only treatment of this subject. Kozo Yamamura, "The Decline of the *Ritsuryō* System," *Journal of Japanese Studies* 1 (autumn 1974): 3–37, analyzes the decline of the Chinese-style system in economic terms.

For the medieval period, again there is a dearth of demographic and economic studies. Asakawa Kan'ichi, *Land and Society in Medieval Japan* (Tokyo: Society for the Promotion of Science, 1965), was the pioneer of research on land tenure and agriculture. Thomas Keirstead, *The Geography of Power* (Princeton, N.J.: Princeton University Press, 1992), discusses the estate system from a postmodern perspective. William Atwell, "Volcanism and Short-term Climate Change in East Asian and World History," *Journal of World History* 12 (2001): 29–98, provides essential data for the period 1200–1699.

Commerce has been examined in some depth. Yamamura, "The Development of the *Za*," *Business History Review* (winter 1973): 438–465, analyzes the rise and fall of the "guild system." Hitomi Tonomura, *Community and Commerce in Late Medieval Japan* (Stanford, Calif.: Stanford University Press, 1992), discusses trade and village life. Yamamura and Kamiki Tetsuo, "Silver Mines and Sung Coins," in J. F. Richards, ed., *Precious Metals in the Later Medieval and Early Modern Worlds* (Durham, N.C.: Carolina Academic Press, 1983), pp. 329–362, and Yamamura, "From Coins to Rice," *Journal of Japanese Studies* 14 (summer 1988): 341–368, have examined the monetization of the economy at this time.

Society

Scholars have evinced much greater interest in pre-1600 social history, particularly as seen through religion and literature. Books examining religious practices throughout this era are Carmen Blacker, *The Catalpa Bow* (New York: Allen and Unwin, 1975), on shamanism, and Ian Reader, *Making Pilgrimages* (Honolulu: University of Hawai'i Press, 2005). Royall Tyler, *The Miracles of the Kasuga Deity* (New York: Columbia University Press, 1990), and Allan Grapard, *The Protocol of the Gods* (Berkeley: University of California Press, 1992), have described and analyzed the Kasuga Cult through the ages. "The Legacy of Kuroda Toshio," *Japanese Journal of Religious Studies* 23 (fall 1996): 217–386, outlines influential interpretations put forth by one of Japan's most famous historians of religion.

Much of the best social history for the ancient period is based on the abundant literature of the time referred to in all these secondary sources. On kinship and women, see the excellent articles by William McCullough, "Japanese Marriage Institutions in the Heian Period," *Harvard Journal of Asiatic Studies* (1967): 103–167; Tonomura, "Black Hair and Red Trousers," *American Historical Review* (February 1994): 138–169; and Margaret Childs, "The Value of Vulnerability: Sexual Coercion and the Nature of Love in Japanese Court Literature," *Journal of Asian Studies* 58 (November 1991): 1059–1079. Joshua Mostow, *At the House of Gathered Leaves* (Honolulu: University of Hawai'i Press, 2004), provides new and important perspectives on courtly gender relations.

There is social history to be mined from work in ancient religion, too. An early but still provocative study, especially on the tie between Buddhism and disease, is M. W. de Visser, *Ancient Buddhism in Japan* (Leiden: Brill, 1935). Paul Groner, *Saichō* (Berkeley: University of California Press, 1984), has written a biography of an important clerical founder. Neil McMullin, "On Placating the Gods and Pacifying the Populace," *History of Religions* (February 1988): 270–293, is an excellent article on the "vengeful spirit" rite.

The social history of the medieval period is intimately bound up with religion, too. The only articles not so defined include Robert Morrell, "Mirror for Women," *Monumenta Nipponica* 35 (spring 1980): 45–75, on the decline of women's status in the fourteenth century and Thomas Nelson, "Slavery in Medieval Japan," *Monumenta Nipponica* 54 (winter 2004): 464–492. Also note Ishii Susumu, "The Distinctive Characteristics of Kamakura as a Medieval City," *Acta Asiatica* (2001): 53–71, and Wakita Haruko, *Women in Medieval Japan: Motherhood, Household Management, and Sexuality*, trans. Alison Tokita (Tokyo: University of Tokyo Press, 2006). Finally, Kaminishi Ikumi, *Explaining Pictures* (Honolulu: University of Hawai'i Press, 2006), treats the class of itinerant storytellers from 1100 to 1700.

Otherwise, studies of sects and religious movements have predominated. James L. Ford, *Jōkei and Buddhist Devotion in Medieval Japan* (New York: Oxford University Press, 2006), and George Tanabe, *Myōe, the Dreamkeeper* (Cambridge, Mass.: Harvard University Press, 1992), have examined the lives of central figures in the Nara sects. Max Moerman, *Localizing Paradise: Kumano Pilgrimage and the Religious Landscape of Premodern Japan* (Cambridge, Mass.: Harvard University Press, 2005), analyzes a major center of Buddhist practice during the medieval age. Bernard Faure, *Visions of Power* (Princeton, N.J.: Princeton University Press, 1996), is an expansive study on Japanese Buddhism. Faure then wrote on Buddhism and sexuality in *The Red Thread* (Princeton, N.J.: Princeton University Press, 1998). The question of a "Kamakura reformation" is ably handled in James Foard, "In Search of a Lost Reformation," *Japanese Journal of Religious Studies* 4 (1980): 261–291, and Richard Payne, ed., *Re-Visioning "Kamakura" Buddhism* (Honolulu: University of Hawai'i Press, 1998). George Elison, *Deus Destroyed* (Cambridge, Mass.: Harvard University Press, 1973), is the definitive study of Christianity in Japan.

Overseas Relations

Ancient and medieval Japan's place in East Asia and the world is a topic requiring much more work. For the ancient era, Bruce Batten, "Foreign Threat and Domestic Reform," *Monumenta Nipponica* 41 (summer 1986): 199–216, is the best examination of the Yamato court's ill-fated intervention in Korea in 663. Batten, *To the Ends of Japan* (Honolulu: University of Hawai'i Press, 2003), has treated Japan's overseas relations more broadly using world systems theory. A fascinating and provocative examination of ancient relations between the courts of Japan and China is Wang Zhenping, *Ambassadors from the Islands of Immortals* (Honolulu: University of Hawai'i Press, 2005). Benjamin Hazard, "The Formative Years of the Wako, 1223–63," *Monumenta Nipponica* 22 (1967): 260–277, is a study of Japanese piracy.

Index

Bold page numbers refer to illustrations.